W9-BMZ-146

Up in the Air

Up in the Air

How Airlines Can Improve
Performance by Engaging
Their Employees

Greg J. Bamber
Jody Hoffer Gittell
Thomas A. Kochan
Andrew von Nordenflycht

ILR Press
an imprint of
Cornell University Press
Ithaca & London

Copyright © 2009 by Cornell University

All rights reserved. Except for brief quotations in a review, this book, or parts thereof, must not be reproduced in any form without permission in writing from the publisher. For information, address Cornell University Press, Sage House, 512 East State Street, Ithaca, New York 14850.

First published 2009 by Cornell University Press

Printed in the United States of America

Library of Congress Cataloging-in-Publication Data

Up in the air : how airlines can improve performance by engaging their employees / Greg J. Bamber . . . [et al.].
    p. cm.
  Includes bibliographical references and index.
  ISBN 978-0-8014-4747-1 (cloth : alk. paper)
    1. Airlines—United States—Employees.   2. Airlines—United States—Personnel management.   3. Airlines—Employees—Labor unions—United States.   4. Industrial relations—United States.
5. Airlines—Employees.   6. Airlines—Personnel management.
7. Airlines—Employees—Labor unions.   8. Industrial relations.
I. Bamber, Greg, 1949–   II. Title.

  HD8039.A4272U583 2009
  387.7068'3—dc22

2008028625

Cornell University Press strives to use environmentally responsible suppliers and materials to the fullest extent possible in the publishing of its books. Such materials include vegetable-based, low-VOC inks and acid-free papers that are recycled, totally chlorine-free, or partly composed of nonwood fibers. For further information, visit our website at www.cornellpress.cornell.edu.

Cloth printing   10 9 8 7 6 5 4 3 2 1

For the late Magdalena Jacobson

Contents

Preface   ix

1. Low-Cost Competition in the Airline Industry   1

2. Developments in the U.S. Airline Industry   15

3. Developments in the Airline Industry in Other Countries   28

4. Industry Trends in Costs, Productivity, Quality, and Morale   61

5. Alternative Strategies for New Entrants: Southwest vs. Ryanair   86

6. The Legacy Responses: Alternative Approaches   124

7. Building a More Balanced Airline Industry   167

Notes   199

Index   215

Preface

We hope that this book will make a contribution to practice as well as to scholarship. The book was made possible by the international research network of the Labor and Employment Relations Association's Airline Industry Council, and in particular by an excellent group of academic colleagues from around the world. We draw on the work of many of them in the book including Michael Barry, Phil Beaumont, Seong-Jae Cho, Geraint Harvey, Laurie Hunter, Byung-Sik Kang, Nancy Brown Johnson, Russell Lansbury, Byoung-Hoon Lee, Robert McKersie, Werner Nienhueser, Sarah Oxenbridge, Judy Pate, Teresa Shuk-Ching Poon, Daphne Taras, Siobhan Tiernan, Peter Turnbull, Joe Wallace, Peter Waring, Lorraine White, Clare Yazbeck, and their colleagues. A series of articles from this network will be published in the *International Journal of Human Resource Management* in 2009.

We are grateful to the practitioners of the Airline Industry Council who have provided data for and feedback on our work including Phillip Comstock, Robert DeLucia, Pat Friend, Jerry Glass, Arthur Luby, Bernhard Rikardsen, Seth Rosen, and Steve Sleigh. We are also grateful to our colleagues in the MIT Global Airline Industry Program including Arnold Barnett, Cynthia Barnhart, Peter Belobaba, John Hansman, James Lee, Amedeo Odoni, Bill Swelbar, and Gerry Tsoukalis who provided data, analysis, insights, and feedback on our ideas.

Several of those mentioned in this preface made helpful comments on the manuscript, as did Peter Cappelli, Stephen Goldberg, Bruce Highfield, Wayne Horvitz, and Terry O'Connell.

Jacalyn Martelli provided expert help in keeping track of the innumerable drafts of chapters, assembling them into a single text (several times), formatting charts and tables, and coordinating schedules between several countries.

In addition, we thank a range of people who contributed in various ways including Tim Bamber, Colleen Barrett, Jeff Brundage, Mark Burdette, Mike Campbell, Martin Daley, Sharon Ford, Rohan Garnet, Ian Glendon, Al Hemenway, Steve Hill, Julian Howe, Alan Joyce, Thom McDaniel, Ian McLoughlin, Toby Nicol, James Parker, Kate Rainthorpe, Ryan Shields, Steven Sun, Donna Towle, Gerry Turner, Adrian Wilkinson, and Jim Wimberly.

We also thank the various other managers, union officials, academics, and others who have shared their views with us. Please forgive us if we have not mentioned your name. There are too many people to name personally and some spoke with us on an anonymous basis.

Our research was facilitated by funding from several sources including the Alfred P. Sloan Foundation, the Australian Research Council, the MIT Global Airline Industry Program, the Social Science and Humanities Research Council of Canada, and the U.S. Federal Mediation and Conciliation Service.

For permission to reproduce or reinterpret data or illustrations, we acknowledge Rigas Doganis (figure 3.1), *Personnel Today* ("British Airways: Examples of Adversarial Employment-Relations Episodes" in chapter 3), and the International Civil Aviation Organisation via Flight Global (many of the tables in chapter 4).

We very much appreciate the guidance and professionalism of Cornell University Press, a leading publisher in our field. Those who have helped us include Fran Benson, Mary-Anne Gilbert, John Raymond, Susan Specter, and their colleagues.

Our good friend and colleague Magdalena Jacobson, former chair of the National Mediation Board and past president of the Industrial Relations Research Association, lost her battle with cancer as we were completing this book. Maggie was a source of inspiration. She put to work principles of our profession that we hold dear: a dedication to public service; an integrity that earned the trust and respect of labor, management, and academic professionals; and a determination to make a difference in people's lives that rubbed off on anyone lucky enough to work with her. We hope that soon we will see a return of the caliber and style of leadership she brought to the airline industry and to the national administration of U.S. labor and employment policies.

Our greatest debt is to our families, who have given us their generous support, as usual, while we worked on this book.

May 2008

Up in the Air

CHAPTER 1

Low-Cost Competition in the Airline Industry

These words from a front-page story in the December 22, 2007, issue of the *New York Times* should serve as a wake-up call to all those responsible for America's air transportation system: "And you thought the passengers were mad. . . . Airline employees are fed up, too—with pay cuts, increased workloads and management's miserly ways, which leave workers to explain to often-enraged passengers why flying has become such a miserable experience."[1] The story goes on to report comments from US Airways' employees in a question-and-answer session with their chief executive officer. The employees' frustrations came through loud and clear about working for the airline with the most passenger complaints and mishandled bags and the lowest rate of on-time arrivals:

> "I hate to tell you but the interiors of our planes smell bad and they are filthy. As an employee I am embarrassed to admit working for US Airways."
>
> "How long do you think the airline will be around the way it's running right now?"

Something is fundamentally wrong when both an industry's workforce and customers report high and rising frustration with the way they are being treated. Can't the industry do better than this? Is it too much to expect the airline industry, or any other industry for that matter, to provide a fair return to investors, high quality and reliable service to their customers, and good jobs for their employees? Measured against these three expectations, US Airways is not alone. The U.S. airline *industry* is failing. In the first five years of the twenty-first century, U.S. airlines lost $30 billion. Four of the largest airlines wiped out their equity investors by going into bankruptcy. In 2008, there were only a few airlines in the world other than those owned by governments whose debt ratings put them above junk bond status. These few included Southwest, Qantas, and Lufthansa. In those five years, U.S. airlines also cut wages by more than $15 billion and laid off one hundred thousand workers. Worker morale fell to all-time low levels. And customer complaints rose to record levels as companies cut the number of flights to fill planes and cut services and frills to save money. With all of this, as well as aging air traffic control technologies, labor problems with and shortages of air traffic controllers, and increased congestion and flight delays, industry commentators in the United States and overseas have expressed worries that a "perfect storm" may be coming.[2]

Is all of this the unavoidable consequence of the 9/11 attacks on New York and Washington, D.C.? To some extent, yes. The sharp drop in air travel after 9/11 made one-time losses and cutbacks inevitable. But it's more than that. This upheaval of losses, layoffs, wage cuts, and bankruptcies echoes previous periods in the early 1980s and early 1990s, highlighting the volatile nature of the industry. Booms are followed by contentious battles about wage increases, which are then followed by busts, accompanied by wrenching episodes of restructuring and concessions, which are followed by booms, as the cycle starts again. By 2006, as some U.S. airlines began to eke out modest profits, employees once again began raising their voices, asking for their fair share of whatever gains might be ahead—and the increasingly volatile up-and-down cycle of the industry seems destined to be repeated.

In each downturn, though, three important stakeholders suffer. Investors lose as company valuations drop and in some cases disappear. Employees, who have substantial firm-specific human capital, especially in an industry such as airlines in which compensation is often linked to firm-specific seniority, obviously suffer from layoffs and cuts to pay or other benefits. Customers suffer much-degraded service levels, as airlines cut back on amenities and delay needed investments in equipment and terminals, and as employees become more and more demoralized.

Yet the most recent upheaval reflects more than just another round of volatility. It also reflects a surge of new entrants that have spread price competition to an unprecedented degree. Around the world, the airline industry is becoming increasingly competitive as markets are deregulated and new entrants with low costs offer low fares. As a consequence, the industry is increasingly driven by cost-cutting pressures. This trend began in the United States after deregulation in the late 1970s; new-entrant low-cost competitors have played an increasing role since the 1990s and have continued to gain market share. They are growing even faster elsewhere in the world.

The annual number of miles flown by all passengers has grown by nearly 200 percent in the United States since deregulation, while the cost per mile has fallen by half, a growth rate and price performance that is not matched by any other relatively "mature" industry. In short, among the stakeholders in the airline industry, customers, especially customers in search of low prices, have been the winners. So if judged solely against the criterion of providing access for more consumers at low prices, airline deregulation would be judged a success. This is important. But while good for consumers' budgets, does increasing price competition necessarily mean negative consequences for investors and employees—and for the service quality that customers experience? Do low fares inevitably mean low-quality jobs? Is volatility a fact of life based on the industry's underlying characteristics? More ominously, will the degradation in human capital caused by lower and more volatile incomes, job security, and morale, along with the increased outsourcing of maintenance and other services, raise concerns about future safety? Are the risks of some type of meltdown in America's air transportation system increasing? Or, can we fashion a more sustainable, less volatile industry that better balances the objectives of customers, investors, employees, and the wider society? And does deregulation necessarily mean the abrogation of government's responsibility to oversee the industry, even as the industry shows clear signs of deterioration and an increasing risk of crisis?

These are reasonable, indeed vital, questions that are too seldom asked. Instead, too many business leaders assume that achieving low costs must mean low wages and no unions. As one veteran airline executive put it when discussing the state of the industry, "It's all about price." Too many union leaders assume that adversarial win-lose relations are the only model for labor-management relations. And too many policymakers accept as an article of faith that an unregulated market in which companies compete autonomously with strategies chosen by executives who are trying to maximize shareholder value is the best way to build an economy in a global marketplace—and the only way to compete. But at least one highly respected veteran airline industry executive, Robert Crandall, the former chief executive of American Airlines, believes the industry has suffered under the watch of government leaders who have been paralyzed by their blind faith in laissez-faire ideology:

> There is no leadership at the federal level. We are in the grips of ideologues. We have had an administration that is convinced the market will solve the problem but the policies that make sense for the overall industry make no sense for the individual airlines and the policies that make sense for individual firms make no sense for the industry. . . . It is a classic case of needing sensible government regulation.[3]

The narrow views of business, labor, and government leaders tend to ignore history, overlook important alternatives and variations, and suffer from a myopic, U.S.-centric view of the world. They forget that American policymakers found it necessary to introduce regulations to stabilize the airline industry in its early years so that the industry could expand in an orderly way to meet the nation's growing need for airline service. The same need for stability led policymakers to bring labor-management relations under the umbrella of a transportation labor law that provided for mediation and other procedures to settle disputes without resort to strikes or other service disruptions and to allow wages to be taken out of competition.

These views also overlook the considerable variation in strategies and practices in the U.S. airline industry. Hidden beneath the bleak results at the industry level are examples of individual airlines, both low-cost entrants and much older or so-called legacy airlines, that have pursued alternative employment practices and achieved more positive results for all of their stakeholders—low prices, high-quality service, profits, relatively good jobs, and less volatility. Two U.S. firms that will feature prominently in our analysis, Southwest Airlines and Continental Airlines, consistently are found in the upper half of the service-quality rankings reported in table 1.1 and have been listed among the 100 best places to work by *Fortune* magazine. The question then becomes whether and how these examples can be emulated to achieve a better balance among stakeholders and reduce volatility across the industry.

Some countries recognize they still have a national interest in balancing the interests of the multiple stakeholders needed to support a sustainable airline industry—one marked by fewer episodic crises and one that doesn't lurch from one extreme to another—even as they move toward greater deregulation and negotiate "open skies" agreements. Around the world there are debates about different "varieties of capitalism," with most Anglo-Saxon countries exemplifying a shareholder-maximizing model of a market econ-

Table 1.1. Service quality comparisons across U.S. Airlines

	Consumer Complaints	On-Time Arrivals	Mishandled Baggage
Southwest	0.3	80.4	6.0
Alaska	0.8	71.5	6.6
JetBlue	0.8	69.3	5.8
Continental	1.1	74.7	5.7
Northwest	1.5	69.7	5.1
American	1.8	69.5	7.4
Delta	1.9	76.9	7.7
United	2.3	71.8	6.0
US Airways	3.4	68.0	8.8

Note: Customer Complaints = complaints per 1,000 passengers, January–September, 2007. On Time Arrivals = Percent total on time arrivals, November 2006–October 2007. Mishandled Baggage = Reports per 1,000 passengers, January–September, 2007.
Sources: Transportation Department and Bloomberg Financial Markets. Reprinted from Jeff Bailey, "Fliers Fed Up? The Employees Feel the Same," *New York Times*, December 22, 2007.

omy, while the Scandinavian and Germanic countries and Japan exemplify a more coordinated-market approach to governing their economies and to balancing the interests of different stakeholders.[4]

There is much to learn from these variations between companies as well as countries. But our research demonstrates that too many airlines, unions, and policymakers have been slow and reluctant learners. This book is an effort to open up the learning process. We do so by considering the trends as new entrants and legacy airlines around the world increasingly compete on costs. We discuss findings from case studies of airlines in the United States and other countries, analyzing the competitive strategies and the employment-relations strategies that airlines have adopted in response to economic pressures, and evaluate the outcomes for customers, employees, and other stakeholders. In particular, we will try to understand the lessons offered by airlines whose managers, unions, and employees have pursued and achieved more constructive relationships that reduce volatility, allow for quicker adaptation to changed conditions, and/or achieve low costs by providing good jobs that engage their workers. We conclude with recommendations for how the industry can better meet the needs of its multiple stakeholders.

Why Are These Questions Important?

One reason we should care about these issues goes to the heart of what citizens in an economy and society should expect from an industry. Most citizens

are consumers and workers.[5] As consumers we expect an industry to deliver
good quality and safe products and services at affordable prices. And as
workers we value good jobs that deliver on what some have called a social
contract—hard work, loyalty, and good performance should be rewarded
with dignity, good wages, and an opportunity to improve our economic security over time. Employment relationships should achieve a balance between
efficiency and equity at work and should respect employees' right to have a
voice in shaping the terms and conditions under which they work.[6] At a more
macro level, the expectation is that wages and standards of living should
improve approximately in tandem with growth in productivity and profitability. This is the essence of the social contract that governed employment relations in the United States for decades following World War II.[7] Wages and
living standards did indeed rise in tandem with increases in productivity over
that period. Unions and companies found ways to both enhance efficiency and
to divide the fruits of their efforts in a more or less acceptable manner. This
tandem movement began to erode in the 1970s and the erosion accelerated
after 1980. Between 1980 and 2005, productivity grew by more than 70 percent while real compensation levels for nonmanagerial workers remained flat.
At the same time executive compensation increased greatly, growing from
about twenty times the average worker's wages in the 1950s to between two
hundred and four hundred times average wages in 2007. Few defend such an
increase on either equity or efficiency grounds.[8] The old social contract has
broken down in the airline industry and more generally across other sectors of
the American economy. Although changes in technology, markets, and the
workforce make it impossible and perhaps even undesirable to return to the
past, can a new social contract be fashioned, one better tailored to the contem-
porary economy and workforce? As employment-relations specialists, we see
this as a critical challenge and responsibility facing the airline industry, labor,
and government leaders.

There is a second concern that we bring to this analysis. Most airlines are
highly unionized in the United States and in many other countries. Research
has demonstrated that many of the traditions and practices of collective bargaining and labor relations that were developed during the twentieth century should be changed to meet the different needs of workers, employers,
and the political economy of the twenty-first century. Yet labor relations in
the U.S airline industry, and in other countries as well, have been painfully
slow to change. Some of the pain that has been endured by the workforce
and the industry in recent years reflects the failures of earlier efforts to
change on a more gradual and consistent basis. Thus, the parties need to

learn from past failures (as well as successes) so that they can avoid repeating past mistakes. The evidence from the experiences of some parties shows there are better, more productive, and more satisfying ways to structure and govern employment relations in the airline industry. But it will take concerted and coordinated efforts from industry, labor, and government to lead the change process.

Beyond these employment-relations concerns, there is another dimension to "why this is important," specific to the airline industry, namely, the externalities and centrality of airlines to most countries and their economies. Airlines are a key part of the transportation infrastructure in most countries. They are important to national and international security. They help generate and support at least four times the number of jobs beyond the direct workers of the airlines and are fundamental to the economic growth and vitality of the communities they serve. Numerous jobs in other industries are facilitated by the direct jobs in airlines, including jobs in: airports, aerospace, tourism, hotels and hospitality, retailing, car hire, security, and many other services. One analysis estimates, for example, that, on a global scale, approximately five million direct airline jobs generate nearly twenty-five million jobs in other sectors. In the United States alone the approximately 450,000 airline jobs are complemented by another four million jobs that together contribute $410 billion to the nation's gross domestic product.[9] A study of one airport (Houston) estimated that airlines and related services accounted for 151,000 local jobs and $24 billion in revenues for local businesses.[10]

Airlines are also embedded in a larger aviation infrastructure that is paid for and supported to varying degrees by local and national governments—air traffic control systems, airports, ground transport, and other facilities. In many countries airlines were or continue to be subsidized directly by national governments and in some cases they serve as iconic sources of national pride. Even in countries such as the United States, with multiple large carriers and an increasing number of new entrants where the possible demise of any single airline is likely to be offset by the growth or entry of others, the strength and sustained performance of the airline industry as a whole is of national concern. Thus, the strategies of individual airlines must be considered in the context of the sustainability of the industry nationally and globally.

We will also explore a question and worry we hear increasingly around the world: Is the American model destined to be replicated elsewhere as other countries open their skies to increased international competition? Or will the cultural and institutional differences between countries moderate how airlines compete, engage their employees, and serve their customers? Alternatively, will American firms be able to compete with airlines that offer higher quality services and/or are more heavily subsidized or protected by their home countries?

The stakes are high and cover a wide range of concerns including the quality of employment relationships, the interests of national economies and societies, and the role of U.S. and international airlines in the global aviation industry.

Our Analytical Framework

Although the focus of our analysis is on the U.S. airline industry, we put the U.S. experience into a global context by drawing on the work of an international network of researchers who have used a similar analytical framework in studying airlines in other countries. We acknowledge in the preface many research colleagues who have conducted studies of airlines based in Australia, Canada, Ireland, Germany, Korea, Malaysia, Scandinavia, and the United Kingdom.[11] By taking such a comparative perspective we avoid presenting the issues raised here as just an American problem, or one limited to American options or solutions. Those responsible for regulating the airline industry and employment relationships in other countries can also benefit from these international comparisons and from a more careful look at variations among companies in the United States. The "American model" is neither as uniform as many assume nor the only way to govern an industry or its employment relationships.

We approach the study of these issues by focusing on the variations in the national institutional contexts, firm-level business strategies, employment policies and practices, and the interconnections between these levels. None of these broad factors are the inevitable result of an "invisible hand" or deterministic force. The competitive environment, for example, is shaped by government policies and actions ranging from the degree and nature of competition allowed among airlines to the security and safety rules governing operations, from labor and employment regulations to the actions of airlines and unions. Thus, we take what has been called a "strategic choice" perspective: government leaders, industry executives, and labor leaders have options for how to compete and how to structure their relationships and these choices have profound effects on the outcomes of interest to investors, employees, customers, and society.[12] To be sure, the options chosen have to take account of competitive realities, technological changes, and other factors that may be outside their control. The task of analysts and decision makers is to understand how external constraints and strategic choices interact to shape the outcomes of concern to the different stakeholders.

Competitive Positions and Strategy

As we analyze the strategies of selected airlines in the United States and in some other countries, we will focus on their employment-relations strategies. At a high level, two basic competitive positions can be identified: legacy and new-entrant airlines, each of which operates with fairly distinct competitive strategies. At a more detailed level, although a range of decisions and dimensions might be relevant to defining competitive strategies, we will focus on how airlines achieve cost competitiveness.

Legacy and New-Entrant Airlines

Legacies (e.g., American, United, British Airways, Lufthansa, Qantas, and SAS) are airlines that were founded long before deregulation and were originally designed to compete in a regulated environment. Most of the new entrants to the industry (e.g., Southwest, AirTran, JetBlue, Ryanair, easyJet, and Virgin Blue) were founded in anticipation of or after deregulation, and were designed to compete in a less regulated environment. For a number of reasons, new entrants tend to have significantly lower costs than legacies—hence, they may also be referred to as low-cost airlines.

First, legacy and new-entrant airlines tend to have distinct product offerings. The legacy airlines have typically been "full service," while most of the new-entrant airlines began by featuring "no frills service." "Full service" airlines offer a range of amenities, such as flying out of primary airports (which are more convenient for many customers), and offering such "frills" as assigned seating, several classes of service, airport lounges, in-flight meals, drinks, entertainment, and baggage transfers between interconnecting flights. Such amenities are seen as important to attracting less price-sensitive business travelers. "No frills" airlines forego most of these amenities as a way to lower costs and thereby offer lower fares to the more price-sensitive leisure travelers that they have targeted, at least initially.

Second, legacy airlines develop one or more hubs to maximize destination coverage and to defend their markets. Relative to the new entrants, this approach incurs the costs of higher airport fees as well as greater congestion and delays, which reduce aircraft utilization. In addition, this approach requires a more diverse fleet of aircraft to service routes of different density, which adds to the costs of maintenance and training.

The new entrants tend to rely less on hubs and are more likely to operate point-to-point route structures instead. They can therefore rely more easily on a single aircraft type, increasing aircraft utilization and lowering the costs of maintenance and training.

Third, due to their age, legacy airlines tend to have older employees and older aircraft than the new entrants, and the higher costs associated with both, such as higher wages due to seniority, higher pension costs, higher retiree health-care benefits, and less fuel-efficient aircraft. Some legacy airlines have also accumulated work rules that limit work flexibility and fleets that include many types of aircraft acquired in different periods. There is more variation in the current age of the newer entrants, however, particularly in the United States where deregulation occurred thirty years ago. Southwest Airlines, the oldest in this category, was founded in 1971, while JetBlue is one of the youngest, founded only in 2000. Outside the United States, Ryanair was founded in 1985 in Ireland, but it was not initially run as a low-cost airline; the other new entrants in the rest of the world are much younger.

Strategies for Cost Reduction

Given that legacy and new-entrant airlines are increasingly competing on costs—because of increasing deregulation and the increase in the number of new entrant airlines—a second critical strategic dimension is how they choose to be cost competitive. One option is to focus on achieving low labor costs by minimizing wages and benefits, keeping staffing as lean as possible, and avoiding unionization or limiting union influence if or when employees organize. Another option is to focus instead on achieving low total costs by increasing employee and aircraft productivity as well as the productivity of other costly assets such as airport gates—for example, by speeding up the turnaround time of aircraft at the gate. We present Ryanair as the prototype new entrant of the former approach and Southwest as a prototype that has adopted the latter strategy. Although these are presented as two contrasting

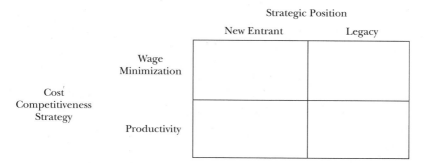

Figure 1.1. Competitive strategies.

or distinct options, in reality most airlines pursue some mixture of the two strategies and can be placed somewhere on a continuum between the two options.

Figure 1.1 lays out a simple two-by-two matrix that we will use to classify legacy and new-entrant airlines according to which of these two strategies dominate their efforts at cost reduction.

Employment-Relations Strategy

Alongside these differences in competitive strategies, we analyze differences in two aspects of employment-relations strategies. In their relationship with employees, airlines can focus either on controlling employee behavior or on engaging their commitment to the goals of the airline. In their relationship with unions, airlines can seek to avoid, accommodate, or partner with them. Both dimensions of employment-relations strategy are depicted in figure 1.2.

Control or Commitment

Airlines and other enterprises have two primary options when it comes to managing their employees. Under the control approach, managers specify what needs to be done and instruct employees to comply with those directions.[13] The workplace is characterized by a fairly rigid hierarchy and narrowly defined jobs. Employees are expected to come to work and just do their job. By contrast, managers following the commitment approach seek to

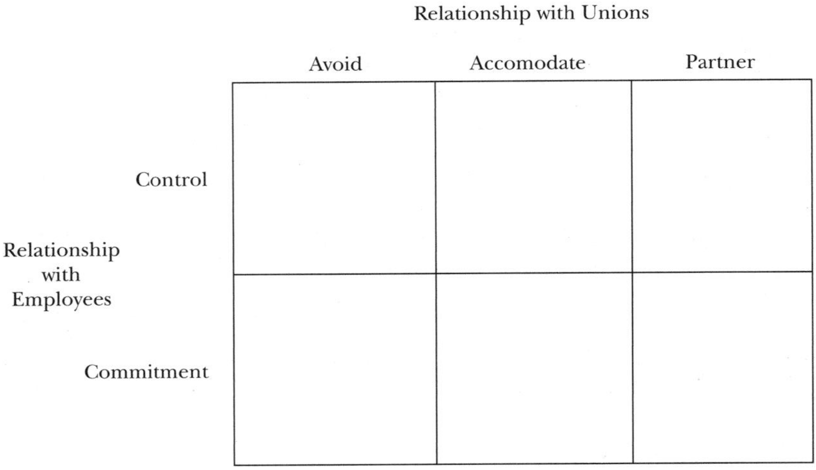

Relationship with Unions

	Avoid	Accomodate	Partner
Control			
Commitment			

Relationship with Employees

Figure 1.2. Employment-relations strategies.

Source: Richard E. Walton, Joel Cutcher-Gershenfeld, and Robert B. McKersie, *Strategic Negotiations* (Boston: Harvard Business School Press, 1994).

generate a deeper, more organic relationship between employees and the organization. Their focus is on engaging employees to understand the interests of the enterprise and its customers and to act accordingly. Employees are encouraged to be committed to the enterprise and its decisions and in return the enterprise promises commitment to the long-term well-being of employees. The commitment approach is usually characterized by greater use of teamwork or cross-functional coordination, higher levels of employee discretion, and more flexible job boundaries.

Avoid, Accommodate, or Partner with Unions

There are also options when it comes to relations with unions. One option is to avoid having employees represented by unions, which can be pursued in two ways.[14] The first is union suppression—voicing strong opposition and aggressively fighting the initial establishment of a union or undermining or challenging the existence of an already established union. The second strategy is union substitution—paying high wages and benefits and providing a work environment that reduces workers' incentives to, or perception of the need to, organize.[15]

Second, rather than avoiding unions, airlines can instead accommodate them, which means that they accept—however grudgingly—the basic legitimacy and existence of unions, negotiate with them at arm's length, and have a contractually based relationship with them.

A third option is to partner with unions, seeking to establish a broader or deeper relationship than is contractually required. Companies and unions are engaged in more continuous communication. Unions are brought into the decision-making process earlier and on a wider range of issues in an attempt to find mutually acceptable solutions to the challenges that are faced by the airline, as opposed to interacting primarily via the negotiation and adjudication of the collective bargaining contract. Partnering can be either formal or informal. In formal or structural partnerships, unions are involved in the governance of the firm, typically through ownership stakes, representation on the board of directors, or formal consultation processes. In informal partnerships, unions are involved through consultation or problem-solving processes that are not built in to the governance structure of the airline.

Stakeholder Outcomes

One of our key questions is how do different competitive and employment-relations strategies induce different outcomes on measures of importance to airlines' various stakeholders? What outcome measures are important? For airlines and investors, important outcomes include productivity, cost competitiveness (relative unit cost levels), and profitability. For customers, an important outcome, in addition to price, is service quality.

It is important to recognize three distinct dimensions of service quality. One dimension involves the level of amenities or "frills," as mentioned above (e.g., assigned seats, free meals, first class, and so forth). A second dimension is "reliability," particularly an airline's on-time and lost baggage performance. The third dimension is "friendliness": how an airline's staff—on the phone, on the ground, in the air—interacts with customers. These quality distinctions are achieved in different ways. Amenities can be imitated via additional investments and higher costs, whereas reliability and friendliness do not necessarily require higher costs but instead stem from superior operational coordination and workforce motivation. Airlines that rate highly on one dimension will not automatically rate highly on the other two. We keep these distinctions in mind in our analyses.

For employees, important outcomes include income levels, employment security, morale, and job satisfaction. This is linked to the idea of human resource advantage and the burgeoning literature on people (employees) as a source of competitive advantage.[16] Some potential sources of competitive advantage (e.g., new planes) can be fairly easily replicated via capital investment, whereas others, such as the reliability or "friendliness" of customer service, cannot be so easily replicated (e.g., will staff use their initiative or "run the extra mile" to help to solve problems that might not always be easily predictable or programmed).[17]

What's to Come

In the chapters that follow, we explore the competitive strategies and employment-relations strategies found in the United States (chapter 2) and in a range of other countries (chapter 3), before and after deregulation. In chapter 4 we analyze recent trends in quality, productivity, and costs, as well as employee outcomes. In chapter 5 we look more closely at selected new-entrant airlines and find a wide range of competitive and employment-relations strategies being used in this segment of the industry. In chapter 6, we examine several legacy airlines and identify the distinct strategies they have adopted to respond to competitive pressures from new-entrant airlines. These chapters each focus on selected U.S. airlines and those based in some other countries. In chapter 7, we summarize the strategies of new-entrant and legacy airlines, and offer lessons about how airlines can and do change their strategies over time in their efforts to compete more effectively.

We offer recommendations, using our historical and comparative analyses to discuss whether a path forward can be identified that can provide a better balance in stakeholder outcomes. We end on a positive note, arguing that if the parties learn from their experiences and from each other, in the United States and other countries, there is a path that deals with the pressures building up in the airline industry, offering hope for a better balance between investor, employee, customer, and societal interests. Key questions are whether and from where the leadership will come to get the industry moving down this path or whether the main parties might not take such action before there is a "perfect storm."

CHAPTER 2

Developments in the U.S. Airline Industry

Labor relations in the U.S. airline industry have often been a high-stakes enterprise. The national interest in airlines was recognized in the 1930s just as the industry was getting off the ground. After lobbying by the Air Line Pilots Association (ALPA), in 1936 the federal government brought airlines under the same labor law, the Railway Labor Act (RLA), that governs railroads, the other large transportation sector deemed worthy of national labor regulation. Thus the basic structure of labor relations in U.S. airlines was born. This structure came to be known as "class and craft" to signify that each occupational group—pilots, flight attendants, mechanics, customer service agents, and so forth—would have its own union and that each airline would negotiate separate agreements with each group. Under this law workers have the right to strike, but only after the government has provided mediation and only after other efforts to reach agreement have failed. The bargaining process under the RLA is described here:

Negotiating in the U.S. Airline Industry

Labor agreements in the U.S. airline industry do not have fixed expiration dates. Instead, they have "amendable" dates. After the amendable date, the provisions of the existing contract remain in effect until the parties reach a new agreement or until they have exhausted the provisions of the Railway Labor Act. New contract terms cannot be

imposed unilaterally and strikes or lockouts cannot be initiated until the parties have progressed through several steps that are regulated by the National Mediation Board (NMB).

If the parties cannot reach a contract agreement on their own through direct negotiations, either side may then apply for mediation services from the NMB. Once in mediation, negotiations continue until an agreement is reached or until the NMB declares an
impasse. At that point, the NMB offers the option of entering into binding arbitration. If
either party rejects the offer of arbitration, the NMB "releases" the parties. Once re-
leased, the parties then enter a thirty-day "cooling-off period," during which time the
existing contract provisions remain in effect. At the end of the cooling-off period, if the
parties still have not reached an agreement, the NMB chooses whether to let the parties
engage in "self-help"—that is, a strike by workers or a lockout or unilateral imposition of
new contract terms by management—or recommend that the president create a Presidential Emergency Board (PEB). The PEB, composed of three neutral experts, is allowed thirty days to deliberate and formulate a recommended settlement. After the PEB
issues its recommendations, another thirty-day cooling-off period begins. Finally, at the
end of the second cooling-off period, the parties are free to engage in self-help. As a final recourse, after the expiration of the second cooling-off period, the president can refer the case to Congress. Congress has the authority to legislate a settlement if it cannot
get the parties to resolve the dispute by other means.

At the same time, Congress sought stability by bringing the airline industry under the authority of the Civil Aeronautics Board (CAB), which regulated the entry of new airlines, the routes individual airlines could fly, and
the prices on all routes. Regulation was motivated by the destructive price
wars that had occurred between large airlines in the early 1930s. But regulation was also motivated by the belief that airlines served two critical national
interests—to provide reliable, safe transportation and to provide help to the
nation in times of war or other crises.

From the 1930s to the end of the regulatory period in 1978 the airline
industry expanded steadily. Just before deregulation, fourteen large airlines,
classified as "major airlines" by the Department of Transportation, dominated the U.S. market, with another twenty-three smaller airlines serving
various regional markets. By 1978, passengers were flying approximately 275
million miles per year. Unions grew significantly from the 1930s to 1978. At
the time of deregulation unions represented about 45 percent of the workforce and more than 60 percent of the nonmanagerial workforce. Labor relations in the airline industry were similar to labor relations in other large-scale
industries at that time. Wages and working conditions were governed by

collectively bargained labor contracts that became filled with comprehensive and complex work rules.[1] The relationship between airlines and their employees was generally at arm's length, heavily regulated by these contracts. Altogether, the airlines of that era fit into the control/accommodation employment-relations categories (see figure 1.2).

Though wages were set through firm-by-firm, craft-by-craft negotiations, cross-firm wage standardization was achieved through pattern bargaining. After one major union-airline pair reached an agreement, negotiators at other airlines felt pressure to match it. Because the Civil Aeronautics Board passed wage increases on to consumers by granting price increases, pattern bargaining worked both for unions and for airlines.

Negotiations were not always harmonious. In 1958 management sought to strengthen its hand in bargaining by forming a "Mutual Aid Pact" in which airlines that gained revenue from increased business because of a strike at another airline would share that revenue with the airline suffering the strike. Northwest Airlines took the prize for collecting the most from this Mutual Aid Pact (Eastern Airlines was second) because it had the worst strike record of all major airlines before the Mutual Aid Pact was abolished in 1978 under deregulation. Thus ended the first major effort at industry solidarity in response to union bargaining power.

How did the large airlines compete before deregulation? Since they could not control prices and had only limited flexibility in choosing routes and even less unilateral discretion in abandoning routes that proved to be unprofitable, they attempted to differentiate on the basis of service quality and economies of scale.

With a few exceptions, there was little effort to turn employment relations or human resources into sources of competitive advantage. Among the legacy airlines, Delta Airlines was the major exception. Delta's historic approach to employee and labor relations involved an implicit commitment to high wages, lifetime employment, and a "family" culture with the intention of substituting for union representation and inducing high levels of service from its employees. Delta followed a commitment/avoidance employment-relations strategy (figure 1.2). For a long time, this approach helped Delta maintain a reputation for delivering high-quality service. Delta's approach also discouraged all employees except its pilots and dispatchers from unionizing. In addition to Delta, two new-entrant firms attempted to turn employment relations into a source of strategic advantage—Pacific Southwest Airlines (PSA) and Southwest Airlines. PSA was founded in 1949 and Southwest began operations in 1971, both as small intrastate operations in California and Texas, respectively. Both were early pioneers of the low–cost airline model, and they adopted innovative, commitment-based employment approaches from the beginning. PSA was taken over by US Airways in 1987. We will discuss Southwest in detail in chapter 5. For now it is sufficient to note that it survived and grew in the regulated environment but operated stealthlike, largely below the radar screen of the large airlines or airline industry analysts. Little was learned by other airlines from the experiences of these two small firms during these years.

Deregulation: The Oscillating Cycle Begins

Deregulation came in 1978 when the Carter administration decided that the industry and its customers would be better served by being more open to new entrants, by ending price regulation, and by gradually relaxing control over the routes airlines could fly and the cities they could serve. For those who led the deregulation effort in the United States, the primary goal was to increase price and cost competition. In 1978, Alfred Kahn, chairman of the Civil Aeronautics Board, told Congress that "competition is the only persistently effective mechanism available to us for holding costs and prices in check, and for stimulating cost, price and service innovations."[2] Although Kahn mentioned service innovations, the emphasis at the time was on cost competition. Nearly thirty years later, Kahn looked back at his efforts with satisfaction and had good reason to do so: average fares measured in price-per–seat-mile had declined by 50 percent (adjusted for inflation) since deregulation, a price decline unmatched by any other mature industry. Only some agricultural industries—egg production, for example—came close to the same price performance, largely due to the increased productivity of both farmers and chickens![3] These highly favorably price trends fueled a dramatic expansion in passenger miles flown, growing from 250 million passenger miles in 1978 to 750 million passenger miles in 2005.

Reflections by the Father of Deregulation

At 89, Alfred Kahn doesn't fly as much as he used to. When he does, he can't help but smile and feel a sense of accomplishment when he sees how crowded the planes are these days. "Sometimes, I even gloat a little bit," he admits.

More than anyone else, Kahn, a Cornell University economist who headed the old Civil Aeronautics Board under President Carter, gets credit for the dramatic lowering of fares over the past 30 years that has powered the explosion of demand for air travel. Last year, a record 745 million passengers boarded flights in the USA.... In 1978, when the Airline Deregulation Act passed, the average air traveler paid 8.3 cents per mile for a flight. In 2006, travelers paid just less than half that.... Kahn estimates consumer saving at $5 billion to $10 billion a year (some estimates are even higher—closer to $20 billion a year).

Kahn says he'll gladly shoulder the blame for today's crowded conditions aboard commercial flights and for what he concedes in many cases is a dramatic reduction in service quality:

> People want both affordable and comfortable transportation. In the old days, you liked the empty middle seat next to you.... But in the old days, you also were paying for that middle seat next to you. You just didn't know it.[4]

[This account was first read by one of the authors while sitting in the company of grumpy and tired fellow passengers early in the morning the night after a cancelled flight due to a combination of congested East Coast traffic, a mechanical problem with the plane, and lack of a back-up crew or equipment to cope with these interacting problems.]

Deregulation introduced a new era of volatility to the industry. The seesaw-like pattern of industry profits and losses since 1978 is illustrated in figure 2.1. The oscillations that correspond to the ups and downs of the business cycle in the U.S. economy have been increasing in magnitude in the airline industry over time. As we will see, labor relations in the industry since deregulation have also followed an oscillating pattern, albeit not always in synch with the oscillations in profits and losses. And, like the profit pattern, the oscillations in wage movements have also increased in magnitude over time.

Many firms entered and exited the industry over the first three decades of deregulation. More than 250 new airlines started up between 1979 and 2005, but more than two hundred of them failed or were bought by other airlines. By 2000, there was a net growth of thirty airlines with operating licenses, not counting foreign airlines with landing rights in the United States. So in effect the number of airline firms operating in the United States grew from thirty-seven in 1978 to sixty-seven in 2000.[5]

The entry opportunity afforded by deregulation led to the creation of some highly visible new players. People Express Airlines was formed in 1981 around the concept of low fares, new employees not tainted by previous experience in the airline industry, and a high-commitment employment-relations model (though its implementation devolved into a dysfunctional version of high commitment, as described in chapter 5). New York Air was formed to compete

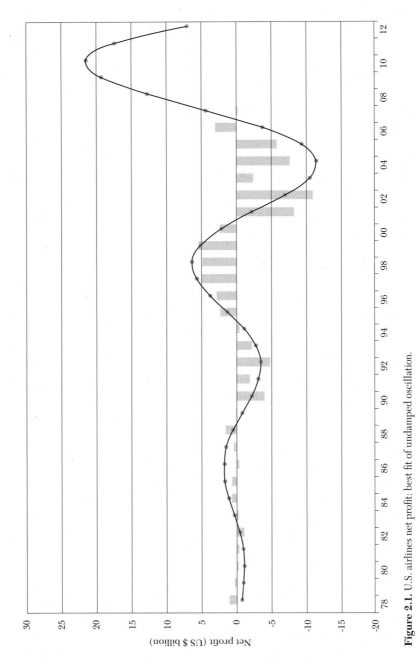

Figure 2.1. U.S. airlines net profit: best fit of undamped oscillation.

Source: John Hansman, MIT Global Airline Industry Project, International Advisory Board Meeting, October 24, 2007.

with Eastern on the lucrative Boston–New York and New York–Washington routes. Both of these new airlines started as nonunion organizations and their executives made it clear that they were determined to avoid unionization in the future. The effect of these lower cost new entrants was to put tremendous pressure on the legacy airlines to find ways to match their lower fares, if only long enough to put these less-well-financed companies out of business.

Initial Responses: Demands for Wage and Work Rule Concessions

The price pressures of the new entrants required some type of employment-relations response from the legacy airlines. Managers at the legacy airlines first approached their unions and demanded wage and work rule concessions. Their demands became very aggressive soon after deregulation for several reasons. First, the industry experienced a severe economic crisis between 1981 and 1983, resulting from a combination of economic recession, rising fuel prices, and rising interest rates that were especially damaging to airlines that had leveraged themselves to buy aircraft to expand in a deregulated context. Second, the August 1981 firing of the striking air traffic controllers by the Reagan administration not only worsened economic conditions in the airline industry (the Federal Aviation Administration forced the airlines to reduce capacity while it hired and trained new controllers) but signaled a hard-line stance against unions in the United States as a whole.[6]

Most unions resisted and refused to grant concessions unless the airline could credibly argue that concessions would reduce the need for significant layoffs.[7] But between 1980 and 1983 a significant number of unions at financially weaker airlines did grant wage and work rule concessions.

In 1983 American Airlines chief executive officer Robert Crandall devised a new approach: set starting wages for new employees lower than those for current employees doing the same job. His argument was that lower average wage costs would enable the firm to grow and therefore the company and the current workforce would be better off. Two-tier wage agreements were thus born. With varying levels of difficulty, almost every other major airline adopted some form of a two-tier wage system by 1986—the first shift in the employment system that was widely adopted by the legacy airlines following deregulation.

By the middle of the 1980s, however, unions began to regain bargaining power. In particular, a strike by pilots at United Airlines in 1985 proved highly effective, much to the surprise of many observers, and demonstrated to the industry that in the absence of the Mutual Aid Pact of the regulated era, pilot strikes were likely to be extremely costly. In fact, despite the aggressive labor relations battles after deregulation, strikes became much more rare than when the industry was regulated (as shown in figure 2.2), mainly because both sides came to realize that strikes were much more costly—in terms of both financial losses and the risk of job losses—than they had been in the regulated era.

Meanwhile, the industry rebounded from the 1981–83 recession, achieving steady growth in traffic and revenues. The legacy airlines adopted innovations unrelated to the employment relationship that proved highly successful in fending off the new entrants, such as hub-and-spoke networks, computer reservation systems, frequent flier loyalty programs, and revenue management systems.[8] Neither People Express nor New York Air survived to reach their fifth-year anniversary. By 1985 both had been taken over and absorbed into Frank Lorenzo's expanding portfolio of airlines. Of the fifty-one new airlines to enter the industry in the 1980s, by 2000 only two of them—America West and Midwest Express (later renamed Midwest Airlines)—had grown to become significant national airlines.[9]

As business conditions improved in the mid-1980s unions began to win wage increases and even whittled away the two-tier systems to the point where by the mid-1990s most airlines were no longer using two-tier systems.[10] But the upturn in the industry and the modest recovery of wages was short lived as another economic slowdown and then recession began in 1990. Some legacy airlines were on the brink of bankruptcy. Two household names, Eastern and Pan Am, went out of business during this period. Between 1990 and 1993 the top nine airlines in the country lost a total of $14 billion. As in the early 1980s, this led to efforts by the legacies to lower their labor costs through wage concessions. In this round of concessions, however, a new approach emerged: providing employees with an ownership stake in the business and seats on the board of directors in return for wage concessions. The early 1990s recession also spawned the emergence of another strategy related to the employment relationship: the shifting of short-haul routes—where the cost disadvantages of the legacies were most pronounced—to regional airlines affiliated with the legacies or to low-cost operations within the legacies themselves. As examples of the former, American Eagle, Air Wisconsin, Comair, and US Air Express expanded to serve American, United, Delta, and US Airways respectively. These turbo-prop and regional-jet operations, which feature lower wages and more exhausting working conditions (though they are generally still unionized), are separately managed but are linked

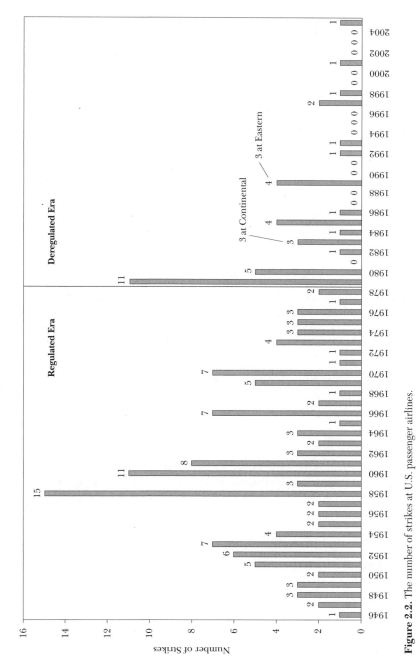

Figure 2.2. The number of strikes at U.S. passenger airlines.

Source: National Mediation Board.

into the legacy airline's route network and scheduling and marketing systems and sometimes share the legacy's brand name.

Still another variant—the start-up of a low-cost operation within a legacy airline itself (a so-called carrier within a carrier)—also involved establishing a separate short-haul operation with lower wage rates and more flexible work rules. Continental Lite (1993) and Shuttle by United (1994) represented the first wave of these efforts and others have been launched since. These subsidiary low-cost operations have not been unilaterally imposed by airlines but rather agreed to via bargaining with unions that accepted such arrangements in an effort to keep the parent airline competitive on short-haul routes and thus to preserve mainline jobs. However, as chapter 6 discusses, most of these carrier-within-a-carrier operations in the United States have been unsuccessful in achieving low enough costs and have not persisted for long.

By the mid-1990s the industry had recovered from recession, traffic and revenues were growing, but the airlines held back from negotiating wage increases. From 1993 to 1997, for example, the profits of legacy airlines increased by 28 percent while the wages paid the typical pilot grew only 7 percent.[11] This delaying strategy would come to haunt the industry as pressures for regaining lost earnings built up within the workforce. These pressures had their impact in 1999 and 2000 as the extended negotiations over pilot contracts at United, Northwest, American, US Airways, and Delta were settled with wage increases ranging from 20 to 30 percent. This produced a surge in labor cost differentials between legacies and new entrants that proved to be unsustainable in the new economic environment that unfolded in the early years of the twenty-first century.

The decade of the 1990s proved to be more successful for new entrants, placing additional pressure on the legacy airlines. The 1990s saw fewer new entrants than the 1980s (thirty-nine as opposed to fifty-one) but more of them appeared poised to succeed, with seventeen still remaining in operation by 2000, and with the founding in 1999 of the best-financed new entrant in all of U.S. aviation history, JetBlue Airways.[12]

Wages and Benefits from Deregulation to 9/11

The "golden era" of stability and wage improvement during the regulatory period ended with deregulation. But the seesaw battles described above only slowly began to erode the relatively high wage positions of airline employees. The bottom on wages would not fall out until the early years of the twenty-first century. Econometric studies of the union wage premium in airlines failed to see much change in the first decade following deregulation. By 1990, however, the wages of airline employees relative to comparable positions in other industries had declined about 10 percent. Then they grew again in the late 1990s before peaking in the first quarter of 2001.[13]

Efforts to Compete on Low Costs and Low Wages: The Lorenzo Legacy

No overview of industry developments after deregulation would be complete without discussion of one labor relations strategy that was influential in the 1980s and early 1990s: Frank Lorenzo's efforts to cut wages and break the unions in the airlines he purchased. In 1981 Lorenzo, who had acquired control of Texas International Airlines in the 1970s, won a hostile bid for Continental Airlines and changed the industry in ways that would come to dominate labor relations over the next decade. He took Continental into bankruptcy and used the bankruptcy law to cancel his labor contracts. In effect, he said to Continental employees, "You can come back to work tomorrow as long as you are willing to work for half of what you were making yesterday."

Caught by surprise, Continental's unions launched a futile strike. By 1985 Continental was out of bankruptcy and competing as the industry's first legacy low-cost, low-wage airline. Meanwhile Lorenzo went on a buying spree, purchasing the remains of a failing People Express and Frontier Airlines and then taking the huge risk of purchasing an ailing Eastern Airlines in the midst of a labor dispute. Following the strategy that worked for him at Continental, Lorenzo demanded pay cuts at Eastern, on top of previous pay cuts employees had just agreed to in exchange for stock and seats on the company board. He then began transferring assets, routes, and the reservation system from Eastern to his parent company. Eventually, in 1989, the mechanics union at Eastern and Lorenzo were embroiled in a strike that would turn out to be a death grip for Eastern. Lorenzo lost control of Eastern to its creditors and the company closed permanently in 1990. Lorenzo was effectively banned from the airline industry when the Department of Transportation revoked his aviation operating certificate for various alleged financial misdeeds.

Over the course of Lorenzo's reign, his companies were involved in seven of the thirteen strikes that occurred in the industry (see figure 2.2). In the pre-Lorenzo era Continental had a reputation for high-quality service; under Lorenzo, its customer-service ratings were consistently below the industry median while the short-term spike in profits it gained from cutting labor costs in 1983 were quickly replaced by losses that brought on a second bankruptcy in 1990. In the end, Lorenzo left his mark on the industry by exacerbating union-management tensions. And his approach demonstrated the risks and consequences of a low-wage, union-suppression, control-based employment strategy.

Twenty-first Century Shocks to the Industry and Employees

The above picture brings us to the turning point in the industry, 2000–2001. While September 11, 2001, the date of the terrorist attacks in New York and Washington, D.C., is often taken as the turning point for the industry. But, as can be seen in figure 2.1, the downward trends that have dominated the industry in recent years began in mid-2000 and were reinforced and deepened in the aftermath of 9/11. In the second half of 2000, the industry began to undergo a fundamental structural shift. Customers began refusing to pay the price premiums that legacy airlines charged over the new entrants, and thus an era of intense price pressure, reinforced by the abrupt declines in traffic following 9/11, produced devastating effects on the legacy airlines and their employees.

Since 2001, wages and benefits at the legacy airlines have been falling and new entrants have steadily gained market share so that by 2007 they accounted for more than 25 percent of passenger traffic in the United States (compared to less than 10 percent throughout most of the 1990s). Between 2001 and 2005 U.S. airline firms lost over $30 billion and employees have endured $15 billion in wage and benefit reductions, as well as 100,000 lost jobs. Four large firms entered bankruptcy: United, US Airways (twice), Delta, and Northwest. Pension plans at all these firms were terminated and turned over to a government insurance agency. So the costs borne by workers in the legacy airlines have been extremely high.

Industry Reconfiguration

Many mergers and consolidations have taken place in the industry over the years since deregulation. In 1986 and 1987, for instance, Delta acquired Western; Northwest acquired Republic; Texas Air acquired People Express, Frontier, and Eastern; and US Air acquired PSA and Piedmont. More recently, American purchased TWA out of bankruptcy in 2001 and America West acquired US Airways out of bankruptcy in 2005 (and adopted the US

Airways name). A bid by US Airways for bankrupt Delta in 2006 failed, but more mergers are likely. For example, as of April 2008, Northwest and Delta have agreed to merge (pending government approval). If that merger occurs, industry observers expect more mergers to follow.

The other dominant development in the industry in the twenty-first century has been the emergence and growth of new entrants with more staying power than the first wave, along with the steady increase in the strength and market share of the original new-entrant airline, Southwest. ValuJet (later renamed AirTran), for example, put significant pressure on Delta by competing in its Southeast regional markets at lower prices with lower costs. JetBlue grew rapidly from its launch in 2001 and has had a similar effect on legacy airlines.

From Stability to Volatility

The picture painted in figure 2.1 of an increasingly volatile industry with oscillations growing in magnitude summarizes what has happened under deregulation. In the 1930s, as the U.S. airline industry was in its takeoff stage, the government stepped in to regulate the industry in an effort to dampen a similar pattern of volatility. Although this ushered in a fifty-year period of steady growth and relative stability, it also led to a pattern of increasing wages and prices and made it nearly impossible for new firms to enter the industry. This changed dramatically with deregulation in 1978. The threat and reality of new entrants and the newfound price competition stimulated innovation and change in employment relations and in the product mix (hub-spoke networks, regional carriers, new low-cost entrants) and services (e.g., frequent flyer programs, e-tickets, online travel and booking options). Employment relations went from being similar across most firms and tied together through pattern bargaining to experimentation in many directions, including wage reductions, two-tier compensation structures, employee ownership plans, union avoidance and suppression, and fledgling efforts at labor-management partnerships. However, none of these efforts have yet emerged as a dominant or stable pattern. Instead, labor relations, like profits, have followed a highly cyclical pattern and one in which the increasing oscillations in wage and benefit movements echo the trends in industry profits. All indications point to the continuation and acceleration of the seesaw pattern in labor relations and perhaps in industry profits and losses, unless something is done to break out of these patterns.

CHAPTER 3

Developments in the Airline Industry in Other Countries

To what extent have airline managers, union leaders, and policymakers in other countries tried different approaches to competitive and employment-relations strategies? Are the volatility and innovation in the U.S. airline industry exceptional or are the strategies chosen in other countries' airlines converging on U.S. patterns? What might policymakers and others in the United States learn from other countries? Do cultural and institutional differences in other countries influence how airlines compete, interact with their employees, and serve their customers? To answer these questions, we will consider selected examples from elsewhere in the world.

Historically, the United States has had the world's largest civilian aviation market. By 2010, however, it is predicted that for the first time in history Asia will be the world's largest aviation market. By 2025, it is predicted that both Europe and Asia will have larger aviation markets than all of North America. These estimates suggest that in 2025 the three largest economic regions will have the following approximate shares of the world's aviation traffic: North America, 25 percent (it was 31 percent in 2005); Europe, 27 percent (29 percent in 2005); and Asia, 32 percent (26 percent in 2005).[1]

Differences between Airlines in the United States and Other Countries

Airlines in other countries are typically different from their counterparts in the United States in three main ways. First, in the post–World War II period most of the legacy airlines in Europe and Asia were at least partly owned by governments, including such leading examples as Aer Lingus, Air France, KLM, Alitalia, British Airways, Lufthansa, Qantas, SAS (Scandinavian Airline System), and Singapore Airlines. Many of these airlines were launched after World War I by entrepreneurs who had been pilots in the war. These new enterprises were often financially unstable, however, and so they failed. In many cases they were taken over by national governments. Such ownership was also encouraged by the bilateral forms of international regulation whereby each country designated its national "flag carrier." Governments wanted airlines that would be financially stable and that would project a good image for their country. Furthermore, after World War II, as in the United States, governments were increasingly aware of the strategic importance of airlines for defense purposes.[2] State-owned airlines, in particular, were potential resources to be mobilized if necessary.

A second difference between U.S. airlines and their foreign counterparts is that, outside the United States, most legacy airlines focus on international flights. This is because, apart from the United States, many other domestic markets are relatively small. Moreover, in Europe, short-haul airlines face serious competition from surface transport, especially the growing high-speed-rail network, while in the United States, by comparison, airlines do not generally face such competition.

Third, the U.S. airline industry was the first to experience deregulation. U.S. entrepreneurs pioneered the development of new-entrant airlines. Most other countries have been slower to deregulate.

In addition to these common differences between U.S. and non-U.S. airlines, we identify two broad categories of context, based on the "varieties of capitalism." This concept distinguishes between two ideal types of institutional context: liberal market economies and coordinated market economies.[3] The United States is a classic liberal market economy. Other English-speaking countries such as the United Kingdom and Australia have broadly similar forms of political economy to that of the United States. These economies can be characterized as ones where firms tend to implement control-oriented employee-relations strategies and cost-competitiveness strategies that focus more on wage minimization than on enhancing productivity.

In contrast with these liberal market economies, the Germanic and Scandinavian countries, for example, have coordinated market economies. Such economies are characterized by interlocking systems of employment relations, training, and education that work together to regulate compensation and employment conditions. Coordinated market economies encourage firms to partner with unions in strategic cooperation and to prevent some of the practices associated with liberal market economies, such as adversarialism and layoffs. In this chapter we will introduce examples of airlines based in liberal market and coordinated market economies and elsewhere. We consider several of these examples in more depth in subsequent chapters.

We focus on the industry in a few European countries. The United Kingdom and Germany are the two largest airline markets in Europe. Ireland is the home of Ryanair, Europe's largest and most prominent new-entrant airline. Three Scandinavian countries share a legacy airline, SAS. In addition, we consider Australia, which has a liberal market economy like those of the United States and the United Kingdom. We also will discuss a few airlines based in Asia and the Middle East.

Regulation and Deregulation

As in the United States, airlines in other countries have been highly regulated. This regulation is overseen by the International Civil Aviation Organisation (ICAO), a United Nations agency. ICAO is an intergovernmental agency. With an imperative to ensure safety, ICAO has developed regulations that cover many aspects of airline operations, including technical, navigational, and resources, including human resources. For instance, ICAO regulations cover the "numbers of flight and cabin crew, their training and licensing, their duties and functions on board and their work loads and schedules."[4] These regulations have limited the issues that can be decided by national-level policymakers, managers, and unions. One unintended side effect of this international regulatory regime has been to limit innovation, as airlines in member countries have simply followed ICAO regulations.

In an attempt to provide a counterweight to the ICAO and governments, the International Air Transport Association (IATA) represents the collective interests of airlines. IATA has operated in effect as a cartel of suppliers. It holds private conferences and has established secret commercial arrangements. This context seemed to encourage a culture of price-fixing and other forms of anticompetitive behavior by legacy airlines.[5] Such price-fixing is illegal under antitrust provisions in the United States and some other countries. Since the 1980s IATA's fare rules have been minimized and largely ignored by most carriers.

If IATA's aim was to maximize members' profits, however, it has not been effective, for the international industry has not generally been very profitable and many airlines have gone bankrupt. Between 1970 and 2000, approximately one third of the world's airlines made a loss rather than a profit. In 2007, airlines' global revenues were $485 billion and their net profits were $5.1 billion. It is forecast that in 2008, airline revenues will be $520 billion and they will make a net loss of $5.2 billion.[6] This is a cyclical industry (see figure 3.1). Profits made by many airlines in boom periods have been wiped out by their losses in recessionary periods. The lack of long-term economic viability of many legacy airlines was long disguised by a high degree of protection, government ownership, public subsidies, and irrational investors. (For some of the latter owning an airline seems to be a national imperative or a form of ego trip.)

The International Transport Workers Federation (ITF) includes 654 unions in 148 countries representing nearly 4.5 million transport workers across many airline occupations (as well as workers from other transport industries). As in the United States, pilots in most other countries are organized separately from the unions that organize other occupational groups. The International Federation of Air Line Pilots Associations (IFALPA) claims to represent more than 100,000 pilots in more than ninety-five countries. ITF and IFALPA represent employees' interests at ICAO and other international regulatory bodies, especially with regard to aviation safety and security.[7]

Under ICAO's umbrella, each country has had its own form of regulatory arrangements for airlines. Toward the end of the twentieth century, the European Union (EU)[8] became more proactive in promoting deregulation, gradually taking over this role from its member states. Before deregulation, the legacy airlines enjoyed monopolies on many domestic routes. On many international routes, there was typically a monopoly, or a duopoly of two legacy national flag-airlines—one based in the home country of each airport, reflecting the numerous bilateral agreements between countries.

The international and national regulatory agencies shape the context for the parties' choices about competitive and employment-relations strategies. These agencies, however, are not generally involved in directly regulating employment relations. For most occupational groups in most airlines, employment relations are regulated by collective bargaining and/or works

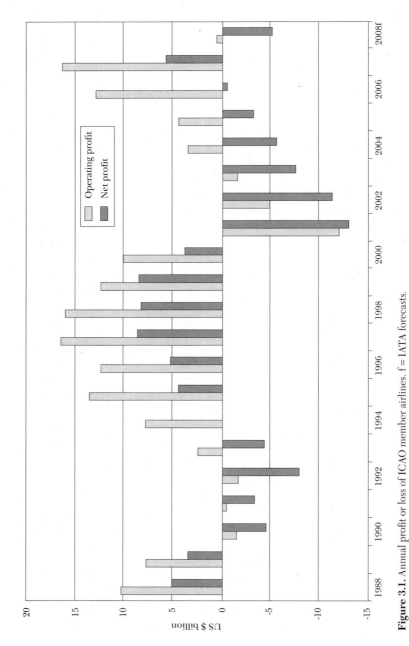

Figure 3.1. Annual profit or loss of ICAO member airlines. f = IATA forecasts.

Source: Rigas Doganis, International Air Transport Association (IATA) and International Civil Aviation Organization (ICAO). The data includes ICAO member airlines.

councils. But in some cases, for example, in airlines that do not recognize unions for collective bargaining, employment relations are determined by managerial prerogative or even by governments where airline staff are in effect government employees.

European initiatives toward deregulation were influenced by the earlier U.S. example of deregulation in the 1970s and the consequent renegotiation of international bilateral agreements between the United States and some European countries.[9] This was not done all at once. The process was much more gradual than in the United States, however, since the EU is a federation of member states, with their own governments, regulatory preferences, and stakeholder interests. The stakeholders include the workers and their unions. Most of the unions are linked in the European Congress of Trade Unions (ETUC), which lobbies the EU directly. The ETUC and unions have more influence over the EU than U.S. unions usually have on U.S. administrations. Such influence is exerted both through direct lobbying and through political parties (e.g., labor or social democratic parties) in which unions have a strong influence.

The EU began to relax airline regulations in the mid-1980s; the process has continued into the twenty-first century.[10] There are continuing debates about deregulation to destinations outside the EU. We offer more detail on the United Kingdom than on most of the other countries, for, like the United States, the United Kingdom is also a liberal market economy. But the United Kingdom has a much smaller domestic market and is also subject to regulatory influences from the coordinated market economies of the European Union.

Liberal Market Economies

Outside the United States, moves toward deregulation and privatization were led by the United Kingdom in the 1980s.[11] This is why, apart from the United States, the United Kingdom, along with Ireland, led the way in launching new-entrant airlines.[12]

The United Kingdom

Typical of a liberal market economy, the United Kingdom has adversarial traditions of employment relations.[13] However, especially since the advent of the post-1997 Labour government, there have been initiatives there to develop partnership arrangements between employers, employees, and unions. Nevertheless, there are at least three obstacles to the establishment of partnership agreements: resistance to the concept; low trust between the parties; and confusion about what partnership is. One influential definition suggests that a genuine partnership ought to feature

- Joint commitment to the success of the enterprise
- Efforts to build trust
- An attempt to address the issue of employment security in exchange for flexibility
- Provision of quality training programmes
- Information sharing and joint problem-solving with managers and employees together, whether in formal consultation or not.[14]

British Airways is the United Kingdom's largest and oldest airline. In 1919, its forerunner company launched the world's first daily international scheduled air service, between London and Paris. There were few passengers, high fares, and tough working conditions. Later, several UK airlines merged to form the original British Airways, which was privately owned. In 1939, the UK government "nationalised" British Airways. In 1974 the government formed a new British Airways by merging its long-haul airline with its shorter haul British European Airways. In the immediate postmerger period, British Airways (BA) was not profitable due in part to a recession. But in order to be privatized in 1987 by the Thatcher government, BA had to become profitable by the mid-1980s. It sought profitability partly by cutting labor costs, by laying off many people.[15] BA has continued to be profitable in most years, though not in the aftermath of 9/11.

British Airways' rhetoric has long included campaigns to foster employee commitment and engagement, saying that "people are our most important asset."[16] Nevertheless, BA periodically launches campaigns to cut labor costs. These two campaigns tend contradict each other. For instance, while BA was advertising its excellent customer service, its attempt to restructure allowances and pay scales for flight attendants prompted a strike in the summer of 1997. BA adopted a tough stance, threatening to sack strikers and to sue them for breach of contract. BA's stance was counterproductive, however. It appeared to be bullying, and turned moderate staff opinion against BA:

> Although only 300 cabin crew joined the three-day strike in July, more than
> 2,000 went on sick leave which resulted in longer-term disruptions through

August. The cost of the strike was estimated at $245 million. The effects on staff morale, service and company reputation (further damaged by the simultaneous introduction of a new baggage-handling system which led to record levels of lost baggage) could not be quantified.[17]

BA has had many other examples of adversarial employment-relations and industrial disruption.

British Airways: Examples of Adversarial Employment-Relations Episodes

- In the week before the terror attacks of 9/11, BA announced eighteen hundred layoffs because of a global economic downturn.
- On September 20, 2001, BA announced it would shed seven thousand jobs in response to falling demand.
- In the summer of 2003 there was a lengthy dispute over the introduction of a new system for clocking-on to work at London's Heathrow Airport, one of the world's busiest.
- A year later, there were days of delays on BA flights associated with a threatened strike involving three thousand check-in staff.
- In April 2005, a female pilot won a sex discrimination case against BA after it refused to allow her to work part-time.
- BA lost more than $80 million in summer 2005 in the Gate Gourmet dispute, where baggage handlers walked out in sympathy with 670 outsourced catering workers who were sacked. BA cancelled nine hundred flights, while delays and cancellations disrupted the travel plans of around 100,000 passengers.[18]
- In November 2005, BA announced it would cut six hundred management jobs by March 2008.
- In January 2006, BA revealed that its pension fund had a massive deficit.
- In the fall of 2006, BA received much public criticism for suspending an employee for wearing a necklace bearing the Christian cross over her uniform.
- In January 2007 BA's stock lost almost $200 million in value after flight attendants called strikes—which were averted at the last minute—in reaction to proposed reductions in pay, pensions, and sick leave.[19]

In the 2001–06 period, BA shed eighteen thousand jobs. Subsequently BA announced, "We will continue to introduce new work practices and efficiencies, which will allow us to run the business with fewer people." BA warned staff to brace themselves for more job losses as it decided to cut costs even further.[20]

BA has followed a paradoxical course between, on the one hand, being willing to endure strikes and implementing cost cutting, and, on the other, trying to foster partnership and employee engagement strategies. When it was privatized in 1987, BA retained its existing collective bargaining arrangements with most categories of its workforce as well as mechanisms for consulting with unions. Following a dispute in 1996, BA has had a formal partnership agreement with the pilots union, the British Airline Pilots Association. However, the union says that BA generally does not honor the spirit of partnership. Moreover, only 54 percent of BA pilots had a favorable view of such a partnership approach. Pilots at other British airlines tended to have a much more positive view of partnership with their airline, even though all but one of those other airlines did not have a formal partnership with the pilots union.[21]

In 2005 BA launched another initiative, the Industrial Relations Change Programme, "to reduce communication barriers and improve understanding."[22] In 2005 more than 1,800 managers and 220 union representatives attended workshops. In 2006 BA stated that "our people want fulfilling and secure jobs, a good working environment, fair reward and personal development. We want them to come to work, do the job well and be flexible." Nevertheless, it is very difficult to maintain and develop a genuine sense of partnership in a context in which there is a continuing emphasis on cutting jobs and benefits.

Since British Airways became a privatized company, in many ways it has been a success story in a highly volatile industry.[23] For years it claimed to be "the world's favourite airline." Nonetheless, as the BBC observed in 2007, "The relations between management and employees seem to have been ossified: . . . there appears to be considerable mistrust of management among employees."[24] Or, as another commentator put it, "staff morale has remained stranded on the runway."[25] Although BA uses the rhetoric of partnership with unions, with employee commitment and engagement, in reality it accommodates rather than partners with unions. Further, in reality it is not yet achieving a consistent high degree of employee commitment; rather, it seems to practice more of a control approach.

Before deregulation, BA had dominated UK domestic and international scheduled aviation from the United Kingdom. Sometimes others challenged BA's dominance of scheduled services, but in a regulated market the new entrants struggled to survive. Either they collapsed or BA bought them.

After winning hard-fought approval from governments on both sides of the Atlantic, a flamboyant pioneer of new-entrant airlines, Freddie Laker, founded Skytrain, flying between London and New York in 1977. This was one of the first international new entrants, and attracted much public support, particularly because it offered low-fare flights. When BA and other airlines colluded to lower their fares in response, the public supported Laker as an underdog. People donated more than $2 million to help keep his business alive. Even so, by 1982 Laker's Skytrain was forced into bankruptcy, after the plane that it used, the DC-10, was grounded and its suppliers withdrew credit. Three years later, the British courts ruled that other airlines had used illegal price pressure. BA and other airlines were ordered to pay Laker about $6 million and settle claims with his creditors. With the benefit of hindsight, Laker said:

> I had 29 airlines ganged up against me. . . . None of them seem to have the idea that . . . perhaps they were spending too much money on aeroplanes and not enough getting the aeroplanes in the air for the right number of hours. I can't see it stopping because the governments seem to love it.[26]

Two years after the failure of Skytrain, another swashbuckling English entrepreneur, Richard Branson, diversified from the record industry to establish Virgin Atlantic as another international new entrant. Branson was inspired by Laker's strategies. Virgin also offered lower fares, but Virgin also promised a high-quality approach. Branson started his airline on the basis that the airline would have to succeed within a year; otherwise, he would exit the market. He started with a one-year lease on a secondhand Boeing 747. To minimize costs if the venture failed, he had a one-year limit on everything associated with starting up. This included limiting initial employment contracts to only one year.[27] He employed pilots who had retired and were already enjoying a pension from British Airways, so they were willing to work for lower salaries.

Although BA again engaged in anticompetitive behavior against its new rival, Virgin Atlantic continued to develop prime long-haul routes from the United Kingdom. It grew into a niche international airline known for its high-quality service, with "frills" that even included in-flight massages. Its marketing was brilliant. As one captain said, "It is a rock 'n' roll airline." Branson held parties for the staff and boasted that while every other airline that Virgin had competed against in 1984 (except BA, which had been supported by the government) had entered bankruptcy, Virgin had survived "thanks largely to the attitude and hard work of its staff—by everyone working well together."[28]

Nevertheless, for its first fifteen years, Virgin Atlantic adopted a union-avoidance strategy. It recognized unions only after it had to do so under the new Labour government, which reformed labor law in 1999. A majority of pilots and flight attendants voted for union recognition. Within a decade, there was a high degree of union density among the pilots, though it was lower among the flight attendants.

Virgin Atlantic survived the 9/11 crisis, but it cut more than twelve hundred jobs on a compulsory basis. Before doing so, it had threatened a larger number of mandatory layoffs, and had proposed to rehire staff selectively on inferior terms. In spite of Branson's joviality, Virgin, like BA, has had an adversarial relationship with the unions that represent its pilots and flight attendants. It accommodated the unions rather than partnering with them. Further, its competitive strategy included trying to minimize labor costs.

Flight attendants in Unite the Union voted to strike to further a pay claim in early 2008. In an acknowledgment that other airlines offer more pay, billionaire Sir Richard Branson provoked outrage when he sent a letter to the homes of the flight attendants that said in part, "For some of you, more pay than Virgin Atlantic can afford may be critical to your lifestyle and if that is the case you should consider working elsewhere."[29] However, after the dispute was averted, he opined: "Our cabin crew are the best flying and continue to provide the highest standards of customer service." The union added: "We now have the opportunity to ensure an improved relationship with Virgin Atlantic in the future."[30]

In 1995 a Greek entrepreneur, Stelios Haji-Ioannou, launched another new entrant airline in the United Kingdom: easyJet. By contrast with the two full-service airlines, BA and Virgin Atlantic, easyJet is a low-cost "no-frills" airline and focuses on short or medium-haul routes in Europe. Sir Stelios (as he became later) launched a series of publicity stunts, such as convincing a UK television network to launch a reality show, *Airline*, that featured easyJet, and wearing a comical orange jumpsuit while handing out free easyJet tickets on the inaugural flight of BA's low-cost subsidiary, Go! (EasyJet later took over Go!)

EasyJet was founded on the principle of maximizing aircraft utilization and no frills. Although easyJet is based in the United Kingdom, it has also developed hubs in other parts of Europe. By 2007, easyJet claimed to be operating more flights per day than any other European airline. It is planning to grow by 15 percent a year for the next few years. It has generally been profitable, but for the six months ended March 31, 2008, it made a net loss of $85.4 million, owing largely to higher fuel costs and integration costs after it acquired GB Airways.[31]

In its early years, easyJet's employment-relations strategy was in the control category, along with union-avoidance. One comparative study found that in 2002 easyJet's pilots had a lower level of job satisfaction and a higher level of turnover than those in five other British airlines.[32] However, by 2007 easyJet had adopted more of a commitment approach, along with a union accommodation strategy. EasyJet's director of people Mike Campbell explained: "We had a belief that in a service industry the people factor can make a difference but we needed to test that in an airline environment. At Southwest we saw that it was possible to run a profitable low-cost airline and still have a strong people culture."[33] Despite being a low-cost airline, by 2008 the pilots union perceived that easyJet's behavior was closer to a partnership approach than that of BA and Virgin Atlantic.

The Republic of Ireland

On the other side of the Irish Sea, Ireland's national flag airline Aer Lingus was founded in 1936.[34] Servicing long- and short-haul routes, legacy airline Aer Lingus flies to British and continental European airports, as well as to the United States and the Middle East.

At Aer Lingus, 92 percent of the workers are union members. In the 1970s and 1980s there were strikes in response to productivity initiatives undertaken by Aer Lingus to cut costs. In 2002, a strike and a lockout involved Aer Lingus and its 530 pilots. Aer Lingus also initiated pay freezes, voluntary layoffs, and reorganizations. Against the background of national attempts to introduce more social partnership (between companies and unions) in Ireland, however, Aer Lingus also introduced employee profit sharing and stock ownership. This was a pragmatic trade-off by the airline in response to union pressures. In each instance of change, Aer Lingus had to deal with the unions, but the extent to which they made concessions was a function of the relative power situation. Before the partial privatization of Aer Lingus in 2006, the unions were in a relatively strong position; subsequently their position was weaker. In early 2007, Aer Lingus tried to introduce change unilaterally. This was criticized by the Irish Labour Court.

Nevertheless, the Labour Court also recognized the need for change, giving the substantive point to the management in its recommendation, but the procedural one to the union. Aer Lingus fits in the accommodate category of union-management relations.

In 1985, as deregulation began, Tony Ryan cofounded Ryanair to compete with Aer Lingus. New entrant Ryanair was based in Dublin and its first international routes were to Britain:

> Ryanair recognized it was going up against a formidable opponent. . . . Aer
> Lingus aircraft were all painted a patriotic green and bore the names of Irish
> saints. It was a steadfast airline with an impressive safety record, and Irish
> people generally believed that they owned part of it.[35]

After a few setbacks for the struggling Ryanair, Michael O'Leary took over its leadership in 1993. He transformed it into a fast-growing and highly profitable low-cost airline. Ryanair's success occurred against the background of changes in government competition policy and a governmental directive to Aer Lingus to give up its landing slots at one of London's secondary airports (Stansted). Also, Ryanair's low fares helped it to grow new business, so it was not simply taking passengers from Aer Lingus.

Nonetheless, with increased competition, chiefly from Ryanair, as well as the impact of 9/11 and other issues, Aer Lingus found it increasingly difficult to operate as a legacy airline, so in 2002 it reinvented itself as a low-cost airline.

Ryanair's employment strategy is to focus on low costs via wage minimization and on employee control. Although Ryanair has denied accusations that it is anti-union, "this claim does not hold up in the face of extensive evidence of union suppression."[36] According to an ITF survey, Ryanair is one of only a few airlines in Europe that does not recognize a union for collective bargaining. It aggressively avoids unions via suppression. This has induced the ITF to launch a web-based campaign (Ryan-be-Fair) that is attempting to mobilize Ryanair workers across Europe to organize. According to the ITF:

> Discontent is never far from the surface at Ryanair, where workers feel mis-
> trusted, marginalised and mistreated. Once again Michael O'Leary's bombast
> and bullying has brought it bubbling to the surface, and he is going to have to
> either accept the consequences or learn to behave like any other normal, civi-
> lised, twenty-first century employer.[37]

Nevertheless, despite taking a tough stance toward its customers as well as its staff, Ryanair, along with easyJet, has become one of the new-entrant airlines leading the growth of the European market for cheap, no-frills flights.[38] Like the flamboyant entrepreneurs Laker, Branson, and Stelios in the United Kingdom, O'Leary has cultivated an image as a kind of popular folk hero. He promotes his new-entrant airline as offering low fares to challenge the high fares of an old legacy monopolist. Branson adopted a similar approach in Australia.

Australia

Australia, like the United States, is a liberal market economy. Although Australia has less than 10 percent of the U.S. population, like the United States Australia has an extensive domestic aviation market. For most of the post–World War II period, the Australian government had a "two airline" policy which meant, in effect, a duopoly. The domestic mainline routes were shared between Australian Airlines (later merged with Qantas) and Ansett. Qantas was founded in 1920 and is Australia's dominant legacy airline. Since it was privatized in the 1990s it has operated profitably in international and domestic markets. Ansett was mainly a domestic airline. The strategic position of both of these legacies was to offer full service. These airlines had relatively high operating costs and fares.

Following several short-lived attempts since the 1980s to start a third domestic airline, Impulse and Virgin Blue both launched airlines in 2000. Branson supported a business plan to develop a Virgin-branded new entrant in Australia. [39] Branson provided a onetime equity investment of nearly $10 million. An Australian Virgin Group executive in the United Kingdom, Brett Godfrey, cofounded Virgin Blue Airlines. He became its chief executive officer and his team saw Southwest Airlines as a role model.

The almost simultaneous launch of Virgin Blue and Impulse precipitated a price war, which temporarily reduced fares to historically low levels. Qantas and Ansett dropped their fares to match the new entrants' start-up deals. Because the legacies had higher costs, the fare reductions were a challenge for all of the airlines. During this price war, Qantas took over Impulse, which it later relaunched as a low-cost subsidiary, Jetstar, and Ansett went bankrupt in 2001, on the day after 9/11.

Despite an experiment with an "accord" policy (a form of government-union social partnership) between 1983 and 1996, Australia still has adversarial employment relations, but to a much lesser extent than the pre-1983 tradi-tions.[40] Both Australia's legacy airlines were highly unionized across all oc-cupational categories. They had a general employment-relations strategy to accommodate unions. In 1989–90 the two legacy domestic airlines, with strong support from the federal government, fought a major dispute for more than six months with the Australian Federation of Air Pilots. This involved a lockout and mass resignations of most of the legacies' domestic pilots.[41]

In the early twenty-first century, in the face of the new-entrant airlines enjoying a 30 to 40 percent cost advantage, Qantas was still accommodating the unions, but its rhetoric was increasingly confrontational. It periodically contemplated "offshoring" various operations to other countries, which had lower labor costs. It established bases in Asia and the United Kingdom, but the outsourcing of much maintenance was limited by opposition from politi-cians and unions. By 2008 Qantas was still maintaining a strong balance sheet, even though it was facing more competition, especially since more new entrants had begun to enter the Australian international and domestic markets alongside Virgin Blue, including Emirates from Dubai, AirAsia from Malaysia, and Tiger from Singapore.

Coordinated Market Economies

In comparison with their approaches when they were state-owned enter-prises in regulated markets, the three legacy airlines discussed above—British Airways, Aer Lingus, and Qantas—have been adopting increasingly tough management tactics in relation to their employees and unions. They con-tinue to accommodate unions, but have not really partnered with them. To what extent do coordinated market economies provide a different context for low-cost competition in the airline industry? Germany and Scandinavia il-lustrate a different context.

Germany

Lufthansa is the legacy airline that has long dominated German aviation. Although the original Lufthansa was born in 1930, the current Lufthansa was reborn in 1955. The German Federal Republic, the state of North Rhine-Westphalia, and the national public-sector railroad each held major stakes in Lufthansa. The reborn Lufthansa also had private shareholders. Since 1966, Lufthansa's shares have been traded on stock exchanges. Lufthansa has involved its employees in profit sharing and has given them the opportunity to choose between cash and preference shares since 1970. When Lufthansa was fully privatized in 1997, employees received more than 3 percent of its shares.

Lufthansa has usually made a profit. Even in 2001, the year of the 9/11 crisis, when many airlines lost money, Lufthansa earned a small profit. Lufthansa has developed into a mega-aviation group with nearly ninety-five thousand employees.[42]

Germany has collective bargaining on wages and working conditions involving unions and employers.[43] Lufthansa's managers are constrained by the German form of social partnership: codetermination. Such German firms are obliged to treat unions as partners. Lufthansa and other companies based in the coordinated market economy of Germany have a two-tier board. The supervisory (upper-level) board appoints, supervises, and advises the executive board. The executive board is responsible for the implementation of corporate strategies and managing the company. The two boards collaborate.[44] The supervisory board has twenty voting members. The ten shareholder representatives are elected by the annual general meeting, the ten employee representatives are elected by Lufthansa employees. Multiple stakeholders (employees, executives, other shareholders) are embedded in the company's structure. This strongly influences Lufthansa's approach to deregulation and the growth of competition from new entrants. In contrast with British Airways, where Lufthansa has outsourced functions, they have remained under the same collective bargaining umbrella. This has been true even in major functions such as maintenance and cargo.

Because of the formal role that labor plays in corporate governance, in contrast to most airlines in other varieties of capitalism, Lufthansa does not have as wide a range of options for adjusting employment conditions and employment-relations strategies in the face of market changes. Lufthansa did reduce labor costs, but it did so in consultation and agreement with the unions, which negotiated job-protection agreements. Thus, unlike some of the U.S. legacies, Lufthansa did not (and probably could not) impose layoffs on its workforce as an early response to changes experienced in its markets. Instead, managers had to share information on market developments and consult with labor representatives about potential strategic responses and the full range of employment-relations issues.

This institutional requirement has fostered a continuing labor-management partnership at Lufthansa. The company's partnership approach facilitated its success in restructuring to become profitable again after its losses and cash-flow problems in the early 1990s' recession. Union and works council involvement in Lufthansa's restructuring ensured that there was no major deterioration in working conditions, nor were there mass layoffs.

To what extent does this different context induce different strategies and behavior from German-based airlines compared with those based in liberal market economies? Drawing on their study of three national airlines, Peter Turnbull and his colleagues argue that in the context of their relatively open markets, the British and Irish legacies have been "permitted, if not compelled, to pursue short-term, cost-minimizing strategies inimical to their labor-management partnerships."[45] By contrast, Lufthansa developed a competitive strategy consistent with and complementary to its partnership approach to labor-management relations, including greater integration rather than outsourcing. Instead of simply cutting labor costs at its mainline airline, Lufthansa launched its own low-cost subsidiary Germanwings in an attempt to respond to the challenge of increasing new-entrant competition. Toward the end of the twentieth century, several new-entrant airlines were launched in Germany in anticipation of deregulation there. Air Berlin is the largest, while others launched there include Hapag-Lloyd Express and Condor.

After 9/11, many U.S. airlines immediately announced layoffs, typically of about 20 percent of their total workforce. Although Lufthansa also suffered a significant loss of revenue following 9/11, it did not implement any layoffs. Rather, managers and unions agreed on other, socially more responsible measures, such as long-term unpaid leave and part-time working, which meant that Lufthansa was able to avoid having to fire people.[46]

Scandinavia

Scandinavia includes relatively small countries: Denmark and Norway, each with about five million inhabitants, and Sweden, with about ten million.[47] From a distance, the three countries may seem to be similar. They have similar forms of government that combine a welfare state with an open market economy. However, there are important differences, in terms of their history, political economy, and development of industry. For instance, there are differences in terms of tax structures and inflation and recession cycles. Sweden has a very high level of payroll taxes for employers, Denmark lacks such taxes, and Norway is in between these extremes. These countries have not joined the single European currency system; there are still varying interest levels and exchange rates between them.

As in other European countries, civil aviation in Scandinavia was developed by private enterprises and it began to grow in the 1920s. World War II stopped developments in Denmark and Norway, which were occupied by Germany, while it continued in a limited way in Sweden, which was neutral. Emerging from the war with scarce resources, the major private airlines, visionary industrialists, and the governments of the three countries decided that a joint effort would be the best way to develop Scandinavian aviation on an international scale. Between 1946 and 1950, they created a pan- Scandinavian airline, Scandinavian Airline System (SAS). SAS was structured as a consortium owned by the three national private airlines, which in turn were listed on the three national stock exchanges. The shares of these three national airlines were half owned by each of the three countries' governments and half by private investors. SAS is still half owned by the three governments, but a holding company owns the three founding airlines; its shares are now listed in parallel on the three stock exchanges.

As elsewhere, civil aviation in Scandinavia was highly regulated. SAS operated the routes to and from Scandinavia, effectively in duopolies with the national airlines of the destination countries. The governments have generally not intervened financially or politically in the governance or operations of SAS, except after SAS overinvested in jet aircraft in the early 1960s.

Labor relations in Scandinavia are broadly based on a tripartite model between employers and unions, with the state shaping the context. In general, the state encourages employment-relations arrangements based on relative moderation by unions, which helps to ensure that industries are profitable and that they provide good jobs. The model is built on a welfare state fully funded by taxes. This eases the direct burden of health care, for example, for employers and employees. However, the context is one of relatively high total labor costs. This induces businesses to improve productivity, to develop innovative products, and to focus on premium consumer markets.

There are national divergences from this general Scandinavian model. For example, Denmark has the most liberalized and employer-friendly legislation. This makes it easier for employers to dismiss employees. Norway's economy is built on rich resources of oil and gas, which leads to higher costs than Denmark and Sweden. Sweden has a huge export industry relative to the size of its economy, and encourages close cooperation between employers and unions.[48] Another important aspect of the Scandinavian model is the representation of workers' interests on companies' boards of directors. This gives employees a voice in their company. Such representation has a long tradition in Sweden, but it has a shorter history in Norway, and is even more recent in Denmark.

Although SAS has adopted a general Scandinavian model for employment relations, it has had to cope with the additional complication of dealing with the three national peculiarities. Complications include, first, pay differentials across national borders; second, concerns about the fairness of the distribution of jobs and resources between the countries; and third, managers who do not understand the inter-Scandinavian nuances in labor relations.

Before deregulation, when SAS was a monopoly in some markets, its employees enjoyed terms and conditions of employment that were more generous than those which generally applied in most other industries. As the Scandinavian countries deregulated the airline industry in the mid-1990s, SAS's lack of international competitiveness became more apparent. SAS's Scandinavian employment-relations model fosters relatively cooperative relations between the main parties. Nevertheless, it was more costly for SAS than the models faced by most other airlines. This reflected SAS's tendency to offer its employees the best of the benefits from each of the three countries.

This tendency became a serious problem for SAS, as competition in national and international markets increased. New-entrant airlines were attracted to Scandinavian markets because of the relative affluence of the population, frequency of air travel in Scandinavia, and the high fares charged by SAS. For a few years before 9/11, SAS focused on expansion. In this period, labor costs increased, but the underlying uncompetitive cost-structure was hidden by growth during the economic boom of the late 1990s.

The increased level of competition became more obvious following the 9/11 attacks in the United States in 2001 and its immediate negative impact on world aviation. The smaller privately owned airlines in Scandinavia reacted quickly to the downturn in the market. They chose various adjustment strategies, from layoffs to other cost reductions. But in accordance with the Scandinavian custom, these were achieved by collaborative discussions between the parties.

After 9/11, then, the decline in profitability of SAS and its dysfunctional structure became even more evident. Expansion as a panacea was replaced by drives to reach agreements to reduce costs with all thirty-nine of its unions. SAS executives saw these agreements as essential for survival, since SAS seemed headed for bankruptcy unless it took drastic action. SAS argued that it had too many pilots and flight attendants, that their productivity was too low, and that their total labor costs were too high. Consequently, SAS stopped recruitment and resorted to layoffs, which affected all categories of staff.

In the 2003 collective bargaining round, the parties at SAS agreed to halt growth in salaries, change working conditions, and reduce the workforce via agreements to promote part-time work and leaves of absence. In the 2004 collective bargaining round, the parties agreed to cut pay by up to 6 percent to be more compatible with the levels paid by competitors and to freeze the "production payment" (the component of pilot salaries tied to the weight and utilization of the aircraft fleet), which was not connected to profitability. If the parties had not agreed to this "production payment freeze," pilot labor costs would have been about 20–24 percent higher. The pay cut defined a lower starting point for subsequent salary discussions. There were also cuts for senior executives whose salaries were reduced by 10 percent.

The parties at SAS also redesigned their time-consuming labor-contract negotiation process. The new negotiation process was subject to a strict timeline, monitored by SAS directors. The targets focused on cost reductions with immediate effect, thus avoiding a protracted confrontation that would take longer to negotiate and that would jeopardize short-term cost savings. It was a painful and demanding process. Nevertheless, most of the negotiations were contained within SAS in a spirit of collaboration and were not featured in the media, nor did they affect customers, for instance, through labor disputes. By 2004, the parties had met the targets by a process of mutual-gains negotiations. By 2008 SAS had achieved multiyear agreements with all of its unions and new principles for cooperation.

SAS, like Lufthansa, and consistent with a coordinated market economy context, implemented relatively gradual cuts in labor costs. SAS also confronted its organizational complexity and its trinational labor-relations model. Its managers and unions realized that they had to develop a new approach to ensure that SAS would survive. The approach had two aspects: decentralizing SAS into subsidiaries and initiating a process for renegotiating labor contracts more quickly than hitherto, all in an effort to foster a "cultural turnaround."

Management advisers strongly recommended radically reducing employment in the original legacy airline, SAS, while simultaneously growing the new-entrant airlines that it had acquired and which had become SAS subsidiaries: Spanair in Spain, Braathens and Widerøe in Norway, Blue1 in Finland, and (though only a minority stake) Air Baltic in Latvia and Estonian in Estonia. Despite such recommendations, SAS chose to give unions a chance to work with the managers to help turn around the airline, in line with the cooperative tripartite norms of Scandinavian society and its political economy. In

2004 the parties agreed on a lower pay scale for new pilots, compared with that for current pilots. The flight attendants unions made a similar agreement two years later. However, these new pay scales were not implemented because SAS was not recruiting new staff. Unlike several airlines in the United States, SAS did not make any major unilateral cuts in its pension plans. In short, SAS's strategy included cost reduction, the avoidance of nonessential costs, and increasing productivity.

After SAS returned to profitability, the unions tried to win back some of the concessions they had made in 2004. There was a short labor dispute in 2006 at SAS, but the parties soon settled it with a compromise contract in which the unions won twelve of their thirty-six claims.

By 2007, the Scandinavian aviation industry was reaping the gains from having restructured and reduced costs, also helped by a favorable business climate. A slight recession unveiled further structural challenges that had been avoided in the earlier restructuring, causing SAS to initiate another cost-reduction program.

The main stakeholders in Scandinavia generally see their employment-relations model as effective, durable, and flexible; this was the case even during the turmoil following 9/11. This perception is shared by most managers and unions at SAS, even though SAS's structural complexity blunted the effectiveness of the Scandinavian employment-relations model. Further, there is usually more of a genuine partnership with unions in the Scandinavian countries when they have Social Democratic governments. Governments formed by right-wing parties tend to be less supportive of such partnerships. This was the case in Sweden after the change of government in 2006, which illustrates that governments do make a difference.

The obligation of managers at Lufthansa and SAS to consult with their employees fosters a focus on longer-term restructuring options. In terms of the cost-competitiveness strategy of these legacy airlines, the so-called rigidities of the German and Scandinavian labor markets encourage managers to choose productivity-enhancing strategies. In such coordinated market economies, the managers have to partner with their employees and their unions. This encourages them to *negotiate* more in responding to market changes, which contrasts with the tendency of most airlines in the United States and other liberal market economies of trying to *unilaterally impose* short-term cuts to labor costs as their first response to market downturns.

Let us move away from Europe to consider other forms of capitalism, which are different again from the liberal market economies and coordinated market economies.

Asia and the Middle East

As noted earlier, by 2025 the Asian civil aviation market is likely to be larger than those of North America and Europe. Asia is a much more diverse region than North America and Europe, with multiple governments and regulators involved in Asian aviation. Although there are regional trade entities, such as the Asia-Pacific Economic Cooperation Forum and the Association of South East Asian Nations,[49] these are much weaker than the European Union and North American Free Trade Agreement.

Asia and the Middle East also include more diversity than the United States and Europe, in culture, religion, race, income level, industry structure, and forms of political economy. While the United States, Canada, and the EU are primarily developed market economies, Asia includes several clusters of economies that are at different levels of development, as reflected by their contrasting levels of gross domestic product per capita. Asia includes developed market economies (Japan, Australia, and New Zealand); more recently industrialized "tigers" (Hong Kong, Singapore, South Korea, and Taiwan); emerging economies (China, India, Indonesia, Malaysia, Russia, and Thailand); less developed economies (e.g., Bangladesh, Pakistan, Nepal, and Vietnam); and oil-rich states (e.g. Brunei, United Arab Emirates, and Iraq). We focus on a few examples: South Korea, Malaysia, and the Emirate of Dubai.

In comparison with the United States and Europe, unions are weaker and more fragmented in Asia and the Middle East, and are not well positioned to press for EU-style social partnership arrangements.

Since the 1970s, airlines have grown even more rapidly in Asia and the Middle East than in North America and Europe. This reflects the rapid growth of Japan, the Asian "tigers," and other economies. Many legacy airlines based in Asia and the Middle East, such as Malaysia Airlines, Singapore Airlines, Thai Airways, and Garuda of Indonesia are government owned. But some, such as Cathay Pacific of Hong Kong, Eva Airways of Taiwan, and Asiana Airlines of South Korea, are private companies. Some of the airlines in this region are not IATA members, so they were not constrained by IATA decisions on pricing and levels of service. This made it easier for them to offer lower fares and better service levels than IATA members.[50]

In recent years, U.S. airlines were preoccupied with the aftermath of the 9/11 crisis as well as the rise in fuel costs. Meanwhile, Asian airlines also had to cope with other serious challenges including the Asian financial crisis (1997), the Bali bombings (2002), the Severe Acute Respiratory Syndrome

(SARS) epidemic (2003), the Asian tsunami (2004), and continuing strife in Iraq and other parts of the Middle East. Such events have had devastating effects on the industry in this region. In some markets, short-term demand fell by more than 30 percent. Nonetheless, in the early twenty-first century, on average Asian airlines were more profitable than those in Europe, which have in turn tended to be more profitable than those based in the United States.[51] The degree of profitability is probably related to the degree of continuing regulation. Asian legacy airlines have enjoyed more protection so far, but this will not last. Bearing in mind the slower movement toward deregulation and the rapid recovery from the Asian financial crisis, Asian-based airlines have generally been profiting from excess demand. Legacy airlines still appear to be profitable in much of Asia, to a greater extent than in the other two regions. This also reflects the lack of practical alternatives to air transport between some of the key cities, given long distances, often separated by sea, as well as poorly developed surface transport infrastructure in some countries.

Many of the factors that allowed Asian airlines such as Cathay Pacific, Singapore Airlines, and Thai Airways to enjoy high profits in the early years of the twenty-first century are diminishing. As markets are being deregulated, new-entrant airlines are growing. There is increasing competition in much of Asia. The challenges that have confronted airlines in the United States and Europe also are increasing in Asia. Accordingly, in an attempt to compete, many of the legacy airlines have been restructuring their operations.

Although there are varying moves toward deregulation in Asia and the Middle East, there is also still lingering protection. In this part of the world, Australia, Japan, and the Philippines were among the earliest countries to start to deregulate their domestic markets. Similar to the development of the industry elsewhere, new-entrant airlines in this region were launched primarily to offer point-to-point services targeting price-sensitive leisure travelers. However, especially after the 1997 Asian financial crisis, several new entrants also focused on business travelers funded by cost-conscious firms.[52] The development of new entrants has been facilitated by moves toward deregulation, privatization of airports, and the economic buoyancy of many countries in the region.

With the tentative start of only a few new entrants after the mid-1990s, new entrants have been developed more quickly in the early years of the twenty-first century. Notable new entrants in the region include Lion Air (Indonesia, 2002); One-Two-Go (Thailand, 2003); Air Deccan (India, 2003); Thai AirAsia, Nok Air (Sky Asia) (Thailand, 2004); Valuair and Tiger Airways (Singapore,

2004); SpiceJet and Kingfisher Airlines (India, 2005); AWAir (Indonesia, 2005); Okay Airways (China, 2005); Oasis (Hong Kong, 2006); and in the Middle East, Emirates Airways (1988) and Etihad Airways (2003).[53] The rapid growth of new entrants was driven in part by a growing demand for air travel in this region, with expected annual growth rates of 8.6 percent for domestic travel and 9.9 percent for international travel[54] between 2003 and 2008 compared with a 4 percent average annual growth rate for the world as a whole.[55]

South Korea

Korean Air and Asiana Airlines dominate the airline industry in Korea; they are still protected by government regulation.[56] Korean Air was established in 1969 after a company purchased the former government airline. Korean Air monopolized Korean air travel until 1988, when the government permitted Asiana to become a second national airline. More recently, two new entrants (Hansung Airlines and Jeju Air) were allowed to enter the Korean market following an "open skies" policy established with China.[57]

In relatively stable operating conditions, the two legacy airlines have developed their policies to manage human resource and employment relations, providing relatively high wages and associated conditions such as fringe benefits, job security, career paths, and extensive training.[58] Both legacy airlines provide a Japanese-style policy of "lifetime employment," where employees are given firm-specific training, opportunities for career growth, and little job mobility (largely due to the duopolistic nature of the Korean industry). This, in part, is due to regulations in Korea that require statutory licenses for jobs as pilots, mechanics, and flight attendants. The lifetime employment policy and associated human resource practices—for example, promotion from within rather than filling vacancies from the external labor market, considerable investment in training, and relatively few rules limiting flexibility in job assignments—reflect a commitment approach to employees. Such practices also support the service-enhancement strategies emphasized by the Korean airlines.

Many pilots are recruited from the Korean air force; however, a shortage of pilots prompted Korea Air to develop a "pilots academy," where pilots are trained and must remain at the company for ten years following training. Flight attendants are usually graduates from Korean colleges.

Both airlines have accommodated unions. Two unions cover most of their workforce: one for pilots and the other for all other employees. The Korean

Air Labor Union, covering all employees except pilots, has usually cooperated with managers. In exchange it has maintained 100 percent membership. The other unions at the two legacies have been critical of management's authoritarian approach to labor relations. The pilots unions have been concerned about the long working hours of their members.[59]

Although the South Korean context is different from either a coordinated market economy or a liberal market economy, it shares some features of each of these "ideal types." For example, there is a high degree of central coordination of the economy, but not much sign of EU-style social partnership.[60] The airlines accommodate unions rather than partnering with them. Employee relations display some elements of a commitment approach (e.g., greater employment security and flexible job assignments), but not the partnering aspects that are characteristic of Germany and Scandinavia.

Malaysia

Malaysia Airlines (MAS) began in 1937 (as a joint initiative between British Airways and shipping companies) to fly between Penang and Singapore. MAS lost nearly half a billion dollars in 2005 when some of its regional competitors reported strong profits. In 2006 the government divided Malaysia's domestic air routes between MAS and new-entrant AirAsia, which meant that these airlines would not have to compete on their home ground.

In December 2001, a few months after 9/11 left the international airline industry reeling, a new Malaysian company led by Tony Fernandes purchased AirAsia. It was then a small underperforming domestic airline, which he bought for only 30 cents—while assuming twelve million dollars in debt. Nevertheless, Fernandes has made AirAsia into one of the world's fastest-growing airlines. For the 2007 fiscal year, it reported a pretax profit of $79 million—more than triple that of 2006—on revenue of $458 million, a 17 percent margin that is third best in the industry, behind only Brazil's Gol and Ryanair. It became profitable by adopting a new-entrant model. Such transformations in Asia are not unusual with certain national airlines reforming as low-cost carriers (as Aer Lingus did) in attempts to remain profitable.[61]

An informed observer refers to Malaysia as having a "stifling regulatory environment."[62] However, after years of protectionist government policy toward MAS, in 2007 the government also endorsed AirAsia's sister company, AirAsia X—a low-cost, long-haul airline. AirAsia X began flying to Australia and other destinations in 2007 and plans to start flying to Europe and the

United States. The Virgin Group bought a 20 percent stake in AirAsia X in 2007.[63]

These Asian new entrants often claim to be implementing the Southwest model. However, AirAsia does not really emulate Southwest. AirAsia does not even accommodate unions, let alone partner with them. Rather, AirAsia emulated Ryanair's employment-relations model. The Malaysian context appears to favor more of a control-style management approach than is typical either in the coordinated market economies or even the liberal market economies, such as the United States.

AirAsia follows a control approach with its employees, for the most part, and avoids unions. Therefore, the ITF has established an Internet forum for AirAsia staff to discuss their working conditions and to campaign for AirAsia to recognize a union to give the workforce a unified voice.[64] This ITF campaign parallels its Ryan-be-Fair campaign.

Although AirAsia has continued to grow, MAS has had to restructure.[65] MAS launched a business turnaround plan that focuses, among other things, on the employment relationship:

> Unleashing talents and capabilities—we are committed to our people. . . . We will work together with our employees to ensure that they have a working environment in which their talents can thrive. . . . We are dedicated to the creation of a company that will be a source of pride and admiration for its employees and indeed all its stakeholders.[66]

The plan cites exemplars from the United States and Europe and calls for

> dramatic staff cuts fuelled by massive increases in labor productivity . . . [and] that in an industry where prices decline by 2 percent per year-on-year on a real basis, continuously rising labor costs—through both wage increases and the natural aging of the workforce—is unsustainable.[67]

MAS's management used to have a position called HR controller for discipline.[68] This symbolizes that MAS adopts a control approach toward its employees. By contrast MAS also accommodates unions. Its chief executive officer thanked unions "for their support and cooperation," while MAS was cutting jobs by 15 percent (a reduction of more than three thousand employees).[69] However, the relationship is not a partnership. The unions are less complimentary about MAS. The ITF, for example, complains that the airline discriminates against women—female flight attendants are forced to retire at forty, while the retirement age for men is fifty-five—in spite of the employment law, the collective agreement, and the union's attempts to challenge such discrimination. Further, flight attendants,

> sixty per cent of whom are female . . . are limited to when and how many children they can have [two], and . . . pregnant women are not redeployed to other duties, but instead are forced to take seven months unpaid leave.[70]

MAS's plan to become "a five-star" legacy airline at a new-entrant cost base in a less regulated environment appears to be more rhetoric than reality. MAS's strategy is like the tougher approaches that often prevail in many airlines in liberal market economies.

The Emirate of Dubai

Dubai borders the Gulf of Oman and the Persian Gulf, between Oman and Saudi Arabia. Dubai is one of the seven emirates (states) of the United Arab Emirates (UAE). The UAE's per capita GDP is on a par with those of leading Western European nations. The UAE has an open economy. Despite largely successful efforts at economic diversification, nearly 40 percent of the UAE's GDP is still directly based on oil and gas output. Dependence on oil and a large expatriate workforce are significant challenges for the UAE.

Dubai has a population of less than 1.5 million people. This emirate is one of the most rapidly developing economies in the world. Dubai's strategic plan focuses on diversification and on creating more opportunities, especially for its nationals, through improved education and increased private-sector employment, as well as by a huge investment in growing its aviation industry.[71]

In 1985 Dubai launched its flag airline, Emirates. It has become one of the fastest-growing airlines and is the eighth largest international airline in the world. Emirates pays no taxes. Contrary to rumor, it pays market rates for fuel. It does, however, have one of the more successful fuel-price-hedging programs in the industry.

Emirates' home airport does not restrict aircraft noise, so that Emirates keeps its planes in the air for fourteen hours a day (compared to eleven hours for many other major airlines). By 2007, it had more than one hundred planes and was planning to have more than 169 wide-bodied planes by 2012. Emirates flies to all the other continents nonstop from Dubai airport. It services more than a hundred destinations in more than sixty countries. In 2007 Emirates announced the biggest aircraft order in civil aviation history, with a commitment for up to 131 Airbus and 12 more Boeing aircraft.[72]

Emirates was the first airline to order the "super-jumbo" Airbus A380 "double-decker" aircraft (it is the largest initial buyer of this aircraft with fifty-eight A380s on order). In 2008 the government of Dubai (Emirates owner) announced that it would set up another airline, which would adopt a more conventional new-entrant low-cost model. Though initially some Emirates expertise would be used to assist the start-up, it was intended that this airline would operate independently.[73]

Emirates faces at least two other growing airlines also based in the Middle East: Etihad Airways and Qatar Airways. Each of them have relatively small local markets, but rely on transferring through their hub traffic between Europe, on the one hand, and Asia (including the Indian subcontinent and Australasia), on the other hand.[74] Nevertheless, Emirates has been very profitable: in 2005 it claimed to be the world's second most profitable international airline. Although it is government owned, Emirates claims that it has not been subsidized by the government.[75] Dubai's open-skies policy provides significant competition for Emirates, with more than 110 other airlines that pass through the airport.

Although it is a new entrant, Emirates is also a national flag airline. Its reported costs are closer to those of Ryanair than to those of British Airways or similar legacy airlines. Profit per seat at Emirates is also as high as Ryanair.[76] Hence in some ways it is also a low-cost and low-fares airline. For instance, on the "kangaroo route" between Europe and Australia, its fares are significantly less than those of legacy airlines such as Qantas. However, Emirates' strategic position is to be a full-service airline that prides itself on offering good customer service. It has quickly become a remarkable competitor and has marketed itself with high-profile sports sponsorships including the world's most watched sporting event—the Fédération Internationale de Football Association (FIFA) World Cup.

Many of Emirates' employment-relations strategies are geared to provide good customer service. Emirates provides benefits to employees including "a competency based approach to performance management, with employees coached and guided on their individual developmental needs," profit sharing and merit pay, comprehensive health plans, and paid maternity and sick leave, among other things.[77] In addition to profit sharing, Emirates has systems to reward good work, and employee participation schemes on an individual basis. Staff members are encouraged to use their experience to provide ideas on improving customer service, efficiency, safety, and cutting costs. These practices suggest a commitment-based approach to managing employees at Emirates.

A very high proportion of Emirates pilots and flight attendants are expatriates (more than 90 percent). Emirates provides support for expatriates' transition to Dubai. Many enjoy the Dubai lifestyle, which includes excellent shopping.[78] However, others find it difficult to adjust to the Middle East culture, leading to a small percentage of resignations and large numbers of commuting staff or broken families.[79]

Dubai is Emirates' only base: expatriate staff members have to live there to work for the company. A few pilots joined Emirates, for instance, after the 1989–90 Australian pilots' dispute (mentioned earlier), while more pilots from Australian legacies joined subsequently.[80]

Unlike their former airlines, which were unionized, labor unions were then illegal in Dubai. In 2006 new laws allowed unions to be established, with citizens allowed to have full membership, but expatriates only associate membership.[81] There have been some concerns with the notion of associate membership, since more than 80 percent of the workforce is expatriates.[82] The proposed single federal union would be given power to enforce standards in working conditions, with separate representatives in each major industry.[83]

Nonetheless, Emirates avoids unions. Further, some have argued that the new laws allowing unions are ineffective, as there are few consequences for employers who break the law. Despite legalizing unions, after several disputes in the construction industry the government banned strikes.[84]

Some argue that the initial success of Emirates in avoiding unions reflects the impotence of unions there.[85] Further, due to Dubai's proximity to India and Pakistan, Emirates is also able to recruit cheap labor from there. Labor accounts for only 18 percent of Emirates' operating budgets, compared to nearly 30 percent of Lufthansa's operating budget.[86]

International Mergers and Alliances

In Europe, there have been a range of intracountry takeovers. Several of the legacies have purchased new entrants to buy out (potential) competitors. Moreover, some of the larger new entrants such as easyJet have taken over smaller ones such as BA's low-cost subsidiary Go!

There was a major merger between Air France and KLM in 2004. This created the world's top airline by revenue (but several other airlines carry

more passengers). Although they are both based in EU member states—
France and the Netherlands—each country has a different institutional
framework, labor and company laws, and different unions representing the
staff. Investors asked, for example, whether the combined management
would be stronger, or would it get caught up in power struggles and politics,
which would militate against this being a successful merger.[87] As Peter Cappelli points out, it is difficult to ensure that mergers are successful: "The
learning curve is steep in . . . mergers, so the companies that do them well
are the ones that do a lot of them," rather than just expanding with one big
merger.[88] Nevertheless, this merger seems to have been successful and to be
benefiting from network coordination, economies of scale, and cost savings
through synergies. Although this combined airline has not yet fully integrated,
Air France KLM has been praised as having a "formidable route system,
healthy finances, and robust growth."[89] By 2008, it was profitable and enjoyed a 48 percent increase in operating income in 2007–08, even though
Air France was hit by a strike.[90]

In recent years Lufthansa took over SWISS, which has remained a
semi-independent airline based in Switzerland, with its own fleet and crews.
In 2008 Lufthansa also announced an aim to take over BMI (British Midland International, the second largest airline at London Heathrow).

Nevertheless, most proposed international mergers have been resisted by
protectionist sentiments. Therefore, so far there has been much less international merger activity in this industry than in many other industries, which
are less likely to arouse strong nationalist sentiments. Mergers have been less
of a homogenizing force internationally than in the U.S. airline industry, or
in other industries such as automobiles, telecommunications, chemicals, or
the news media. In spite of the financial difficulties experienced by many
airlines, especially during cyclical downturns, there have been only a few
intercountry mergers. However, there may be more, because competition
and fuel prices have been increasing and the national flight treaties are being
consolidated, for instance, into Australia-U.S. and EU-U.S open skies agreements, as well as EU-wide and other international treaties. This is reducing
the regulatory barriers to crossborder mergers. Yet the successful implementation of such mergers still confronts formidable challenges. So far international homogenization in the airline industry outside the United States has
generally not taken place via mergers, but rather through imitation, competitive pressures, and strategic alliances.

Such alliances are an important means by which airlines can influence
product markets, rather than simply being influenced by markets. If an airline

can improve its market situation, this can reduce pressure on labor costs. Aviation markets are tough (see figure 3.1); there is cyclical demand and labor costs are a major component of total costs. Therefore, if an airline is able to improve its market situation, it may be less likely to adopt a tough strategy with regard to employment relations, labor costs, wage-minimization strategies, and layoffs.

Different alliance structures can lessen or heighten the impact of the market. To this end, the larger, older, and more fully integrated Star Alliance (between Lufthansa, SAS, United Airlines, and others) has more potential than the relatively less-integrated Oneworld Alliance (between British Airways, Qantas, American Airlines, and others). This is another favorable factor in the coordinated market economy cases of Lufthansa and SAS, but a missed opportunity in the liberal market economy case of British Airways.[91] Thus, although alliances are most visible as marketing platforms, they also have implications for employment relations.

Relationship with Employees: Control or Commitment?

Deregulation was more gradual in Europe than in the United States and has been even more gradual in Asia. Accordingly, airlines were generally slower to focus on cutting costs in Europe, and even slower in much of Asia.

An obsession with maximizing shareholder value has been less prevalent outside the United States. In the post–World War II period, most of the main legacies in other countries were partly or fully owned by governments, were highly regulated, and were seen as providing a form of *public* transport service. However, since the 1980s, many of these airlines have been privatized and their markets have been at least partially deregulated. Against this background, especially in the liberal market economies, legacy airlines have generally been increasingly concerned with maximizing shareholder value, mainly in the short term. Consequently they have tended to become tougher employers, with cost-competitiveness strategies that have focused more on wage minimization. One paradox is that the rhetoric from several of them (e.g., British Airways) has emphasized the importance of fostering employee commitment and exhorting employees to offer good customer service, while they simultaneously seek to reduce employees' compensation or benefits. Such airlines were not reaping the potential advantages of developing partner relationships with their workforce and their unions.

In terms of their relations with employees, while some non-U.S. airlines have adopted a "low-road" control strategy, including Ryanair and AirAsia, others have continued to provide reasonably good jobs for their employees (a "high-road" commitment strategy). Although there are exceptions, many non-U.S. airlines have continued to aim to provide high-quality service to their customers (in terms of "frills"), as well as a return to investors, to a greater extent than has been typical among the U.S. legacies. At least in part, this reflects the slower pace of deregulation in most other countries compared with the United States. Nonetheless, only a few of the non-U.S. airlines discussed here have tried to turn employment relations into sources of competitive advantage. As one experienced airline captain put it:

> Why don't more airlines learn from Southwest? If other airlines were to follow Southwest's example, really trying to engage their staff and partnering with their unions, they could provide a better service to their passengers and be more profitable.[92]

The differences with most other U.S. airlines' management styles are particularly evident in the cases of Germany and Scandinavia. Those coordinated market economies have an institutional context of encouraging a partner approach to employees and unions and the other stakeholders to a greater extent than in any of the other countries discussed. This is symbolized by a quarterly report, in which Lufthansa stated that "it is our incentive to continue to see profit growth and bring joy to our shareholders, clients and employees in equal measure."[93] Such rhetoric is not empirically testable. But the above examples of airlines' behavior in coordinated market economies implies that they may usually pay attention to such a balanced three-way incentive and to maintaining a partner approach, more than those in other types of economies.

Ryanair (and AirAsia) exemplify the antithesis of such a partner approach. The former has followed an aggressive union-avoidance strategy. This happened even though Ireland, at a national level, has fostered notions of social partnership more than the United Kingdom or Australia. Ryanair has been able to pursue a ruthless low-cost strategy, because it is in effect a "greenfield" operation. In response to growing competition from Ryanair, Aer Lingus attempted to reduce its labor costs and to become more like a new entrant. But it was more constrained by its established bargaining arrangements and the unwillingness of workers and their unions to give these up.

Virgin Blue decided at its inception to accommodate unions in all categories of its workforce. Because it also wished to provide a friendly service, albeit with not all of the full-service "frills," Virgin Blue also fostered a relationship with flight attendants, in particular, that was a form of commitment approach. It adopted such an approach despite the prevailing antiunion policies in Australia under its 1996–2007 conservative government, which tended to encourage more of a control approach. This exemplifies that enterprises have scope for exercising strategic choice, in spite of the institutional context.

By 2007, easyJet was also trying to adopt a commitment approach. However, there was more institutional support for such an EU-style approach in the United Kingdom under the post-1997 Labour government than there was in Australia under the conservative government of the time.

Airlines in such liberal market economy contexts receive less encouragement for partner strategies than those in coordinated market economies. This is illustrated by the behavior of most of the legacy airlines in the United States, as well as in the United Kingdom (British Airways), Ireland (Ryanair), and Australia (Qantas). Further, those that do adopt partner strategies may have more difficulty sustaining them in liberal market economy contexts. In contrast, firms operating in the coordinated market economies of Europe are less likely to adopt union-avoidance and employee-control strategies and when they do they are less likely to be sustained. So the varieties of capitalism framework does provide some, but not complete, explanatory power in framing the strategic responses of firms.

The institutional context alone does not determine enterprise behaviour. There is still scope for airlines to make choices, as shown by the contrasting people-management strategies of Ryanair and Southwest.

Chapters 5 and 6 will discuss in more detail the employment-relations strategies of such new entrants and legacies in Europe and Asia, as well as those in the United States. But, first, in Chapter 4 we explore recent trends in costs, productivity, service quality, and employee morale for legacy airlines and their new-entrant competitors.

Industry Trends in Costs, Productivity, Quality, and Morale

The growth of low-cost competition initiated by new entrants and the other changes introduced by legacy airlines in the early years of the twenty-first century are transforming the airline industry in fundamental ways. In this chapter we summarize a large body of data to take stock of the results of this transformation. Our focus is on variations and changes in costs, productivity, quality, morale, and labor-relations outcomes in U.S. firms where the data are most readily available. Where possible we compare trends in the United States with those in Europe and Asia.

What has happened to the cost differential between legacies and new entrants over time as low-cost competition has overtaken the industry, moving beyond the new entrants to include the legacy airlines as well? Has restructuring by the legacy airlines narrowed the gap?

But before turning to the data on unit costs, it is important to acknowledge the role of differing "stage length"—the average length of flights flown—on unit costs. Longer stages reduce unit costs because the fixed costs of airport slots, ground crews, and so forth can be spread over longer flights. For these reasons, as shown in figures 4.1, 4.2, and 4.3, most airlines in both the United States and around the world have moved to increase their stage lengths, though legacy carriers tend to fly longer stages than new entrants. U.S. legacies have increased their stage lengths from 979 to 1,173 miles since 2000 (a 20 percent increase), while their new-entrant competi-

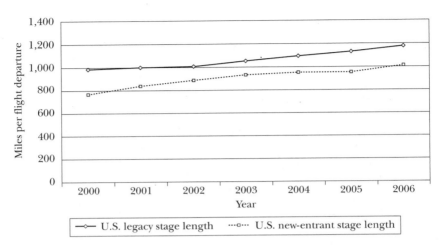

Figure 4.1. Stage lengths for U.S. legacy versus new-entrant airlines. Legacy: Alaska, American, Continental, Delta, Northwest, United, US Airways. New entrant: AirTran, ATA Airlines, JetBlue Airways, Southwest, Spirit.

Source: U.S. Department of Transportation, Form 41.

tors have increased their stage lengths even more, from 768 to 1,004 miles (a 31 percent increase), resulting in a convergence toward more similar stage lengths for the two sectors. In Europe, the legacy airlines have increased their stage lengths from 1,086 to 1,243 miles (a 15 percent increase), while the new entrants have moved more aggressively into longer haul flying with stage lengths increasing from 559 to 679 miles (a 22 percent increase), resulting in a convergence toward more similar stage lengths for these two sectors, as also was observed in the United States. When we include Virgin Atlantic with the European new entrants, flying primarily transatlantic routes with an average stage length of 3,759 miles in 2006, the stage length of European new entrants far exceeds that of their legacy counterparts. In Asia, legacy airlines have moved toward longer haul flying with stage lengths increasing from 1,024 to 1,188 miles (a 16 percent increase), and while we don't have comparable data for the Asian low-cost sector, we expect that stage lengths have been increasing here as well. Given the cost and productivity advantages of longer haul flights, these trends toward longer average stage lengths should help airlines in both sectors to reduce their unit costs. Even so, unit costs have risen in both sectors, as we will see.

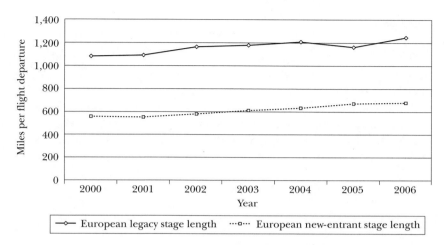

Figure 4.2. Stage lengths for European legacy versus new-entrant airlines. Legacy: Air France, British Airways, Iberia, Lufthansa. New entrant: Air Europa, easyJet, Ryanair, Spanair.

Source: International Civil Aviation Organization.

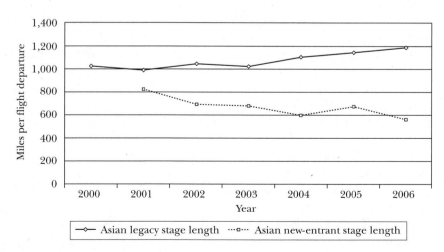

Figure 4.3. Stage lengths for Asian legacy versus new-entrant airlines. Legacy: Air China, Asiana, Korean Air, Malaysia Airlines, Thai Airways. New entrant: Virgin Blue, Air Asia.

Source: International Civil Aviation Organization and company documents.

Cost Trends

Unit costs are a critical driver of success in an era of low-cost competition.[1]
Although total unit costs are ultimately what determine an airline's ability to
offer low fares while remaining profitable, airlines have tended to focus on
the labor component of total costs when engaging in cost reductions. Why?
Perhaps this focus on labor costs as a source of cost reductions is due to the
view that labor costs are more controllable than other costs, further reinforced by a managerial mind-set that portrays employees more as a cost than
as a source of value.

United States

Data in figure 4.4 indicate that labor unit costs dropped dramatically for the
legacy airlines between 2000 and 2006 from $.039 to $.032 per seat mile, a
reduction of 18 percent, while labor unit costs for the new-entrant airlines
crept up slightly from $.024 to $.026, an increase of 8 percent. Declining labor unit costs for the legacy airlines can be attributed to bankruptcies undertaken in the wake of September 11 at United, US Airways, Delta, and
Northwest and demands for labor cost savings made by management to
avoid bankruptcy at American and Continental. The slight upward trend in
labor unit costs for low-cost airlines can be attributed to the aging of the
workforce, as well as a greater ability to reward workers in the wake of September 11 given a relatively rapid bounce back from the crisis.[2] The labor
cost gap between the legacies and the low costs thus narrowed from $.015
per seat mile to $.006 per seat mile (reducing a 38 percent cost advantage to
only 19 percent). Thus, the legacy airlines are close to achieving parity with
the new-entrant airlines on labor costs. See figure 4.4 for trends in U.S. labor
unit costs.

But when we look at total unit costs, we see very different trends. Total
unit costs rose for U.S. legacy airlines over the 2000 to 2006 period from
$.105 to $.135 per seat mile, an increase of 29 percent, despite the fact that
these airlines had reduced their labor unit costs by 18 percent over the same
period (see figure 4.5). By contrast, new-entrant airlines experienced moderate increases in total unit costs from $.085 to $.096, a 13 percent increase.
Despite reductions in labor costs at the legacies, the new entrant cost advantage over this time period grew from $.020 to $.039 per seat mile. Looking at
the legacy numbers from another perspective, nonlabor costs at the legacy

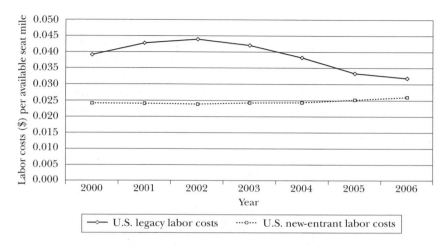

Figure 4.4. Labor costs for U.S. legacy versus new-entrant airlines. Legacy: American, Continental, Delta, Northwest, United, US Airways. New entrant: AirTran, ATA Airlines, Frontier, JetBlue Airways, Southwest, Spirit.

Source: U.S. Department of Transportation, Form 41.

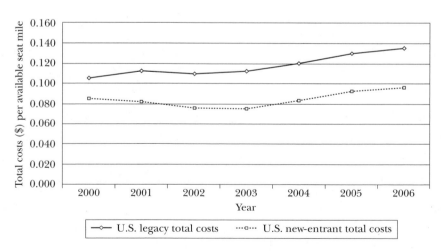

Figure 4.5. Total costs for U.S. legacy versus new-entrant airlines. Legacy: American, Continental, Delta, Northwest, United, US Airways. New entrant: AirTran, ATA Airlines, Frontier, JetBlue Airways, Southwest, Spirit.

Source: U.S. Department of Transportation, Form 41.

airlines increased during this time period from $.066 (.105-.039) to $.103 (.135-.032) per seat mile, or by 56 percent. *While achieving an 18 percent decrease in labor costs, the legacy airlines experienced a 56 percent increase in their nonlabor costs.*

A substantial component of this total unit cost increase comes from fuel, of course. Jet fuel prices increased almost 400 percent (391 percent to be exact) between 2000 and May 2008 when the cost of oil reached $125 a barrel.[3] Legacy airlines have been hit harder than the new entrants by these rising jet fuel prices. At a unit cost level, these costs increased by 129 percent for U.S. legacies compared to increases of 67 percent for new entrants (see figure 4.6). Perhaps due to their initial cost disadvantage and their slower growth in recent years, legacies have been less likely than the new entrants to replace aircraft and thus fly older, less fuel-efficient aircraft. Financial constraints have also prevented the legacies from purchasing fuel-hedging contracts to shield themselves from fuel price increases to the same extent as new entrants have. As a result, U.S. legacies went from a slight advantage in fuel costs per available seat mile in 2000 ($.001 less per seat mile) to a distinct disadvantage in 2006 ($.007 more per seat mile).

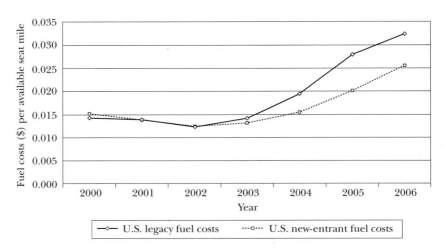

Figure 4.6. Fuel costs for U.S. legacy versus new-entrant airlines. Legacy: American, Continental, Delta, Northwest, United, US Airways. New entrant: AirTran, ATA Airlines, Frontier, JetBlue Airways, Southwest, Spirit.

Source: U.S. Department of Transportation, Form 41.

In addition to the jet fuel increases, as legacies have increased their stage lengths to avoid growing competition from low-cost airlines in their short-haul markets, they have been forced to pay increasingly large fees to regional airlines to feed passengers into their long-haul flights. Thus the legacy cost-reduction strategy of increasing stage length has had some hidden costs. These fees are included under total costs in a category called "transport-related expenses," and are far greater for the legacy airlines (see figure 4.7). Transport-related expenses increased from $.004 to $.026 per seat mile for the U.S. legacies and from $.000 to $.002 for the U.S. new entrants, increasing the transport-related cost disadvantage of the legacies from $.004 to $.024 per seat mile.

This increase in transport-related costs is the biggest single contributor to the widening of the cost gap between U.S. legacies and low-cost airlines. But transport costs also skew total costs for U.S. legacy airlines in the following sense: the legacies incur some (though certainly not all) of the costs of the seat miles flown by their regional partners without getting credit for having flown those seat miles. When we remove these transport costs from total costs, the total cost trends look different. Instead of a cost gap that increases from $.020

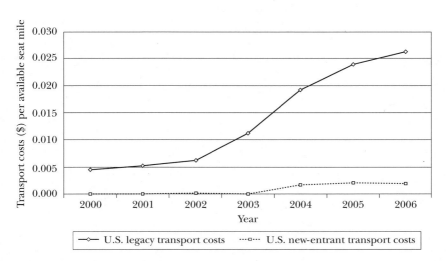

Figure 4.7. Transport-related costs for U.S. legacy versus new-entrant airlines. Legacy: American, Continental, Delta, Northwest, United, US Airways. New entrant: AirTran, ATA Airlines, Frontier, JetBlue Airways, Southwest, Spirit.

Source: U.S. Department of Transportation, Form 41.

to $.039 per seat mile, we see a nontransport cost gap that has remained constant at $.016 per seat mile. Even when both fueling and transport-related expenses are removed from total costs, the remaining nonlabor cost advantage of the new entrants has increased between 2000 and 2006 (from $.002 to $.003 per seat mile), though not nearly so much as when these other expenses are included. Overall, the bottom line is that nonlabor costs at the legacies have increased while labor costs have declined, such that their total cost disadvantage has increased rather than decreased over time.

On the other side of the income statement, the legacy airlines earn higher unit revenues due to their higher fares, which are justified in part by the higher level of amenities and services they provide. These premiums compensate in part for their higher unit costs (figure 4.8 shows recent trends in unit revenues for the U.S. legacies and new entrants). Looking at recent trends, we see a nearly consistent revenue differential between the two sectors over time, with a slight increase in the differential from $.014 to $.020 per seat mile (see figure 4.8). So the increasing total cost disadvantage of the U.S. legacy airlines is counterbalanced in part by an increase in their revenue advantage. Figure 4.8 also suggests that legacy airfares are no lower today than they were in 2000 and that new-entrant airfares are only slightly

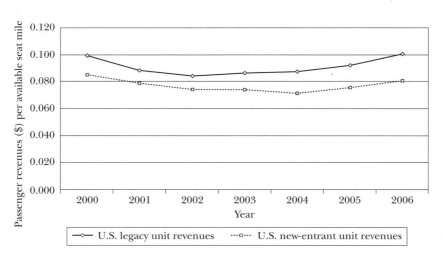

Figure 4.8. Passenger revenues for U.S. legacy versus new-entrant airlines. Legacy: American, Continental, Delta, Northwest, United, US Airways. New entrant: AirTran, ATA Airlines, Frontier, JetBlue Airways, Southwest.

Source: U.S. Department of Transportation, Form 41.

lower, questioning the extent to which low-cost competition has resulted in lower fares for customers over the past seven years. The fare reductions of the 1990s have slowed down considerably in the 2000s, due in part to the need to pass increased fuel costs on to customers.

Europe

To what extent are these trends found outside of the United States? Due to data limitations, we can only observe total unit cost trends in Europe and Asia. Total costs have increased from $.111 to $.157 per seat mile, a 41 percent increase in total costs for the European legacy airlines from 2000 to 2006, and from $.084 to $.111 per seat mile or a 32 percent increase in total costs for the European low-cost airlines over the same period (see figure 4.9 for total unit costs trends in Europe). Because we do not have access to sufficiently comprehensive labor cost data for airlines in this region, we are not able to observe differences in the trends for labor versus nonlabor costs for European airlines. But the bottom line is similar to what we have seen in the United States—namely, total unit costs in Europe remain higher for the legacies and in addition these costs are rising more rapidly than they are for the new entrants.

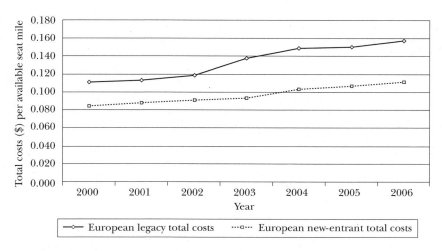

Figure 4.9. Total costs for European legacy versus new-entrant airlines. Legacy: Air France, British Airways, Iberia, Lufthansa. New entrant: Air Europa, easyJet, Ryanair, Spanair.

Source: International Civil Aviation Organization and company documents.

Asia

Similar patterns are observed in Asia. Total unit costs have changed from
$.100 to $.136 per seat mile for a 36 percent increase in total costs for the
Asian legacy airlines from 2000 to 2006. For the Asian new entrants, total
costs have decreased 3 percent from $.068 to $.066 per seat mile from 2001 to
2006 (see figure 4.10 for total unit cost trends in Asia). Because we do not have
access to sufficiently comprehensive labor cost data for airlines in this region,
we are not able to observe differences in the trends for labor versus nonlabor
costs for Asia airlines. Still, the bottom line is similar in Asia to the United
States and Europe—total unit costs remain higher for legacies than for new
entrants, and that cost gap is expanding rather than shrinking over time.

Summary of Cost Trends

Total unit costs across these three regions, first for the legacy airlines and
then for the new entrants, are summarized in table 4.1. Comparing across
sectors and regions, the European airlines have the highest costs in each re-
spective segment. The U.S. and Asian legacies are basically tied for second at

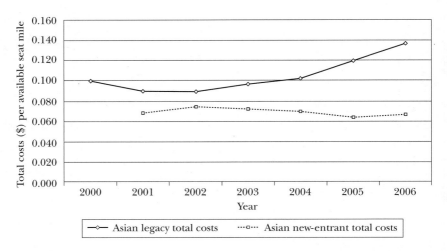

Figure 4.10. Total costs for Asian legacy versus new-entrant airlines. Legacy: Asiana, Korean
Air, Malaysia Airlines, Thai Airways. New entrant: Virgin Blue, Air Asia.

Source: International Civil Aviation Organization and company documents.

Table 4.1. Cross-regional comparison of total unit costs (2006)

	Total unit costs ($/available seat mile)		
	Legacy Airlines	New-Entrant Airlines	New Entrant/Legacy (%)
Europe	.157	.111	71
United States	.135	.096	71
Asia	.136	.066	49

Source: U.S. data from U.S. Department of Transportation, Form 41; other data from International Civil Aviation Organization and company documents.

$.135 and $.136 respectively. But the Asian new entrants have by far the lowest costs with the U.S. new entrants falling somewhere in between their European and Asian counterparts. These comparisons have been of somewhat academic interest in the past given the constraints on competition between U.S., European, and Asian airlines. With the current wave of deregulation opening up competition across these regions, however, these cross-regional cost comparisons are taking on increased practical significance.

Total unit costs have increased more quickly for legacy airlines than for new entrants in each region, despite increasing efforts in both sectors to engage in cost competition and the dramatic reductions in labor costs among U.S. legacy carriers. These trends call into question recent analyses claiming that the two sectors are converging and that the distinctions between legacies and new entrants are increasingly irrelevant.[4] Although there are important differences within each of the two sectors, the two sectors still remain quite distinct.

Aircraft and Employee Productivity Trends

Aircraft Productivity

The increases in total costs reported above have occurred despite the fact that, at least in the United States (where we have relatively complete data), airlines have enjoyed substantial increases in both aircraft and labor productivity in recent years. As can be seen in figures 4.11 and 4.12, aircraft productivity has increased substantially between 2000 and 2006 for both U.S. legacies and new entrants based on two distinct measures: average block hours per aircraft day and available seat miles per aircraft day. Block hours are the hours that aircraft spend away from the gate in revenue-producing mode. These revenue-producing aircraft hours have increased from 10.2 to

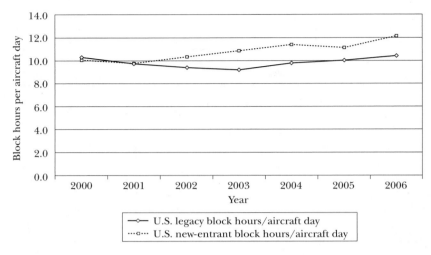

Figure 4.11. Block hours per aircraft day for U.S. legacy versus new-entrant airlines. Legacy: American, Continental, Delta, Northwest, United, US Airways. New entrant: AirTran, ATA Airlines, Frontier, JetBlue Airways, Southwest, Spirit.

Source: U.S. Department of Transportation, Form 41.

10.4 for legacy airlines and from 10.0 to 12.2 for new entrants, moving the new entrants from a 2 percent productivity disadvantage in 2000 to a 17 percent productivity advantage in 2006. This new-entrant productivity advantage has been achieved despite the shorter stage lengths of new entrants, but it has been helped along by the convergence toward more similar stage lengths that we observed at the start of this chapter.

The second measure of aircraft productivity, available seat miles per aircraft day, is driven by aircraft size in addition to stage length. On this measure, U.S. legacies have traditionally outpaced the new entrants due to their larger aircraft as well as their longer stage lengths. The legacies retained their advantage on this measure, but their advantage decreased from 116,479 to 55,393 available seat miles per aircraft day due to faster productivity growth among the new entrants.

Labor Productivity

Labor productivity has increased even more dramatically than aircraft productivity among U.S. airlines, and more dramatically than in either the

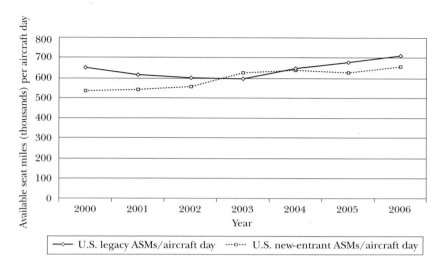

Figure 4.12. Available seat miles per aircraft day for U.S. legacy versus new-entrant airlines. Legacy: American, Continental, Delta, Northwest, United, US Airways. New entrant: AirTran, ATA Airlines, Frontier, JetBlue Airways, Southwest, Spirit.

Source: U.S. Department of Transportation, Form 41.

1980s or 1990s. For U.S. airlines as a whole, labor productivity measured as available seat miles per employee has increased 35 percent between 2000 and 2006 (see figures 4.13 and 4.14). The increase in labor productivity has been more rapid in the new-entrant sector, increasing the labor productivity advantage for new entrants relative to legacy airlines from 224,000 to 344,000 additional available seat miles produced per employee. Labor productivity measured as passengers per employees has also increased over this seven-year period by 27 percent. Even on this measure, the labor productivity advantage of the new entrants has expanded rather than contracted, from 626 to 738 additional passengers served per employee.

Employment

The increases in labor productivity at the legacy airlines have been achieved in large part through reductions in employment, increases in hours worked (especially for pilots and flight attendants), and leaner staffing of both ground and flight operations. The net result of these changes has been a decrease of about 130,000 jobs at the U.S. legacies between 2000 and 2006, a 32 percent

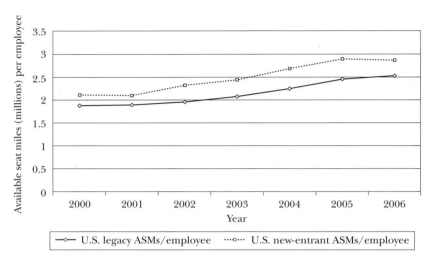

Figure 4.13. Available seat miles per employee for U.S. legacy versus new-entrant airlines. Legacy: American, Continental, Delta, Northwest, United, US Airways. New entrant: AirTran, ATA Airlines, Frontier, JetBlue Airways, Southwest, Spirit.

Source: U.S. Department of Transportation, Form 41.

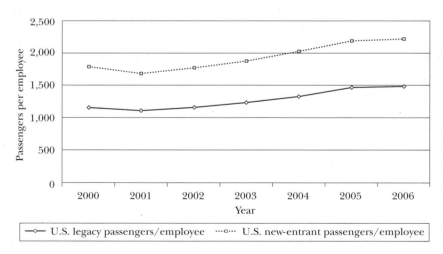

Figure 4.14. Passengers per employee for U.S. legacy versus new-entrant airlines. Legacy: American, Continental, Delta, Northwest, United, US Airways. New entrant: AirTran, ATA Airlines, Frontier, JetBlue Airways, Southwest, Spirit.

Source: U.S. Department of Transportation, Form 41.

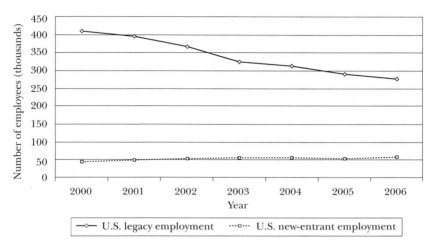

Figure 4.15. Employment for U.S. legacy versus new-entrant airlines. Legacy: American, Continental, Delta, Northwest, United, US Airways. New entrant: AirTran, ATA Airlines, Frontier, JetBlue Airways, Southwest, Spirit.

Source: U.S. Department of Transportation, Form 41.

reduction in employment in this sector. Increases in labor productivity at the new entrants have, on the other hand, been achieved in the context of employment growth that supported business expansion, with an increase of about 15,000 jobs at the U.S. new entrants between 2000 and 2006, constituting a 34 percent increase in employment in this sector (see figure 4.15 for employment trends among U.S. airlines). But the large percentage gains in employment in the new-entrant sector are far outweighed by the losses in the much larger legacy sector. The net result of these shifts is that 115,765 jobs (26 percent of employment at the airlines in our sample) have been lost since 2000.

Summary of Productivity Trends

Overall, productivity has grown substantially in the U.S. airline industry over the past seven years, driven in large part by increases in labor productivity. In labor productivity and one key measure of aircraft productivity, the legacies have fallen further behind their new-entrant counterparts. Recalling that the U.S. legacy airlines achieved dramatic reductions in labor unit costs relative to U.S. new-entrant airlines over this period, these productivity numbers suggest that the convergence in labor unit costs occurred despite the fact that the legacies have fallen further behind in labor productivity and that the labor cost convergence we observed has been driven mainly by reductions in employee wages and benefits.

Service Quality Trends

Despite the importance of low costs for competing in an era of growing price sensitivity by customers, service quality also plays a role in successful competition.[5] Recall that in chapter 1 we identified three distinct components of service quality in the airline industry: amenities or frills, reliability, and friendliness. In this section we focus on the reliability and friendliness dimensions of service quality, where reliability is measured by on-time and baggage handling performance, and friendliness is reflected, albeit imperfectly, by the number of customer complaints.

One reason that service quality matters is that customers shy away from airlines that perform poorly on service quality rankings, though not as much as we might expect—indeed, some industry observers suggest that airline passengers appear to have very short memories and pay more attention to costs than quality when booking their travel. But there is a second reason for airlines to care about service quality that is equally if not more important in the current era: poor quality drives up costs. A core principle of total quality management (TQM) is that poor quality (in the form of low reliability) is costly, and that the same attention to process excellence that yields low costs also yields high quality.[6] Indeed, this is one of the fundamental lessons that Toyota taught the global auto industry in the 1980s.[7] This TQM principle would lead us to expect higher service quality as costs are reduced, but only if costs are reduced through underlying process improvements rather than through slashing and burning the workforce.

What do the data tell us? Looking over the past five years, key quality indicators show deterioration in overall service quality, as noted in chapter 1 and as lamented in the popular press.[8] See figures 4.16, 4.17 and 4.18 for trends in U.S. service quality. After system capacity reached the breaking point in 2000, on-time performance and baggage handling improved post-9/11 when passenger loads were lighter due to the decline in travel, but then both took a dive once again after 2003, recently reaching near record low levels. Indeed, flight delays in the first half of 2007 were reported to be the worst since 1995, the earliest period for which the Department of Trans-

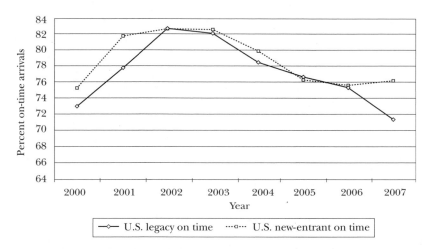

Figure 4.16. On-time performance for U.S. legacy versus new-entrant airlines. Legacy: American, Continental, Delta, Northwest, United, US Airways. New entrant: AirTran, ATA Airlines, Frontier, JetBlue Airways, Southwest.

Source: U.S. Federal Aviation Administration, Air Travel Consumer Report.

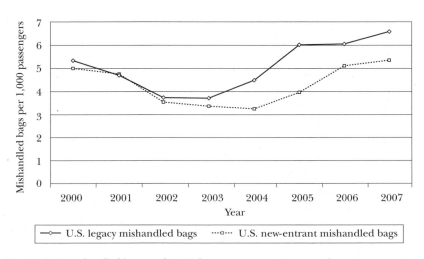

Figure 4.17. Mishandled baggage for U.S. legacy versus new-entrant airlines. Legacy: American, Continental, Delta, Northwest, United, US Airways. New entrant: AirTran, ATA Airlines, Frontier, JetBlue Airways, Southwest.

Source: U.S. Federal Aviation Administration, Air Travel Consumer Report.

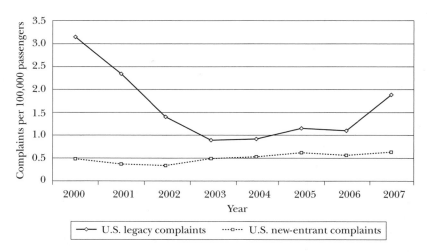

Figure 4.18. Customer complaints for U.S. legacy versus new-entrant airlines. Legacy: American, Continental, Delta, Northwest, United, US Airways. New entrant: AirTran, ATA Airlines, Frontier, JetBlue Airways, Southwest.

Source: U.S. Federal Aviation Administration, Air Travel Consumer Report.

portation has comparable data.[9] Passenger complaints also came down post-9/11 when passenger loads were lighter and stayed relatively low until 2007 when complaints spiked, particularly for the legacy airlines. Consistent with the TQM principle of lower costs and higher quality, the data also suggest that the new entrants as a whole have achieved higher quality (in the sense of friendliness and reliability, not frills) than the legacy airlines. Though the differences are not large, the pattern is fairly consistent over time and across each of the key measures.

Looking within the legacy and new-entrant sectors provides further insight regarding the relationships between costs and quality. Table 4.2 shows total unit costs, total unit costs net of transport costs, and labor unit costs for individual U.S. airlines in 2006. Interestingly, in each sector the airline with the highest labor costs also has some of the lowest total costs. In the new-entrant sector, Southwest has the second lowest total costs (after Jet-Blue) and the highest labor costs. In the legacy sector, American has the lowest total costs and the highest labor costs. One potential interpretation, to be explored in our case study analyses in chapters 5 and 6, is that these airlines are building employee commitment to reduce total costs rather than adopting a narrower focus on reducing labor costs.

Table 4.2. Cost performance for U.S. legacy and new-entrant airlines (2006)

Total Unit Costs ($ per available seat mile)		Total Unit Costs— Transport-Related Costs ($ per available seat mile)		Labor Unit Costs ($ per available seat mile)	
U.S. New-Entrant Airlines					
JetBlue	.079	JetBlue	.078	JetBlue	.021
Southwest	.088	Southwest	.088	AirTran	.022
ATA	.097	ATA	.097	Frontier	.024
AirTran	.097	AirTran	.097	Spirit	.026
Spirit	.104	Frontier	.098	ATA	.028
Frontier	.109	Spirit	.104	Southwest	.034
U.S. Legacy Airlines					
American	.125	Continental	.105	US Airways	.029
United	.132	Delta	.106	Delta	.030
Continental	.135	United	.108	Continental	.031
Northwest	.137	US Airways	.109	United	.031
Delta	.138	American	.110	Northwest	.032
US Airways	.146	Northwest	.118	American	.037

Source: U.S. Department of Transportation, Form 41.

The two lowest-cost airlines in the new-entrant sector—Southwest and JetBlue—also delivered the highest service quality for passengers in 2006 though each had one area of relative weakness (baggage handling for Southwest and on-time performance for JetBlue). In the legacy sector, however, the correspondence between low costs and high quality is less apparent.

A final trend to note in service quality is the rate of flight cancellations, which we take as an indicator of strain on system capacity. As airlines compete on costs, they tend to reduce normal levels of excess capacity in the system to produce higher utilization of aircraft and labor. This reduction in excess capacity leaves a smaller margin for error, resulting in the need to cancel more flights. Spikes in flight cancellations can also result from conflicts between labor and management. If contentious contract negotiations stall, employees may begin working to rule and declining overtime assignments, leading to flight cancellations because the airlines' systems rely on overtime and lean staffing. Looking at recent trends (figure 4.19), we see that flight cancellations were highest in 2000, a year in which the system was considered to be stretched to the limit and experienced significant labor conflict, before they dropped steeply in 2001 and 2002 due to the decline in

Table 4.3. Quality performance for U.S. legacy and new-entrant airlines (2007)

Consumer Complaints (per 100,000 customers)		On-Time Performance (%)		Baggage Handling Errors (per 1,000 customers)	
U.S. New-Entrant Airlines					
Southwest	0.26	Southwest	80.1	AirTran	4.06
Frontier	0.66	Frontier	77.6	JetBlue	5.23
JetBlue	0.78	AirTran	76.8	Southwest	5.87
AirTran	0.83	JetBlue	70.1	Frontier	6.16
U.S. Legacy Airlines					
Continental	1.09	Delta	76.9	Northwest	5.01
Northwest	1.43	Continental	74.3	Continental	5.33
American	1.65	United	70.3	United	5.76
Delta	1.81	Northwest	69.6	American	7.25
United Airlines	2.25	American	68.7	Delta	7.60
US Airways	3.16	US Airways	68.7	US Airways	8.47

Source: U.S. Federal Aviation Administration, Air Travel Consumer Report. ATA and Spirit not available for 2007.

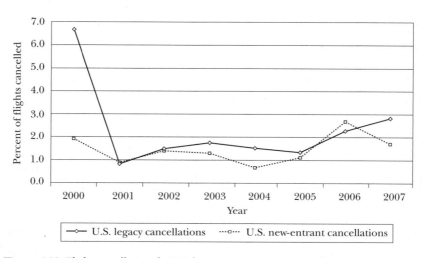

Figure 4.19. Flight cancellations for U.S. legacy versus new-entrant airlines. Legacy: American, Continental, Delta, Northwest, United, US Airways. New entrant: AirTran, ATA Airlines, Frontier, JetBlue Airways, Southwest.

Source: U.S. Federal Aviation Administration, Air Travel Consumer Report. December data only.

passenger volumes post-9/11. Since then, however, flight cancellations have been creeping back upward and in June and July of 2007 they reached historic records, as aircraft were stretched to capacity limits and as downsizing resulted in fewer employees available to step in when their colleagues reach legal limits on flying time.

Employee Morale

Reducing costs primarily on the backs of labor has not only put service quality at risk but has also contributed to a decline in employee morale (as indicated in the survey data reported in figures 4.20 and 4.21). These data come from surveys of over 150,000 pilots and flight attendants across a sample of thirty airlines in the United States from 2000 to 2007. Employees were asked about the degree of confidence they had in how management was running their airline and for their views on the overall morale of the workforce. Both indicators show precipitous declines since 2001. Favorable (positive or very positive) views of how management is running the airline declined from a peak of nearly 80 percent shortly after 9/11 to 20 percent in 2007. Morale has followed a similar path but has plummeted even further.

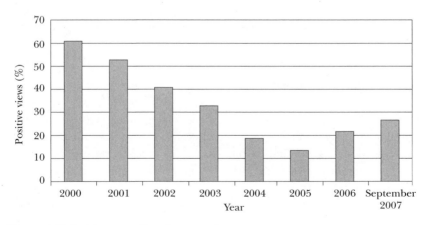

Figure 4.20. Positive views of employee morale.

Source: Wilson Center for Public Research. Based on 150,674 interviews conducted with pilots or flight attendants from January 1, 2001, to September 20, 2007. The specific question read as follows: "How would you describe, in your own words, the pilot [flight attendant] group's morale?"

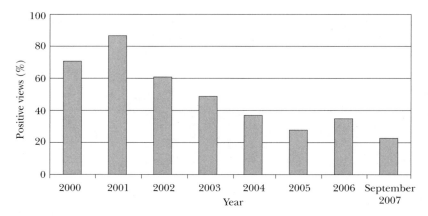

Figure 4.21. Positive views of how management is running the airline.

Source: Wilson Center for Public Research. Based on 150,674 interviews conducted with pilots or flight attendants from January 1, 2001, to September 20, 2007. The specific question read as follows: "How would you describe, in your own view, how [company name's] management is running the company?"

The percentages responding that morale was high or very high fell to under 15 percent by 2005, and then recovered to around 25 percent by 2007.[10] Although employees seemed to understand airlines' initial reactions to 9/11, including the layoffs, the sustained job losses and concessions over the next several years have led to increasing cynicism among employees regarding airline management.

Labor Negotiations and Conflict

Another dimension of performance in the airline industry is the time required to reach new labor agreements. Because U.S. airlines are covered by the Railway Labor Act and its procedures for minimizing service disruptions, negotiations in the U.S. airline industry have tended to drag out for extended periods of time. The average length of time required to reach new labor agreements for U.S. airlines from 1984 to 2002 is summarized in table 4.4.[11] For the industry as a whole, it took 13.8 months on average to reach these agreements; for the legacy airlines it took an average of 17.6 months. Moreover, contract delays increased over this time period. Our estimates indicate that the time required increased by approximately nineteen days each year between 1984 and 2002.

Table 4.4. Time to reach labor agreement in U.S. airlines (1984–2002)

	Number of Standard Contracts	Mean Number of Months to Reach Agreement	Standard Deviation	Minimum	Maximum
All Airlines	205	13.8	13.3	−11.5	72.1
Legacy Airlines Only	89	17.6	15.4	−11.5	72.1

Note: These numbers include standard contracts only, no midterm negotiations or initial contracts. All airlines include legacy, new-entrant, and regional airlines.

Source: Andrew von Nordenflycht and Thomas A. Kochan, "Labor Contract Negotiations in the Airline Industry," Monthly Labor Review (July 2003): 18–28; with data courtesy of Airline Industrial Relations Conference.

Negotiations that drag on for a long time have two very negative consequences. First, given the cyclicality of this industry, the underlying economic conditions often change so that negotiators find themselves attempting to agree on wage increases (or decreases) that no longer reflect the economic conditions of the day or those coming in the future. Employees in 1999 to 2000, for example, argued for retroactive "catch-up" wage increases to reflect the booming industry conditions of 1995 to 1999 just as industry experts were looking ahead and seeing a market decline around the corner—and they were right to see it coming. The second problem is that delays irritate rank and file employees and increase conflicts associated with either a strike threat or uses of the National Mediation Board procedures. These conflicts reduce productivity and service quality and thus exact real costs on both economic performance and customer service.[12]

Impact of Employment Relations on Firm Performance

As the data presented above indicate, U.S. airlines, particularly the legacies, put enormous energy into reducing their labor costs in the years since 2000. The question therefore arises of whether the focus on reducing labor costs is an appropriate strategy for returning these firms and the overall industry to a position of sustained profitability and improved service. We addressed this question in a large quantitative study linking different aspects of employment relations to firm performance (service quality, employee productivity, aircraft productivity, and profit margins from operations) for the twelve largest U.S. airlines operating between 1987 and 2002.[13]

We found that unionization per se (the percent of a firm's labor force unionized) was not significantly associated, positively or negatively, with firm performance. For achieving firm performance over time, the *quality of the employment relationship* mattered most, as measured by the presence of a positive workplace culture and low levels of conflict in labor negotiations. High-quality employment relationships predicted high levels of service quality, labor productivity, aircraft productivity, and operating margins. We found that wage reductions negotiated in concessionary periods before 2001 resulted in short-term but not sustained increases in productivity and profit margins and also produced reductions in service quality. These results suggest that labor cost reductions may be necessary from time to time, but by themselves will not achieve or sustain high levels of performance for firms or even customers, much less for employees. Our results clearly suggest that strategies seeking to build commitment and harmonious labor-management relations have a higher likelihood of achieving desirable performance outcomes than those that focus on control, union avoidance, or drawn-out, conflictual negotiations.

Summing Up Competitive Trends

Together, the data presented in this chapter paint a mixed picture of competitive trends in the industry. Total unit costs have risen for both new- entrant and legacy airlines in all regions, with the exception of the new entrants in Asia. Astonishingly, these increases in total unit costs in the United States have occurred *despite* large increases in labor and aircraft productivity and cuts in employee pay and benefits. Deep cuts in pay and benefits at U.S. legacy airlines have nearly closed the labor-cost gap with new entrants. However, the total cost gap between legacies and new entrants has actually increased. One reason for this may be that while the legacies were focusing on cutting labor costs, new-entrant airlines were focused on increasing their labor and aircraft productivity and improving their quality performance.

When these data are considered in light of our research on how the employment relationship drives firm performance, it is clear there is more work to be done. Labor cost reductions may have been a necessary condition for survival at some airlines, but they are far from sufficient for fostering a return to sustained profitability. Labor cost reductions can even be counterproductive when they are carried out in a way that allows total costs to grow and service quality to decline. When service quality declines, costs can rise even further due to the costs of service recovery, while revenue premiums may decline. The bottom line is that reducing labor costs is not sufficient and at some point becomes counterproductive for reducing total costs.

Although in this chapter we have compared cost, productivity, and quality trends between new-entrant and legacy airlines in different regions of the world, we have not observed the employment relationships *inside individual airlines* that influence the ability to achieve high levels of productivity and service quality. Our case studies in the following two chapters explore alternative approaches to the employment relationship to show how different approaches can be established and sustained over time, first focusing on the new entrants, and then on the legacy airlines.

CHAPTER 5

Alternative Strategies for New Entrants: Southwest vs. Ryanair

New-entrant airlines that compete on costs are transforming the global airline industry. Their low-cost competitive strategies are the most visible part of their impact. Although less visible, their employment-relations strategies are also transforming the industry. This chapter considers the variations in the employment-relations strategies we observed among new entrants in the United States and other countries. We first describe the employment-relations strategy of Southwest Airlines, based on employee commitment and union partnership. Southwest is the longest-surviving new entrant and a prototype that many other firms have looked to as they entered the industry. We then contrast the Southwest approach with another prototype, Ryanair, a firm that has chosen to compete on low costs by taking a diametrically different—control/avoidance—approach to employment relations, and with AirAsia, a new entrant that has followed key elements of the Ryanair employment-relations strategy. We also consider hybrid new entrants that have taken Southwest's commitment-based approach and paired it either with Ryanair's union-avoidance approach (JetBlue and WestJet) or with a union-accommodation approach (easyJet, AirTran, and Virgin Blue). We conclude by considering what is at stake for firms, employees, and customers if one of these models diffuses to become the dominant model in the airline industry of the future.

The Commitment/Partnership Strategy

Southwest Airlines

Founded in 1971, seven years before deregulation, Southwest Airlines is the oldest of the "new entrants." In 2004 Southwest became the largest airline serving the domestic United States and has been continually profitable each year other than its first year, an unusual feat in the postderegulation U.S. airline industry. According to a 1993 government report, Southwest's success over time has created pressures for other airlines to change:

> Southwest is having a profound effect on the airline industry. Southwest's much lower operating costs are making it the dominant airline today in the sense that Southwest, more than any other airline, is causing the industry to change. Other airlines cannot compete with Southwest in the same manner as they do with each other.[1]

Southwest's competitive strategy was based from the start on achieving high levels of employee and aircraft productivity and low unit costs through rapid turnaround of its aircraft at the gate. Rapid turnarounds at Southwest were supported by standardization of aircraft and by offering a single class of service and open seating. But rapid turnarounds also require high levels of coordination across the functions involved in flight departures, including pilots, flight attendants, mechanics, ramp agents, gate agents, operations agents, and so on, to maintain a rigorous schedule and get the aircraft on its way without delays, customer complaints, or lost baggage (see figure 5.1). Coordination of the flight departure process at Southwest tends to be characterized by frequent, timely, problem-solving communication between functions, supported by relationships of shared goals, shared knowledge, and mutual respect, a form of coordination that is especially appropriate for work that is highly interdependent, uncertain, and time-constrained.[2] This form of coordination, known as relational coordination, has enabled Southwest to achieve high levels of employee and aircraft productivity while also achieving reliable performance relative to its competitors (figure 5.2 illustrates the dynamics of relational coordination). Table 5.1 shows the relationship between relational coordination and airline performance, where airline performance is an index of quality metrics (on-time performance, baggage handling performance, and

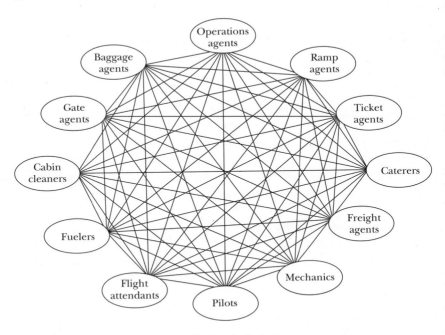

Figure 5.1. Employee work groups involved in the flight departure process.

Source: Jody Hoffer Gittell, *The Southwest Airlines Way: Using the Power of Relationships to Achieve High Performance* (New York: McGraw-Hill, 2003).

customer satisfaction) as well as efficiency metrics (aircraft turnaround time at the gate and employees per passenger enplaned).

The high levels of relational coordination found at Southwest can be attributed to a distinctive set of human resource management practices that focus on building shared goals, shared knowledge, and mutual respect between distinct employee workgroups.[3] Southwest used the hiring process to identify relational competence in addition to functional skills, and it used the training process to further build relational competence. In the *hiring process*, for example, prospective employees were asked to take an incident from their previous work experience when they had a conflict with another employee, and explain how they handled it and what the repercussions were. Selectors tried to identify prospective employees who demonstrate awareness of other people and a respect for their work, as well as the willingness to do what it takes, over and above one's area of functional specialization, to ensure a successful outcome. The *training process* built

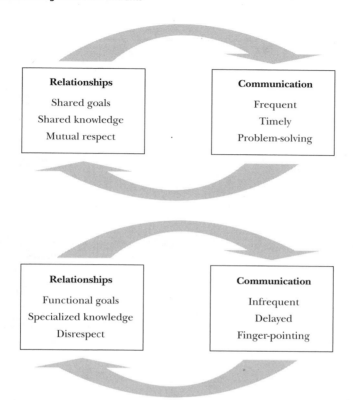

Figure 5.2. Alternative dynamics of relational coordination.

Source: Jody Hoffer Gittell, *The Southwest Airlines Way: Using the Power of Relationships to Achieve High Performance* (New York: McGraw-Hill, 2003).

on this foundation. For example, each employee received on-the-job training from a training coordinator who explained not only the tasks to be performed but which other functions were impacted by those tasks and the significance of each task in achieving Southwest's overall goals. This approach to hiring and training was consistent with *job design* at Southwest, which was based on functional specialization with flexibility around the boundaries of jobs. Job descriptions laid out a set of tasks that were specific to the particular job function, then concluded with broader language such as "and whatever else is needed to ensure a successful operation." One manager explained:

Table 5.1. Relational coordination as a predictor of airline performance

	Flight Departure Performance				
	Turnaround Time	Staff Time per Passenger	Customer Complaints	Lost Bags	Late Arrivals
Relational Coordination	−0.21***	−0.42***	−0.64***	−0.31*	−0.50**
	(0.000)	(0.000)	(0.000)	(0.042)	(0.001)
Flights/Day	−0.19***	−0.37***	−0.30***	0.13	−0.22+
	(0.000)	(0.000)	(0.000)	(0.287)	(0.065)
Flight Length, Passengers,	0.79***	0.45+	0.13	0.12	−0.54**
and Cargo	(0.000)	(0.081)	(0.188)	(0.471)	(0.001)
Passenger Connections	0.12**	0.19**	0.09	0.13	0.00
	(0.004)	(0.008)	(0.329)	(0.287)	(0.987)
R^2	.94	.81	.69	.19	.20

Note: This table shows the impact of relational coordination on flight departure performance. Relational coordination, coordination carried out through relationships of shared goals, shared knowledge, and mutual respect, is measured as the percentage of cross-functional ties that are "strong" or "very strong," based on an employee survey. Flight departure performance includes quality—customer complaints, mishandled bags, and late arrivals—as well as efficiency—turnaround time per departure and staff time per passenger. Exact definitions of performance and product measures and details regarding the sample are reported in Jody Hoffer Gittell, *The Southwest Airlines Way: Using the Power of Relationships to Achieve High Performance* (New York: McGraw-Hill, 2003).

All models are random effects regressions with site/month as the unit of analysis (n=99) and site (n=9) as the random effect. Statistical significance is denoted: +p<0.10 *p<0.05 **p<0.01 ***p<0.001, and suggests the certainty that a change in relational coordination will produce a change in performance, where a smaller p-value suggests a higher certainty. R^2 denotes the percentage of the variation in performance that is explained by the model.

We train people to do a specific function and we train them very well. They are exposed to other functions in their training, but we don't cross-utilize." An employee elaborated: "We are not like People Express [a US airline in the 1980s that was known for cross-utilization]. Each person has a specific job, but part of the job is to help the other person. Then it's easier to work in a more efficient manner.

To support coordination, Southwest assigned an operations agent to serve as a *cross-functional team leader* for each flight departure. This team leader coordinated the information flow around each departure, coming into face-to-face contact with most functions and ensuring that all parties were on the same page. Southwest also invested heavily in *frontline supervisors* (one supervisor per ten to twelve frontline employees, relative to ratios of 1:20 and 1:35 found in other U.S. airlines) based on the long-held philosophy that "the most influential leaders in our company—aside from [the CEO]—are the frontline supervisors." Higher levels of supervisory staffing gave Southwest supervisors responsibility for fewer employees, enabling them to engage actively in coaching and feedback and to relieve workloads at peak times.

To counteract the tendency toward blaming others when things went wrong, Southwest developed a distinctive approach to *performance measurement* in the form of team delays, allowing multiple functions to take responsibility for a given delay so that the onus is removed and the focus can turn to problem-solving rather than the assignment of blame. In addition, Southwest used *conflict resolution* proactively as an opportunity to build a shared understanding of the work process among participants in different functions who may not fully understand each other's perspective. Frontline employees were encouraged to resolve conflicts among themselves whenever possible. Supervisors and managers were encouraged to resolve unresolved conflicts by bringing employees together in meetings that were initially called "come to Jesus meetings" then renamed "team building meetings." The ideal in these meetings was that "a light goes on" and both employees understand the other's point of view in a way that is enriching to them and their ability to work effectively together. The worst-case scenario was that "it blows up in your face," which was sometimes taken to indicate that neither employee was a good fit for Southwest.

Amid the intensity of work at Southwest, there was a concern for *work/family balance*. Employees were encouraged to work hard while at work but also to be themselves and to have fun. As a station manager said, "We always ask people in an evaluation if they are having fun in their job. If they are, there is a good chance they are doing well." Employees were also encouraged to take time off to renew themselves and to maintain their family and community commitments. According to Jim Wimberly, former executive vice president of operations, "It is an intoxicating business. We love the business and this company. We all need to make sure it stays intoxicating and not addictive." Connection to family was further strengthened by the practice of sending letters home to employees and by stepping in to provide help when crisis hits individual employees and their families. Libby Sartain, former vice president of people, pointed out that

> people at Southwest care about one another's families. We recognize deaths and births. We help in times of tragedy. . . . We hire people who have worked for other airlines who say they never received anything at home from their former employers, that they never were acknowledged in a personal way.

Another element of the Southwest model was a commitment to *employment security*. Southwest has deliberately avoided layoffs throughout its thirty-six-year history, even during severe downturns, in the face of the post-9/11 crisis, and in the face of significant automation of customer service functions. According to Herb Kelleher, cofounder and former chief executive officer of Southwest:

> Nothing kills your culture like layoffs. Nobody has ever been furloughed at Southwest and that is unprecedented in the airline industry. It's been a huge strength of ours. It's certainly helped us negotiate our union contracts. We could have furloughed at various times and been more profitable but I always thought that was shortsighted. . . . Not furloughing people breeds loyalty. It breeds a sense of security. It breeds a sense of trust. So in bad times you take care of them and in good times they're thinking, perhaps, "We've never lost our jobs. That's a pretty good reason to stick around."

Unlike some other new entrants, Southwest has not sought to avoid unionization or even to keep unions at arm's length. On the contrary, Southwest's leaders invited union organizing from the start and have strived for *partnership with union representatives*. The result of this strategy is that Southwest is the most highly unionized airline in the United States (currently about 88 percent) with some of the lowest conflict levels in the industry, having suffered only one strike in its thirty-six-year history (with its mechanics in the early 1980s) and having achieved over the years some of the shortest times to negotiate contracts in the industry.[4] President Colleen Barrett explained Southwest's approach:

> We treat all as family, including outside union representatives. We walk into the room not as adversaries, but as working on something together. Our attitude is that we should both do what's good for the company. . . . [Unions] have their constituency, their customer base. We respect that. We have a great relationship with the Teamsters and they have a reputation for being really tough negotiators. We try to stress with everybody that we really like partnerships.

This partnership approach does not eliminate conflict, however. A recent conflict between Southwest and its flight attendants union moved dangerously near the brink of a strike, with a breakdown of respectful communication. Ultimately the conflict was resolved in a way that strengthened the relationship, according to Thom McDaniel, president of the flight attendants union, a local of the Transport Workers Union:

> Gary [Kelly, the new CEO] and Laura [Wright, the CFO] have tried to create a more constructive dialogue. We have a quarterly labor briefing, when profits are reported. Gary talks, then Laura talks. So many more doors are open. The credibility we got . . . has created a much better relationship. I think the company is back on track. . . . Through that conflict we strengthened the relationship. We still walk a tightrope between advocacy and cooperation. But I don't think it would have happened if "the girls" hadn't stood up for themselves.

It is worth mentioning that from the beginning, Southwest's pilots formed an independent union called the Southwest Pilots Association (SWAPA), which has maintained its independence despite the industry's movement toward representation by the Air Line Pilots Association (ALPA). Some observers charge that Southwest has been able to maintain a consistent partnership with its pilots over the years because of SWAPA's independent status. We would simply observe that most of Southwest's unions are not independent, and that Southwest has nevertheless maintained long-term partnerships with them. Moreover, other airlines have independent pilots unions, such as the Airline Pilots Association (APA) at American Airlines, and this fact has not been sufficient to bring about a long-term partnership between American and its pilots. So it seems that independent, "in-house," or employer-specific unions are neither necessary nor sufficient for achieving a long-term sustainable partnership. In addition, given that Southwest pilots and other employee groups are now among the highest paid in the industry, it is hard to argue that they have not benefited from their choice to engage in a long-term partnership with their employer.

Together, Southwest's human resource management practices form a particular type of high-performance work system that is focused on building connections with and among employees—we call it a *relational work system*. To support and maintain these management practices over time, Southwest Airlines has maintained a relatively conservative growth strategy and strived to maintain a strong balance sheet with low debt levels. Southwest set a growth target of 10 to 15 percent per year and remained committed to that target even when the demand for its low-cost product would have enabled far more rapid growth and even when investment analysts chastised Southwest for its conservative approach to financing and growth, as regional director Matt Hafner explained:

The experts always think we need to expand at a more rapid pace. What these so-called experts express is their desire for Southwest to jump at opportunities at a more rapid clip. Apparently growth excites investors. [But] nobody is pushing us. That could never happen.

Slower growth enabled Southwest to build high levels of operational capability, with high levels of employee productivity and commitment and high levels of aircraft utilization that generated the basis for both sustainable low fares and reliable service outcomes, which together were a recipe for customer loyalty. As Kelleher explained in 2000:

> Most people think of us as this flamboyant airline, but we're really very conservative from the fiscal standpoint. We have the best balance sheet in the industry. We've always made sure that we never overreached ourselves. We never got dangerously in debt, and never let costs get out of hand.

These financial reserves have enabled Southwest to avoid layoffs throughout its history, including the Gulf War crisis in the early 1990s and even during the industry crisis following the attacks of September 11, 2001. More recently, the automation of customer service functions has led to overstaffing, but rather than conduct layoffs, Southwest responded with an aggressive "Go Where We're Growing" policy, encouraging employees to move into other functions and sometimes to new cities. As customer service agents moved into flight attendant and ramp agent jobs, training requirements increased and, for a time, certain quality metrics suffered, particularly baggage handling.

While Southwest's unit costs are nearly the lowest in the U.S. industry on a stage-length-adjusted basis, its labor unit costs have become among the highest due in part to the short-run effects of its no-layoff philosophy in the wake of automation and due in part to its philosophy of "sharing the wealth" with employees. As Kelleher told employees in 1994, when Southwest began to face significant low-cost competition from other new entrants, "We want to reduce all of our costs except our wages and benefits and profit-sharing. This is Southwest's way of competing, unlike others who lower their wages and benefits." Southwest's current chief executive officer, Gary Kelly, expressed the same philosophy. When challenged by the *Wall Street Journal* regarding Southwest's relatively high labor costs, he responded:

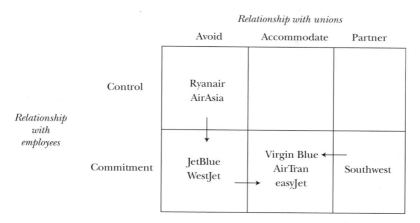

Figure 5.3. Employment system dimensions.

It's true, our employees are well paid. They've produced the most efficient, most profitable airline with the best customer service, and they deserve to share the wealth. . . . Our people know what the airline industry environment is like. I'm confident that they will do what it takes to keep Southwest on top. I would consider it a failure if we have to go to our employees and tell them to take a pay cut.[5]

Rather than viewing its employees as a cost to be minimized, Southwest viewed its employees as partners in reducing costs and producing value. Southwest therefore epitomizes in many ways a high-road strategy, striving for a two-way commitment with its employees and partnership with their union representatives (see figure 5.3 for Southwest's position in our employment system matrix).

In 2007 Southwest was entering a new stage in its development as the U.S. airline paying the highest wages and benefits. As such, the pressure to contain the rate of growth in wages will intensify in the years ahead. Will it maintain the positive workplace culture and low levels of labor-management conflict that have proven to be clear advantages for it? This may depend on whether the company and its employees' unions can find ways to link wage and benefit increases even more closely to changes in performance than they have done in the past.

As we will show in this chapter, several new entrants have sought to emulate Southwest's commitment approach to the employment relationship. But few if any of the other new entrants that we discuss have implemented all aspects of Southwest's approach, particularly its partnership with unions.

The Control/Avoidance Strategy

Ryanair

Ryanair is a large, fast-growing, and profitable new entrant based in Ireland. It has led a transformation of the European airline industry and, like Southwest, it is now influencing new-entrant airlines all over the world. In the late 1980s, Irish officials adopted a two-airline policy, making decisions on routes that would enable Ryanair to better compete with Aer Lingus, for example, by allowing Ryanair to fly into Stansted, a secondary airport near London. Michael O'Leary, then a young accountant working as the personal assistant of owner Tony Ryan, began to influence the direction of Ryanair in 1988 after being appointed to its board of directors. He argued that Ryanair did not have a clear strategy for how and where to grow, and that it was lacking in cost discipline. O'Leary recommended to Ryan that it be closed down, but instead was persuaded by Ryan to turn it around in return for a promised 10 percent of profits and 25 percent of any profits earned in excess of two million euros.[6]

This arrangement set the stage for a contentious period of employment relations at Ryanair. The company then had 450 employees. They had been given shares in the company and had agreed not to join a union on the grounds that they would have influence on how the company was run. There were brief work stoppages in Ryanair's early years at various stages, but these were quickly dealt with.[7] Some of the early attempts to unionize Ryanair seemed to have been dealt with by the company firing the people involved. As part of O'Leary's new deal with Ryanair, pilots were asked to take substantial pay cuts, changes in working conditions, and relocation to new bases with no help with their relocation costs. Of Ryanair's sixty-five pilots, forty-eight were represented by the Irish Airline Pilots Association (IALPA), which argued that Ryanair's senior pilots were already paid only about half of what Aer Lingus's senior pilots were paid, even before pay cuts were made. Ryanair's answer was to hire pilots from the Romanian state airline Tarom. Because they were on work permits and had no ties to IALPA, they could be expected to comply without negotiation with the demands of management. When Ryanair's Irish pilots objected to renewing the work permits of the Romanian pilots, the former were threatened with being fired.

In addition to a punitive approach toward union representation, this incident illustrates a control approach to human resource management at Ryanair, using threats of firing to control employee behavior rather than working to generate commitment to shared goals. Other human resources practices at Ryanair also contrasted sharply with those at Southwest. In contrast to Southwest's focus on balancing work and family, Ryanair's approach was characterized instead by high stress and long work hours:

> Everyone at Ryanair worked long hours. One former employee said it was like being on a treadmill constantly moving at a frenetic pace. "Ryanair felt that it owned you. You were hands-on all the time but there was no direction." Reservations staff worked from eight till eight every day including weekends. Cabin crew could work twenty-seven days in a row without a day off.[8]

Long work hours were seen as a sign of commitment at Ryanair. According to one staff member, "The idea was to recruit a vibrant start-up team, burn them out, then get rid of them and put in a fresh team."[9]

A former manager confirmed that Ryanair works people hard, with cabin crew working four flights per day while facing the additional pressure of making sales to get commission. He noted that there was a tension between the high turnover of cabin crew and the existence of a pool of young people willing to work for Ryanair. The company did not encourage cabin crew to leave, but neither did it try to stop them from going. Because Ryanair had bases in different countries, it was even easier to replace cabin crew with large numbers of potentially willing workers from Eastern European countries. For example, there has been a significant increase in employees from Latvia. To compensate employees for their hard work and to keep unions out, Ryanair paid a competitive rate and also offered stock options to some employee groups. Still, due to the stress, turnover was relatively high.[10]

The stress of working at Ryanair was exacerbated by passenger abuse (known in the United States as "air rage"), brought on by serious quality problems that may reflect disgruntled employees, a too-rapid growth strategy, and a lack of capacity to handle that growth:

> Staff who handled customer grievances were constantly under pressure and won much sympathy from their colleagues. "It was growing too fast," one said. "There was no proper infrastructure and it was constantly taking on more

than it could cope with." "Everywhere you went you were associated with Ryanair," said another. "People would walk up and verbally attack you about problems."[11]

Also in contrast with the Southwest approach were the relatively strict boundaries between jobs found at Ryanair. According to a former employee, at Ryanair people focus on doing their own jobs and don't "interfere" with each other. There was no clear policy to understand other jobs and departments in the airline. Ryanair did not have the flexible job boundaries that were encouraged at Southwest; instead Ryanair employees were told "this is your job, do what you're paid for . . . get the plane turned around." However, management did hold parties to try to bring people together from different departments in an informal way. The young average age of the workforce meant that these events often resulted in the formation of interdepartmental relationships and even marriages.[12]

Similar to leaders at Southwest Airlines, chief executive officer O'Leary could be seen helping on the front line from time to time, whether loading bags or checking in passengers, and would engage in informal activities such as soccer with frontline staff. He professed to have the greatest respect for Ryanair's frontline workers and presented himself as "one of the guys." But unlike Southwest, whose human resource management practices focused on conflict resolution and problem solving rather than blaming, Ryanair's human resource practices relied more heavily on fear of retribution or termination. O'Leary was feared in meetings for his attacks on staff in front of their colleagues.[13] A former manager characterized O'Leary as seen by employees as "aggressive." He was unsure whether employees liked O'Leary or felt a sense of loyalty toward O'Leary or the company. Employees did respect O'Leary because they knew he worked hard, although some employees reportedly begrudged him because he made a lot of money when the company went public.[14]

Nonetheless, because of the high levels of unemployment in Ireland in its earlier years, Ryanair had little problem attracting applicants for positions. At one point when Ryanair was hiring fifty flight attendants, six thousand applications were received. But as unemployment declined in Ireland, Ryanair increasingly looked to Eastern Europe to meet its staffing needs.

Ryanair has continued to maintain its nonunion status, but this status has required active resistance to organizing efforts. In 1998, baggage handlers in the Dublin airport sought union recognition and failed. In 2001, pilots sought union recognition and they also failed. Ryanair has also faced a number of victimization and harassment charges by employees:

A senior Ryanair pilot . . . alleged intimidation and harassment because he was seeking to use normal industrial relations procedures in his dealings with the airline, and to have his concerns represented by IALPA. [The pilot] alleged that he and seven other pilots were written to indicating the 15,000 euros training costs would have to be paid back to the company if Ryanair was "compelled to engage in collective bargaining with any pilot association or trade union" anywhere in Europe. This case was settled out of court with assurance given to [the pilot] on his continued employment and a contribution of 200,000 euros being paid to his legal costs by Ryanair.[15]

Ryanair responded by charging various unions with intimidating Ryanair pilots through their posting on a website, a case that went to the Irish High Court. The judge ruled against Ryanair, saying, "The only evidence of intimidation related to the conduct of the airline." The judge went further to say that "there are occasions . . . to say things that I found extremely difficult but which could not be left unsaid," describing the evidence brought by Ryanair's senior management as "baseless" and "false." He further described the actions of Ryanair as characterized by "despotic indifference," "sneering disregard," a "façade of concern," and "unburdened by integrity."[16]

New evidence regarding safety issues associated with pilot fatigue surfaced in 2006, reflecting Ryanair's high stress and long work hours' management approach. According to IALPA, Ryanair treats fatigue "simply as a control issue, that if somebody is fatigued they've lost a day and you go after them to try and get the day back. You put a system in place that would intimidate people and will provide a disincentive for people to report fatigue, so therefore it gets swept under the carpet."[17] Ryanair has experienced some success in defending its approach in court, however.[18]

The pilots unions and the International Transport Workers Federation (ITF) run public relations campaigns against Ryanair. ITF's campaign, Ryan-be-Fair, includes an "Appeal for Fairness" petition, which argues that "employees deserve respect and the right to make a free choice about joining together with their co-workers for a unified voice in their workplace."[19] But such campaigns have not hampered Ryanair's growth, which is fueled by continuing high demand for low-cost air travel across Europe. According to IATA, Ryanair carried 40.5 million international passengers in 2006, more than any other international airline that year.[20]

Siobhan Tiernan, Joe Wallace, and Lorraine White have summarized the Ryanair approach to employment relations:

Unions are opposed using simple mechanisms such as replacing unionized workers where necessary, demanding individual undertakings affecting the right of unionization and using the law to avoid collective bargaining. . . . Ryanair also eschews human resource management, and uses considerable indirect labor in the form of agency workers. It makes widespread use of outsourcing, using its negotiating position to attract favorable terms. All of this is consistent with a low-cost business model where the key focus is on keeping costs down and employees [are viewed as] one cost among others.[21]

Despite stark differences from Southwest's employment relations strategy, Ryanair tried to emulate certain elements of Southwest's competitive strategy. In particular, it adopted Southwest's strategy of picking city pairs with potential high volume, and serving those city pairs with high frequencies at very low fares, to dominate the competition on a route-by-route basis. It also copied Southwest's quick turnarounds of aircraft to achieve high aircraft and employee productivity. But Ryanair's leadership neglected two of Southwest's most critical lessons: first, that the airline could be superior on both fares and customer service, and second, that it could do so by putting employees first. As a result, although profits have been substantial at Ryanair, there have been considerable costs to customer service and to employees. Although its reliability measures (on-time and baggage handling) are now reasonably good, Ryanair continues to have problems and negative publicity about its treatment of employees and customers, as well as the service experience more generally.

In sum, Ryanair's approach to employees is based on control rather than commitment and its approach to unions is to avoid them. We therefore place Ryanair in the top left corner of our employment system matrix (see figure 5.3), a position opposite to that of Southwest.

AirAsia

New-entrant AirAsia is one of the most prominent airlines in Asia's fast-growing market with an employment relations strategy and a competitive strategy that resembled Ryanair's.[22] Conor McCarthy, former director of group operations at Ryanair, was one of AirAsia's nonexecutive directors who was instrumental in assisting owner Tony Fernandes in remodeling AirAsia into a low-cost airline.[23]

Accordingly, following Ryanair, AirAsia did not provide additional on-board services ("frills") as part of the fare. Instead, food, drink, and AirAsia-branded merchandise could be purchased onboard. Like Southwest and many other new-entrant airlines, AirAsia sought high aircraft productivity through the rapid turnaround of aircraft. Typically, the turnaround time for a Boeing 737 or an equivalent aircraft (seating approximately 148 people) was twenty-five minutes with refueling or sixteen minutes without refueling. Aircraft utilization has grown at AirAsia from 10.1 hours per day in 2001 to 12.1 hours per day in 2005. Increasing stage length is one way to improve aircraft utilization, due to the time-consuming nature of ground time. However, AirAsia improved its aircraft utilization even while its stage lengths became shorter, suggesting that it had found ways to speed up the turnaround process on the ground.

As a result, AirAsia was one of the most cost-efficient low-cost airlines in the world. In 2001, the airline's operating costs were 4.6 cents per available seat kilometer, but by 2005 it had cut this to just 2.2 cents.[24] In terms of reliability, AirAsia's published record was impressive. However, according to a former manager the published data are rather superficial and open to manipulation such as rescheduling delayed flights so that published statistics do not reveal delays.

Similar to Ryanair, AirAsia's management approach was based primarily on control and compliance. A former manager explained that

> [AirAsia has] a wishy-washy approach to employment where the boss decides most of the time. . . . They have an HR department but it is very lean and mean. People are not very oriented in human resource management—they are what I call "Human Remains." There are no policies—many of the positions [Tony Fernandes] decides and there is no system for pay [levels] or a pay scale because it's all designed by him. So it is very much a coercive setup. If you look at systems of thinking it's very much a prison approach."

This management style is illustrated by the number of dismissals that have been contested at AirAsia under Malaysian labor law.

In the hiring process, AirAsia selected for strong communication skills and "good looks" in addition to technical competency. The resources invested in hiring are minimal relative to AirAsia's high rates of growth, and particularly given the high labor-turnover rates. Hiring policy was often based on "get them in fast and now." This practice corresponded with the dramatic growth in staffing levels, which increased almost tenfold from the company's takeover in late 2001 until the end of the 2005 fiscal year, from 241 to 2,016 employees.[25] AirAsia's human resource management department was not always involved in the hiring process and there was a minimum of training resources invested in each new employee. Training was conducted to ensure the new hires had the functional skills required to do their job, but there was little in the way of training for soft skills such as communication, conflict resolution, and other teamwork skills.

Pilot pay was comparable to that at Malaysia Airlines although AirAsia paid less money into employees' pension funds and provided no meal allowance. Despite these differences, AirAsia was successful in recruiting formerly retired pilots of Malaysia Airlines, especially after it had successfully lobbied the Malaysian government to lift the retirement age for pilots. Wages for all employee groups had not changed significantly in the last five years:

> In the first year of take-over Tony gave staff an annual increment. That was the last so far—none during the last four years. I got a 7 percent increment after the first year but after that we never heard of any more because Tony said we were coming up to listing [an initial public offering of stock] and fuel prices are on the increase, we are expanding and this is why I say the BS [bullshit] factor comes in a lot. And as Asians we are not the complaining culture, unlike the Western people who will . . . tell you off. Asians will tell you off behind your back.

AirAsia had a group profit-sharing plan, a fairly commonplace feature of pay policies in Malaysia and Singapore. In addition to this plan, when AirAsia was listed on the Main Board of the stock exchange in 2004, it established an employee share ownership plan (ESOP) in which the initial plan was to allow employees to purchase discounted stock up to 5 percent of the firm's value. Other employment benefits were similar to the industry average. Promotion did not reflect seniority as was the industry norm including at Malaysian Airlines, but rather was at the discretion of the chief executive officer.

However, certain indications suggested movement toward a commitment strategy. AirAsia established a training academy in 2005 and stated in its annual report that "there are comprehensive training modules to ensure that the AirAsia 'culture' is instilled into every employee and to ensure our customer service quality maintains its highest standards."[26] Although there were some signs that AirAsia's hiring and training processes were not keeping pace with its growth, other signs suggested that AirAsia was attempting to put into place the means to build its human resource infrastructure.

Job design at AirAsia was similar to that of Southwest in that employees were assigned to functionally specialized jobs but were expected to go beyond those jobs to do what was needed to ensure a successful operation. Job design at AirAsia was described more specifically as being a "split egg" role where 70 percent of staff time was dedicated to a specific functional role and the remaining 30 percent was spent responding to situational issues where staff was expected to "think on their feet." An example of this is during the departure process when flights are delayed. Customer service staff normally coordinated departures, but in the event of delays all employees assisted to solve the problems. Although functional flexibility was expected, however, it was not clear whether the mechanisms were in place to support it.

Fernandes emphasized the importance of communication with employees as part of his goal of building high levels of employee loyalty at AirAsia. But communication tended to be top down, with no channels for employee voice. In addition to communicating to staff via e-mail, Fernandes typically organized a monthly staff forum at a hotel. These were designed to be fun events to motivate staff but, according to a former manager, there was little attempt to seek the views and suggestions of staff. Moreover, there were no systematic or formalized conflict resolution procedures. Fernandes has complained in a published interview that his biggest challenge is

> to get people to think. At AirAsia, we want 4,000 brains working for us. My biggest challenge is to get people to talk, to express themselves, to get people to challenge me and say "Tony, you're talking rubbish." That's what I want, not people who say "Yes, sir." The senior management doesn't have all the answers. I want the guy on the ramp to have the confidence to tell me what's wrong.[27]

One observer noted that this lack of open expression undermined the culture that Fernandes claimed to be building:

> [AirAsia is] not the big happy family that Tony talks about. You . . . must understand that Tony is very Western so you have candidness and frankness. In the Asian culture no way is someone going to tell their boss, "Hey, you are an idiot," and so forth—they will tell others. So what kind of happy family are we talking about?

Despite some attempts to move toward a commitment strategy, these attempts were undermined by control-oriented management practices that were inconsistent with such a strategy. Furthermore, AirAsia continued to emulate Ryanair's union-avoidance strategy. At AirAsia, union "is a dirty five-letter word to the CEO himself—he doesn't like to hear it." A former manager at AirAsia predicted that unionization is likely to occur because there is a lack of trust between management and the workforce and employees are working well beyond the maximum number of hours per week permitted under Malaysian labor law.

In short, AirAsia's approach to employment relations is more consistent with the model exemplified by Ryanair than with that of Southwest Airlines. AirAsia aims for a strong culture in which employees are loyal to the company, but its control-oriented management practices appear to be inconsistent with such a culture. Given AirAsia's opposition to unions and its control-oriented management practices, we place AirAsia in the upper left-hand box of our employment system matrix, along with Ryanair (see figure 5.3), though the arrow pointing downward indicates that AirAsia says that it wishes to move toward more of a commitment-based model.

The Commitment/Accommodation Strategy

Some new entrants have adopted hybrid approaches, borrowing from Southwest's commitment-based approach to the employment relationship but seeking to maintain more traditional bargaining relationships with unions (Virgin Blue, AirTran, and easyJet), or seeking like Ryanair to avoid unions altogether (JetBlue Airways and WestJet). In this section we analyze the commitment/accommodation strategy, and in the following section we analyze the commitment/avoidance strategy.

Virgin Blue

Virgin Blue is an Australian new entrant that initially followed the Southwest model.[28] It also learned from other new entrants, including WestJet. Virgin Blue's original leadership invested much effort in its human resource management practices, claiming that its success relied on happy, motivated, and committed staff. It particularly focused on recruiting, selecting, inducting, and training the most appropriate people to join Virgin Blue. Virgin Blue used "targeted selection" as a recruitment strategy.[29] According to Bruce Highfield, Virgin Blue's first general manager of people, "When we recruit we look for people who are genuinely interested in making somebody's journey or someone's life at work more interesting. We call it 'Virgin Flair.'" Successful applicants were subject to a series of individual and group interviews, role-playing, medical and drug examinations, and other tests depending on the position for which they applied. Customer service applicants were tested on customer service and teamwork behaviors. They were then offered either a position in a training center and a start date or placed on a waiting list until a position became available.[30]

Virgin Blue recruitment staff were trained to understand the notion of "psychological type" and to look for both rational and emotional intelligence in interviewees. First and foremost, Virgin Blue sought to employ workers with optimistic attitudes. It looked for two key qualities—an achievement-oriented attitude and an ability to influence others to be achievement oriented. Virgin Blue looked for people who treated guests with respect, even when things in their personal lives were going badly. Virgin Blue's initial share offering explained that "people who pay only a dollar fare to Virgin Blue still expect the "full banana," i.e., good service. Virgin Blue likens the concept of Virgin Flair, among other things, as akin to self-awareness or self-control. Virgin Blue also says 'it's a great marketing tool.'"[31] Virgin Blue placed emphasis on recruiting people who had the right attitudes and aptitudes, rather than recruiting primarily on the basis of their industry experience. This new entrant sought to avoid traditional airline notions of functional specialization that would hamper employees from cooperating across work boundaries.

Like Southwest, Virgin Blue had traditional areas of job specialization but with flexibility around the boundaries of these jobs. Labor costs were reduced by ensuring that its crew members were skilled in a variety of areas and were flexible about the roles they worked in.[32] To encourage flexibility, the airline had broad job descriptions—areas of specialization were similar to those in the rest of the industry, but with the understanding that people would go beyond their jobs to help others as needed. In his induction talk to new recruits, chief executive officer Brett Godfrey typically said, "We don't know the meaning of the word demarcation." He and other managers illustrated this by occasionally helping to load bags and, when traveling, by helping to clean the plane.

As well as broadening the expertise of employees, this strategy has implications for productivity. For instance, team members had a practical knowledge and understanding of other job functions and could assist in other departments during busy periods. As staff members gained experience of each section they could apply that knowledge to whatever job they were working in. Baggage handlers tend to have a higher injury rate than most other jobs in the industry, but in view of the cross-training strategy, injured workers could be rehabilitated while working in another less physically demanding department (e.g., the call center).

According to a union representative, Virgin Blue puts "a lot of time and effort into training people." In order to support cross-functional coordination and flexibility, Virgin trained employees not only in their immediate area of functional expertise but also to have an awareness of the big picture. As one manager commented, "It's that old dilemma again: Do we employ a person to lay bricks or to build a cathedral? We want cathedral builders!" Consistent with this approach, Godfrey meets with employees during orientation and encourages them to be problem solvers, then follows this up with a stream of further communications with staff (e.g., via lavish staff parties). He exhorts them to try new things to solve problems and not to be worried about making mistakes, except in the field of safety where there is no scope for compromise.

Like Southwest, Virgin Blue aimed to achieve cost savings primarily through efficient work practices rather than through reducing pay and benefits. For ground workers, there were few differences in pay between Virgin Blue and legacy airline workers in Australia, though Virgin's work rules were far more flexible. In addition to pay, Virgin Blue gave all employees $1,000 worth of shares when the company's shares were floated. Still, like many high-commitment employers, Virgin Blue took the view that monetary rewards were not sufficient to achieve high levels of employee commitment. According to Highfield:

> No one really comes to work just to get paid. People come to work to satisfy a range of personal needs and have fulfillment about them. So when a company can fill an individual's needs, that's when you get maximum [performance] power.[33]

As at Southwest, Virgin Blue also invested a great deal in frontline leadership, giving its supervisors a span of control of only about five frontline employees.[34] This narrow span of control enabled supervisors to engage in coaching and feedback at a personal level. As Highfield put it:

It's very much about relationships at work, and it's very much about how they're handled and how our performance feedback is given to them. . . . Australians don't like to be publicly recognized. They do like to be recognized, but they like it to be done in private and they like it to be from someone they respect and from someone who they genuinely believe has some idea about what they actually do.

Therefore, Virgin Blue did not reward employees using public recognition schemes. Instead, it focused on behavioral performance monitoring, and shared the results with employees. For instance, at the end of each trip, cabin crew supervisors logged on a database a behavior-monitoring report for each member of the cabin crew on the flight. Then cabin crew and supervisors could review their performance on the database, track trends in their performance, and read the comments made about their behaviors.

In addition to high levels of staffing for frontline leadership, Virgin Blue implemented other innovative methods for communicating with employees, for example, "pulse surveys" of employee attitudes and "pep talks" via DVDs. These were designed to inform employees about the company's direction as well as to provide answers in an attempt to preempt too much gossip. Virgin Blue also conducted weekly meetings in which thirty employees met with management to brainstorm and discuss any issues concerning employees. These were rather like the "pocket meetings" used at JetBlue Airways and the meetings that easyJet was beginning to implement at the time of our research. Virgin Blue also encouraged employees to use its e-mail system to communicate directly with each other.

Virgin Blue tried in many respects to emulate the human resource management practices developed by Southwest Airlines. Like Southwest, Virgin hired for relational qualities as well as for technical expertise, though unlike Virgin Blue, Southwest extended these criteria to pilots and mechanics as well as to customer service functions. Like Southwest, Virgin Blue achieved a high degree of flexibility in its work organization. Also like Southwest, Virgin strived to achieve cost reductions by partnering with its employees rather than through reductions in wage and benefits, while maintaining the view that monetary rewards alone are not sufficient to motivate employees.

In common with Southwest, Virgin Blue also recognized unions from its inception as a new-entrant airline. Virgin aimed to recognize "the most appropriate unions" to work with, expressing a preference for working with unions that understood the differences between new-entrant and legacy airlines. Initially Virgin Blue was envisaged as a new entrant that would have only a few routes and check-in options. It was a much smaller airline with less complicated processes than those at the big legacies. Virgin Blue recognized unions that supported efficient work practices and would not seek to enforce traditional demarcations.

For example, the new entrant preferred a union that would not fight for its check-in staff to have equal pay to that of legacy airline check-in staff. Virgin argued that its check-in process was easier as most of its tickets were booked online, whereas the Qantas check-in process was more complicated and involved a dozen different screens.

In essence, Virgin was seeking flexible relationships with its employees and their unions. Its cooperative approach helped to build trust between Virgin Blue, its employees, and unions, and avoided lingering conflicts that may have arisen about the issue if it had opposed unions. Initially Virgin Blue approached the Transport Workers Union (TWU) to cover all Virgin Blue employees. However, the TWU did not want to organize flight attendants and, following its previous experiences with pilots, was reluctant to organize Virgin Blue pilots. Nevertheless, the TWU agreed to cover the rest of Virgin Blue's employees. Hence the flight attendants were organized by the Flight Attendants Association of Australia (FAAA).

Before Virgin Blue was launched, the Australian Federation of Air Pilots (AFAP) sought to represent the pilots. After Virgin negotiated with AFAP, these parties made an initial two-year enterprise bargaining agreement (an Australian term for union contracts). They have subsequently negotiated further agreements. AFAP claims to organize about 80 percent of the pilots.[35]

Virgin Blue therefore works with only three unions and negotiates three contracts, in contrast with Qantas, which deals with at least sixteen unions and has a workforce that is covered by forty-eight separate contracts.[36]

According to a Virgin executive, it took the unions some time to realize that Virgin Blue was a new-entrant airline and therefore not directly comparable with legacies.[37] The unions representing the ground workers and flight attendants say that they have generally had good relationships with Virgin Blue.[38] According to the TWU, they had to raise a Virgin issue only once during the previous five years at the Industrial Relations Commission. The TWU explained that generally it has settled issues with the company through negotiation and consultation at the local level. The TWU has initiated industrial action with Virgin Blue only once, which resulted in the establishment of what it calls "rules of engagement," which in its view have since been followed.

In its early years, Virgin Blue followed a far more aggressive growth strategy than Southwest. Whereas Southwest's annual growth rates in its first five years of operation were 75 percent, 1 percent, 17 percent, 42 percent, and 27 percent, then leveling out to an average of 15 percent per year, Virgin Blue's growth rates were between 100 and 200 percent for its first five years. It had not initially planned to grow so quickly, but its rapid growth was opportunistic, following the collapse of Ansett in 2001 when Virgin Blue had been flying for only a year. As a result, Virgin Blue had won a third of the Australian domestic market share by its fourth year. Despite this rapid growth, Virgin Blue managed to maintain relatively low unit costs, about 35 percent lower than Qantas, as well as high levels of operational reliability, with on-time performance consistently higher than that of Qantas.

Unlike most legacies, including Qantas (which is more profitable), and despite the rise in fuel costs, Virgin Blue has not resorted to layoffs so far. It has stated that laying off staff would be only a last resort. Since it has invested much resources in them, Virgin Blue values retaining employees. When there is a dispute between an employee(s) and a supervisor or the company more generally, the company tries to settle the problem and rekindle the individual's confidence in the company. The three recognized unions can raise issues on behalf of their members with Virgin Blue.

Virgin appears to have the necessary mechanisms in place to maintain a commitment-based relationship with its employees and a partnership with its unions. However, after some changes in its ownership and top management, Virgin Blue changed its approach, at least with respect to union partnership. The original management spoke of engaging the unions early on to identify mutual-gains solutions for Virgin Blue and its workers. However, in 2007 the draft contracts that it negotiated with the pilots and with the cabin crew were both overwhelmingly rejected in staff ballots. Although it does not appear that the new management team is seeking union avoidance, nor is it seeking to partner with them.

Virgin Blue is still seeking to promote a commitment approach especially with regard to its flight attendants and other staff who interact with customers. In accord with a Singapore Airlines precedent, AFAP had suggested that Virgin should agree to a generous profit-sharing bonus scheme with the pilots at Virgin. AFAP held that this would help to win the pilots' commitment and induce them to moderate their salary claims. However, Virgin was willing to make such an arrangement only with its senior executives, with a much more modest bonus scheme for the pilots.

In short, Virgin's current relationship with unions is based on accommodation. We therefore put Virgin Blue in the lower middle box of our employment system matrix (see figure 5.3) with an arrow pointing from the right, reflecting Virgin Blue's migration from its early informal partnership toward a more traditional accommodation strategy.

This matrix facilitates discussion, but it is of course a generalization. For example, if we had space here for a more detailed analysis, including a separate focus on different occupational groups, we would put Virgin Blue's relations with the ground workers union (TWU) closer to the partner box than its relations with pilots union (AFAP), which has more adversarial relations with the airline, and so is not as close to the partner box.

easyJet

A decade after the launch of Ryanair, easyJet was launched in 1995 in the United Kingdom. EasyJet has grown rapidly. Like Ryanair, easyJet followed the Southwest competitive strategy of having relatively frequent, low-cost flights on high-density city pair routes, with an operating strategy of quick turnarounds of aircraft at the gate to achieve high aircraft and employee productivity. According to Mike Campbell, easyJet's director of people, "Our turn time at the gate is twenty minutes. We used to build in longer flight times as a buffer to get the on-time arrivals. But that can really mess up the operations so we don't do that as much anymore."[39]

EasyJet seeks to differentiate itself on operational excellence and service quality as well as low costs. According to Campbell:

> We are low, low cost . . . [but] we also want to be known for our operational excellence—our on-time performance must be the best in the world. We'll continually drive down cost per seat and [increase] our profit per seat. [Overall], our customer proposition is low cost with care and convenience.[40]

The unit costs of easyJet were about double those of Ryanair though still below those of the legacy airlines, while its reputation for reliability and customer satisfaction was better than that of Ryanair.[41]

Differentiating itself from Ryanair, in recent years easyJet has followed much of Southwest's employment-relations strategy, seeking to achieve employee commitment. Campbell explained: "Our people proposition is that we aim to be a great place to work. We measure our success at delivering that by looking at how people feel, which we measure through our annual survey and what they do through employee attendance and retention."[42] EasyJet sought to keep its pay in line with that of other employers, paying less than the legacy airlines, but more than Ryanair. According to Campbell, easyJet's policy was that pay is important but not ultimately what drives satisfaction: "If we don't treat employees well, no amount of compensation can make up for that."

Human resource practices at easyJet included a strong focus on performance measurement and the use of pay for performance. For example, Campbell said:

> Flight attendants get 50 percent in base pay, about 38 percent based on the sectors they fly, 8 to 9 percent commission on onboard sales (they earn 10 percent of sales on board as a team, and 3 to 4 percent depending on if the company hits its profit target). Pilots get 80 percent in base pay, 5 to 10 percent based on length of service, 5 percent based on the sectors they fly, and we proposed 4 to 10 percent bonus based on company performance.[43]

Pilots initially did not agree to the company's pay-for-performance proposal:

> [Pilots] are a risk-averse group, which is a good thing. We want that in pilots. But they didn't go for the bonus based on performance. They didn't trust how it was being measured. Turns out if they had, they would have done very well in the last round. Their representatives now support it, and we think they will too in the next round. We are starting with a bonus based on company performance, then we hope to move to a bonus based on directly controllable performance—on-time, fuel utilization, etc. But first we have to build up credibility and trust with them.[44]

Managers were also paid based on performance, taking into account a range of measures such as people (employee satisfaction and retention), contribution per seat, cost per seat, and so on. Performance measures have the potential to divide workers as well as motivate them, however, which is why Southwest has sought to create cross-functional performance measures to support relational coordination and reduce the tendency toward blaming others. Many of easyJet's performance measures appear to follow this principle.

Similar to Southwest, easyJet hired for teamwork in addition to hiring for functional expertise. Campbell explained easyJet's approach to hiring pilots:

> We want their technical expertise, but we also want them to be part of the team, responsible for working closely with the cabin crew. We also want them to be responsible to the customer. We know they can have a tremendous impact on how customers perceive us. So we need to recruit, select, and develop people who have business acumen in addition to their technical or functional skills.[45]

Although these hiring ideas were not new, Campbell explained, they had not been fully implemented when he joined the airline in 2005:

> We've had the concept of Orange Wings before, a vision of what it means to be a crew member in easyJet, but have never truly taken it beyond the concept stage: doing sensible things to help the overall operation. We've just been introducing elements of understanding the big picture, focusing on attitude and behavioral competence, refreshing what we've always done and most importantly keeping everyone involved. Between the CEO and the management team at least one of us attends every induction program for new starters and every recurrent training.[46]

EasyJet's approach to job boundaries was similar to Southwest's. EasyJet employees had specialized jobs, but at the same time were encouraged to cross functional boundaries to help others as needed:

> If someone says that isn't my job, they are not an easyJet employee. We are uncomfortable with very defined job descriptions. In the early days, if we had a problem, it was simple. Someone would just step in to help. Now it's harder. We're bigger. We need to remember to ask: What can I do to help? Clearly there are specific areas of technical competence that require specific skills and training, but I'm talking beyond that. . . . People fairly comfortably step in. But still, we're not there yet. It's more a journey.[47]

To achieve the goal of everyone helping others as needed, people needed to be better trained in understanding the big picture, according to Campbell:

> The challenge is getting people to understand there is a whole set of processes that operate in parallel, not in sequence. We need everyone to consider how

they can contribute to the whole. It's *The Fifth Discipline* by [Peter] Senge, real systems thinking. It's also consistent with what we read about successful low-cost airlines like Southwest. It's the ability to manage every element successfully, not just one thing. It's a lot of little things put together.[48]

Similar to Southwest, easyJet management believed that frontline leadership was important, though this belief had not yet been translated into action:

We now have four thousand people, one thousand pilots, eighteen hundred cabin crew, and the rest of headquarters [all ground operations are outsourced, as is common in Europe]. They rarely see each other. We are trying to figure out how to connect. Base managers are critical. In a volume business, you can usually centralize the decision making, but not in this business. Frontline managers are critical. We don't do enough. Two people in charge of a base is not enough. We need to understand that role better.[49]

Another communication tool that easyJet management had developed was regular meetings between top management and frontline employees, according to Campbell:

Each member of the executive team has adopted a base to focus on, to talk about our strategic goals—and to listen. I have Liverpool and Bristol and will visit them once a quarter. It's like our back-to-the-shop-floor program. The senior management team will operate with the crew on board. We'll help out, sell, clean. We learn things that way.[50]

EasyJet's growth was part of the value proposition it offered to employees. Growing at a steady rate of 15 percent per year, easyJet was able to offer job security and opportunities for promotion:

Job security has not been an issue. Our growth has been such that we've always been recruiting. We will be hiring about 450 pilots this year and eight hundred to nine hundred cabin crew. We are planning to do 15 percent growth per year over the next six to seven years and beyond. . . . This means we have lots of promotion opportunities. This is one of our big attractions relative to the flagship [legacy] airlines. Pilots can get lots of flying hours and more opportunities to progress. We also have a point-to-point network that gets most of them home every night.[51]

EasyJet's approach to its unions is harder to characterize given that it has changed over time. EasyJet was highly unionized with two unions representing its flight attendants, one that represents call center employees, and one that represents the pilots. Ground handling functions were outsourced. But the early labor/management relations at easyJet were adversarial; the company initially refused to recognize the British Air Line Pilots Association (BALPA) for collective bargaining, despite extensive union membership within the company.[52] BALPA was able to secure recognition from easyJet in 2001, following a change in the UK Employment Relations Act in 1999, but the memory of adversarial industrial relations at easyJet was not easily overcome.

According to a 2002 survey of unionized pilots, easyJet pilots were the least satisfied of all pilots in the United Kingdom. EasyJet pilots reported that they were particularly dissatisfied with their relations with management (95 percent dissatisfied) and with the management of industrial relations problems (97 percent dissatisfied). Schedules were one aspect of the discontent. To cite two examples:

> A second captain who had previously flown with a different UK airline commented on the "inadequate roster system" operated by easyJet, which meant that he was "almost always tired." A newly recruited first officer . . . maintained that although he was "happy at first," after ten months with the airline he believed that his quality of work life was "inadequate." He claimed that pilots at the airline were being "worked off their feet" and that flight rosters were organized in a reactive manner: "I object to driving for an hour [to the airport] to fly two sectors. This wastes time and money and saps morale." The gravity of this issue was expressed in August 2002 when easyJet pilots threatened industrial action against the airline.[53]

Even in 2006, Campbell acknowledged that these scheduling problems had yet to be fully overcome:

> There were problems bubbling around the network, which manifested themselves in pay negotiations but in reality probably had little or nothing to do with pay—more around lifestyle than pay—typically rostering stability. We just weren't listening. . . . There have been some difficulties with the trade unions, some relating to differing agendas, some to do with me being new—relationships are key, but really the key is the relationship with the employees.[54]

Yet there were signs of positive change. An IALPA source in 2006 contrasted Ryanair's approach to pilot fatigue to that of easyJet and Aer Lingus: "[The IALPA representative] pointed to easyJet as having a corporate culture where fatigue is treated as genuine. Their attitude is 'it exists and it's a danger to the operation, [so] we better find out what causes it and try and minimize it.' "[55] In view of this and of Campbell's claim that management is trying to build trust with the pilots to sell the idea of performance-based pay, it would appear that easyJet is developing a commitment approach toward its employees with the rhetoric and management practices appropriate to sustain such an approach. Further, we conclude that easyJet has moved from a union-avoidance strategy to one of accommodating unions. We therefore put easyJet in the lower middle box in our employment system matrix (see figure 5.3) and we include an arrow alongside easyJet to indicate that its position has recently changed.

AirTran

Founded in 1993 in the United States, AirTran became a significant player in 1997 when it merged with ValuJet, another 1993 new entrant that was known for high levels of outsourcing and that was popular with investors until it experienced an air crash in 1996 that killed all passengers and crew on board. ValuJet was saved from likely demise by its merger with the smaller AirTran.

AirTran has developed an approach to hiring that is similar to Southwest's, emphasizing functional skills as well as relational competence. Training also included a focus on the links between individual job performance and the airline's overall financial performance, and the importance of achieving high levels of customer service and efficiency: "Employees are repeatedly exposed to the concept that customer service pays their next paycheck."[56] Like Southwest, AirTran has been proactive with cross-functional conflict resolution. Also like Southwest, AirTran had clear job specialization with the expectation of flexibility between jobs as required by day-to-day operational circumstances. However, the Southwest approach to training that focuses on the link between individual jobs and the overall work process was less evident at AirTran. AirTran also put more focus on choreographing the departure process than Southwest had, resulting in greater standardization of operations.[57]

AirTran sought to keep pay and benefits near, but slightly below, industry averages in an effort to keep costs below competitors,[58] even though pay cuts at the legacy airlines made it difficult to keep pay at or below the industry average. Several AirTran employee groups were unionized—pilots, flight attendants, and mechanics— while the others attempted to organize but had failed so far. AirTran has adopted a strategy of accommodating its unions, in contrast to Southwest's partnership approach. Chief executive officer Joe Leonard characterized his approach to labor relations as "keep it simple and say no a lot."[59]

Like Southwest, AirTran has followed a relatively conservative growth strategy, aiming for a steady 20 to 25 percent annual rate of growth, and along with Southwest and JetBlue was one of the few airlines to avoid layoffs after September 11. Leonard wants to continue providing job security while tying it to the need for high productivity.

With these policies, AirTran has achieved low total unit costs equal to those of Southwest, adjusted for stage length, and just above those of Jet-Blue, with labor unit costs that are the lowest in the industry. AirTran succeeded in reducing these costs over time as its primary competitor, Delta Airlines, reduced its costs. Its quality outcomes have been above average for the industry, and have sometimes exceeded those of Southwest and JetBlue. Customer complaints in 2007 were 0.83 per 100,000 customers, better than the industry average of 1.39 but worse than JetBlue's 0.78 and Southwest's industry-leading 0.26 complaints per million passengers. AirTran's on-time performance in 2007 was 77 percent, between Southwest's at 80 percent and JetBlue's at 70 percent. And AirTran was first in baggage handling performance at 4.06 lost bags per thousand passengers, ahead of JetBlue at 5.23 and Southwest at 5.87.

AirTran's employment strategy is positioned in the lower middle box of our employment system matrix (see figure 5.3) to signify that it focuses on achieving commitment from its employees while carrying out a traditional arm's-length bargaining relationship with its unions.

The Commitment/Avoidance Strategy

JetBlue Airways

JetBlue has been a success story in many respects. As one industry commentator noted in 2004: "There seems to be a 'JetBlue is a Great Airline' story once a week."[60] JetBlue was founded in 2000 by David Neeleman who had helped to build a small low-cost airline called Morris Air in the late 1980s before selling it to Southwest. Neeleman became part of Southwest's management team for a brief period but was seen as a poor fit with the Southwest culture and was asked to leave. He was involved with the development of WestJet, which became Canada's most successful low-cost airline. Then after his noncompete agreement with Southwest expired in 1999, Neeleman started JetBlue, a new type of low-cost airline with a more luxurious on-board experience. As Neeleman explained:

> We're a new kind of low-fare airline, with deep pockets, new planes, leather seats with more legroom, great people and innovative thinking. With our friendly service and hassle free technology, we're going to bring humanity back to air travel.[61]

With initial financing of $130 million, making JetBlue the best-financed start-up airline in the United States, Neeleman put together a management team that drew several members from Southwest, including its original chief financial officer and vice president of human resources. Despite certain differences in its competitive strategy, JetBlue sought to emulate Southwest in many respects, particularly with its focus on people as the key source of competitive advantage. Although JetBlue prided itself on its technological innovations, Vince Stabile, senior vice president of people, pointed out, "Anything technological, someone can beat you on. What they can't beat us on is our people."[62] Consistent with JetBlue's Southwest roots, employees were put ahead of the customer: "We worry about crew members first, rather than the customer. We can trust that if the leadership really worries about crew members, then crew members will worry about the customer."[63] Similar to Southwest, JetBlue supported this philosophy with heavy investment in hiring and training, as Stabile explained:

> We focus on hiring people who are as good a match to the culture as they are to the skills required for the job; it's a true 50/50 balance. We give them the right kind of initial introduction as well as training so that they've got all of the tools that they need to do their job. However, we give them a lot of latitude in decision making, so that what we do is provide leadership and guidance rather than rules, and then when people mess up we treat it as a coaching opportunity rather than a disciplining opportunity.[64]

Despite these parallels, some important features distinguish JetBlue's human resource strategy from Southwest's. First, despite the stated intent that frontline supervisors would serve as coaches, there was relatively little support for frontline leadership at JetBlue in the early years:

> We began hearing fairly frequently that "my leader/manager/supervisor is not very good." Rather than clean them out, we realized that we're the ones that really dropped the responsibility. Because in many cases, people were in leadership roles for the first time, particularly people internally, promoted from within. We were basically promoting great performers, but not giving them the tools that they needed to transition.[65]

To address this shortcoming, JetBlue developed a leadership institute based on its Principles of Leadership.

Second, JetBlue differed from Southwest in its relatively weak focus on building teamwork between different functions. There seemed to be an expectation that such teamwork would just happen by itself if people were selected with the right values, without the need for additional supports or structures. JetBlue's experience, however, contradicted that expectation. According to Al Spain, former senior vice president of operations:

> Horizontal communication is a challenge as we've grown. It's an example of growth necessitating the development of more structure. There's a lot of camaraderie in general, but as we've gotten bigger the informal network for communication stops working. There is a tipping point, and we definitely see an opportunity there for more structure.[66]

To address this weakness, one solution JetBlue considered was to institute a team leader for each flight departure, an innovation at Southwest that was not widely recognized or emulated in the industry. According to Spain:

> We don't have the Southwest-style team leader now, but we are about to institute the flight coordinator position. It is a function of growth. It worked fine previously. When we were doing forty to fifty departures per day, people were able to informally take care of it. When you get larger, also exacerbated by the number of irregular operations, you realize that having a single point of contact with final responsibility for getting a particular flight pushed and off makes logical sense for us.[67]

JetBlue differed most dramatically from Southwest in its approach to unionization. Like Ryanair and AirAsia, and like easyJet initially, JetBlue executives saw unions as undesirable. According to Ann Rhoades, JetBlue's original senior vice president of people, "We are not like Southwest Airlines in this respect. Herb [Kelleher of Southwest Airlines] invited the unions in from day one. We prefer to operate without unions. . . . Not having a union creates a team environment."[68]

JetBlue's leaders argued that unions would undercut teamwork, despite having known personally that the most highly unionized airline in the U.S. industry—Southwest—was highly effective in its use of teamwork.[69] Of greater concern was the apparent belief among JetBlue's founders that teamwork would somehow emerge simply from the absence of unions, perhaps explaining the relative lack of structures to support and build teamwork. Although JetBlue remained nonunion, it did establish formal agreements with certain employee groups—pilots, technicians, and dispatchers. Interestingly, these were the work groups that are predominantly male, whereas the predominantly female work groups—customer service, reservations agents, and cabin crew—did not have formal agreements. And JetBlue leadership was adamant that the agreements that were made were achieved not through negotiation but through discussion, as Stabile explained: "There is no bargaining process. It is all about dialogue, not about negotiation. We look for people's input, but we do not have an actual bargaining process, for compensation, for benefits, or for anything else."[70]

JetBlue's relatively aggressive growth strategy also differed from that of Southwest, with early growth rates of 159 percent, 68 percent, 52 percent, and 28 percent. Despite these high growth rates, JetBlue maintained a strong balance sheet with low levels of debt, in part due to being a well- capitalized start-up.

JetBlue's quality performance has been very strong overall—in 2007, only AirTran had better baggage handling performance, and only Southwest and Frontier had lower levels of customer complaints. But its on-time performance was below the industry average. Although its unit costs have been the lowest in the industry, its labor unit costs were also among the lowest, suggesting that, unlike Southwest, lower wages and benefits may be a significant part of its cost advantage, an advantage that is difficult to sustain over time and perhaps especially for an airline with a commitment strategy. Its aircraft turnaround times were forty-five minutes for medium haul flights, compared to thirty minutes for similar flights at Southwest. Even allowing that JetBlue flies larger aircraft, its aircraft are only 26 percent larger (156 passengers per flight versus 130 for Southwest), while its turn times are 50 percent higher for comparable flights.

In early 2007, JetBlue experienced severe operational difficulties. Though clearly weather-related, these difficulties brought its operational capabilities and its rapid rate of growth into question. According to one account:

> Vulnerabilities from its rapid growth came starkly into public view in mid-February when thousands of passengers were stranded for hours during an ice storm at JFK. The planes were unable to take off or return to gates because of stormy weather and traffic gridlock.[71]

These delays reverberated through JetBlue's network and employees and managers were taken aback by the slow pace of the recovery. Neeleman apologized repeatedly and soon afterward stepped down as chief executive officer.

JetBlue's employment strategy is in the lower left corner of our employment system matrix as seeking commitment along with union avoidance (see figure 5.3).

WestJet

WestJet is a Canadian low-cost airline launched in 1995 by western Canadian entrepreneurs who explicitly adopted certain aspects of the Southwest competitive model. WestJet founders raised $8.45 million from eleven investors, and as the launch of the airline became more likely, they were able to offer major equity stakes to additional investors, including—ironically—the Ontario Teachers' Pension Plan, Canada's largest union pension fund (24 percent equity for a $10 million investment), and American David Neeleman, the founder of JetBlue. A consultant to Morris Air and ValuJet also offered advice during this start-up phase.[72] By 2004, WestJet had gained almost one third of the Canadian domestic market largely at the expense of the dominant incumbent, Air Canada. Like Southwest, WestJet featured significantly lower prices than its competitors combined with frequent and friendlier, albeit no-frills, service. Other features borrowed from Southwest included a short-haul route structure, secondary airports, and a single aircraft type.

Some of WestJet's employment practices were similar to those of Southwest. Like Southwest and JetBlue, WestJet rejected some of the traditional terminology of human resource management, preferring instead to operate a People Department with a vice president of people and a manager of people.[73] Like Southwest, WestJet encouraged a casual style and an expectation that employees would work outside of their functional specialization as needed to ensure operational success in terms of its key performance indicators. At WestJet, the founders are known as the Big Shots, and human resource management policies are shunned; instead, WestJet offers "Promises." Unlike Southwest, WestJet adopted a relatively flat structure with relatively few supervisors per frontline employee.

To emulate the casual, chatty, and relaxed service style of Southwest, WestJet hired customer service personnel without previous industry experience, but with a positive and enthusiastic attitude about customer service. In 2002, 130,000 people competed for two thousand jobs with WestJet. With such a large labor pool, only the best prospects were chosen. The mantra was "Hire for attitude, train for skill." The customer orientation was evident. Whereas Air Canada had a complicated automated call-in system for reservations and information in which it was virtually impossible to speak with a real person, WestJet's policy was that customer service agents answer phones after one ring. Whereas Air Canada customer service agents explained Air Canada's torturous policies to irate customers, WestJet agents tended to adopt a problem-solving attitude.

Although the salaries were intended to be significantly lower than at rival unionized airlines, 20 percent of pay went into WestJet stock with the company matching the contributions. This differed from the Southwest plan, in which 15 percent of the company's pretax operating income was shared with its staff, provided that one quarter of the profit shares went into purchasing Southwest stock. The WestJet compensation plan differed from Southwest in two respects: WestJet did not offer a pension plan, and base wages were less than the industry median wage. More than 86 percent of WestJet employees were shareholders, however. The company called these employee owners "WestJetters" and called its annual reports "owners' manuals."

Unlike Southwest but similar to JetBlue, WestJet did not have a seniority-based system. Instead, WestJet developed a point system for bidding on vacations and other valued perks. Each employee was given a fixed number of points per year, which could be used to bid for desirable periods of time off. This allowed WestJet to meet employees' particular work-life balance needs without a seniority system.

Although the company tried to reduce status distinctions, pilots were treated particularly well. Of WestJet's outstanding share options, nearly 87 percent were held by pilots. In 2004, the company offered 3.7 million share options to pilots. Not all pilots wished to put their investments in WestJet shares, however.[74]

Along with Virgin Blue, easyJet, Virgin Blue, and JetBlue, WestJet provides evidence that a commitment approach to employee relations can be
replicated by other airlines besides Southwest. Unlike Southwest, WestJet
actively avoided union representation by its employees, though it had not yet
faced significant organizing efforts. WestJet's employment strategy is positioned in the lower left corner of our employment system matrix as seeking
commitment from employees along with union avoidance (see figure 5.3).

Southwest vs. Ryanair vs. Hybrids—Which Model Will Dominate?

We have seen that two of the most successful new-entrant airlines in the
world are following contrasting employment-relations strategies. Southwest
has pioneered a commitment-based strategy based on high levels of relational coordination across employee groups, while engaging unions as partners. The Southwest commitment/partnership strategy features distinctive
human resource practices that support relational coordination and commitment. Ryanair is a classic example of a control/avoidance strategy, with an
approach that relies to a significant extent on controlling workers through
fear and burning them out and replacing them over time.

Among our new-entrant case studies, the commitment strategy for managing employees has been adopted more often than the control strategy,
thanks in part to the influence of Southwest. Virgin Blue, AirTran, easyJet,
JetBlue, and WestJet each appear to have learned important lessons from
Southwest's commitment strategy. Despite the longevity and success of
Southwest's union-partnership strategy, this partnership strategy appears to
have attracted few followers among new entrants. Although Ryanair's ruthless control approach to human resource management has attracted relatively few followers, Ryanair appears to have been more influential than
Southwest with respect to union strategies. Among our case studies, union
avoidance (AirAsia, JetBlue, and WestJet) and union accommodation (Air-
Tran, easyJet, and Virgin Blue) are more common approaches toward union
relations. Most new entrants that we observed were therefore hybrids of
Southwest and Ryanair.

The failure to imitate Southwest's successful union partnership approach
may be due in part to the widespread misperception of Southwest as a nonunion airline, rather than as a highly unionized airline with successful union
partnerships. It may also stem from the view that Southwest doesn't have
"real" unions, due to the fact that its pilots are represented by a company-

specific union called the Southwest Pilots Association rather than by the better known Air Line Pilots Association. But as we pointed out above, Southwest has built sustained partnerships with all of its unions, most of which are well-known international unions, not only with its pilots. In addition, other airlines with company-specific pilots unions, like American Airlines, have not achieved sustained partnership with them. Thus, company-specific unions are neither necessary nor sufficient for achieving sustained partnership over time. We would cite instead four factors in successful partnership that we have seen at work at Southwest Airlines: (1) a belief that employees can be trusted to choose their own representatives; (2) a respect for unions and the value that they can bring; (3) constant dialogue to keep all parties focused on what is good for the company; and (4) proving over time that what's good for the company will also be good for the employees.

It is not yet clear whether the Southwest or Ryanair model will prove to be more influential or more sustainable than the other. But the consequences for the three stakeholders highlighted in chapter 1 are relatively clear. So far, both approaches have generated good returns to their investors. Southwest and Ryanair have both been consistently profitable. But the consequences for employees and customers are starkly different. Southwest is consistently rated as one of the best employers in America and employees have prospered financially in tandem with investors, as well as benefiting from stable, rewarding work. Ryanair employees have not shared in the success of their employer to the same extent, but instead have been embroiled in conflict about wages and union organizing and have experienced high levels of turnover.

Southwest has performed at or near the top of U.S. airlines in service quality over the years, while Ryanair has lived up to its stated goal of simply moving people from one place to another with low fares, and with little regard for customer service. So the stakes involved in the diffusion of these two models are clear, even though it is not yet clear which model—or combination of models—will dominate the industry in the years ahead.

CHAPTER 6

The Legacy Responses: Alternative Approaches

One industry insider referred to legacy airlines as "dinosaurs." But unlike the dinosaurs, the legacies are certainly not extinct. Many of them are reinventing themselves. Although new entrants have become an increasingly significant segment of the airline industry, most of the industry's revenue, passengers, and employees are still generated, flown, and employed by large legacy airlines. Thus the impact of the new-entrant airlines on the industry's employment relations comes not only directly from their own practices but also indirectly, from the reactions of the legacies to the rise of low-cost competition.

In chapter 2 we discussed the development of the dominant employment paradigm in the United States since deregulation. The dominant paradigm has remained a control/accommodation approach. Within this paradigm, the industry's wage negotiations have been adversarial as well as volatile, with management and labor exploiting swings in bargaining power as the industry has cycled through ups and downs. In addition, the general direction of wages has been down, with employees often losing in the drive to meet increasing low-cost competition. However, there have been noteworthy variations from the dominant paradigm, which this chapter discusses in more detail, asking two main questions: What alternative practices or approaches have been tried? And which practices seem to have been more effective than others?

We discuss four deviations from the dominant paradigm. The first is the union-suppression strategy pursued by Frank Lorenzo, whose high-profile battles helped set the strongly adversarial tone in the early days of the industry's deregulation. The second is the strategy of a low-cost operation inside the legacy airline. The third is the employee stock ownership plan (ESOP), in which employees (or more accurately, their unions) participate in the governance of the firm via collective stock ownership and representation on the board of directors. And the fourth involves creating a higher commitment relationship with employees.

Union Suppression: Frank Lorenzo at Texas Air, Continental, and Eastern

We briefly introduced the labor relations strategy made famous by Frank Lorenzo in chapter 2. We discuss it in more detail here to contrast it with strategies followed at other airlines in the 1980s and 1990s and particularly to compare it with what followed at Continental after Lorenzo's departure. Lorenzo had acquired a midsized airline, Texas International, in the early 1970s and was eager to seize the opportunity offered by deregulation.[1] One of his first moves after deregulation was to create a corporate holding company, Texas Air, as the parent of Texas International, and then launch a subsidiary low-fare airline, New York Air. New York Air was nonunion and hired relatively inexperienced employees to keep wages 30 percent lower than those at Texas International. This so-called double breasted tactic[2] anticipated the low-cost operations later launched by other legacies but was done unilaterally and was bitterly yet futilely opposed by the unions at Texas International.

However, Lorenzo was more infamous for his tactics at Continental Airlines. He acquired Continental in a hostile takeover in 1982, ultimately winning out in the courts against an attempt by Continental's management and employees to buy the firm via an ESOP. Before and after the takeover, Continental was in financial difficulty. Lorenzo quickly initiated layoffs and demands for wage cuts. Agreements for modest cuts or deferrals were made with all but the mechanics union, which went on strike in August 1983. But Continental hired replacements, the pilots crossed the mechanics' picket lines, and rather quickly the strike was "utterly broken."[3] Continental never bothered to settle with the union and instead began rebuilding a nonunion mechanic base.

Lorenzo then asked the pilots—who had just helped break the mechanics strike—for a *halving* of their wages. When the pilots refused, Continental filed for bankruptcy in September 1983. Unlike "normal" bankruptcy filings, which represent the failure of all attempts to rescue a company, Continental used bankruptcy as a strategic maneuver to reduce its labor costs by abrogating its labor contracts. It then invited employees to return to work at about 50 percent of their previous wages.

These actions prompted the pilots and flight attendants also to go on strike, but enough employees returned to work and sufficient replacements were hired that Continental was able to maintain a small but growing operation. Continental never came to terms with these striking unions either and eventually they were decertified. Lorenzo had successfully busted Continental's unions.

By 1985, Continental emerged from bankruptcy. However, its performance remained subpar from 1985 to 1990. Its profitability lagged major rivals and was more often negative than positive. It was routinely last or next to last among the major airlines in reliability rankings (on-time percentage and lost baggage rates). And, as shown in figure 6.1, it experienced a customer complaint rate consistently above the industry median, with shockingly poor results in 1987 and 1988. By 1990, as the industry entered another down cycle, Continental was back in bankruptcy.

Meanwhile, back in 1986, Lorenzo's next major target was another financially troubled legacy airline, Eastern Airlines, which was already embroiled in contentious labor relations. In the face of Lorenzo's takeover offer, Eastern's pilots and flight attendants agreed to wage cuts to stave off the acquisition. But failing to reach agreement with its mechanics, Eastern accepted Lorenzo's offer. As at Continental, Lorenzo soon made demands for enormous pay cuts. Partly to gain negotiating leverage, he also began transferring Eastern's valuable assets—planes, routes, and a reservations system—to Texas Air and its other subsidiary airlines. Lorenzo also began strike preparations as a first step in the suppression of Eastern's unions. Again as at Continental, he planned to take a mechanics strike first, hoping to lure pilots across the picket lines.

By this time, however, the unions were more prepared. They counterattacked on and off the job, delaying flights, reporting safety violations to the Federal Aviation Administration, and running an anti-Lorenzo public relations campaign. And when the mechanics strike came in March 1989, all the unions honored the strike.

With the strike, Lorenzo put Eastern into bankruptcy. But it was quite different this time. For one thing, recent legislation had made it harder to abrogate labor contracts. (Congress passed the bankruptcy reforms in large part in reaction to Lorenzo's strategy at Continental.) Furthermore, by 1990 the industry was heading into a downturn that pushed all of Texas Air, including

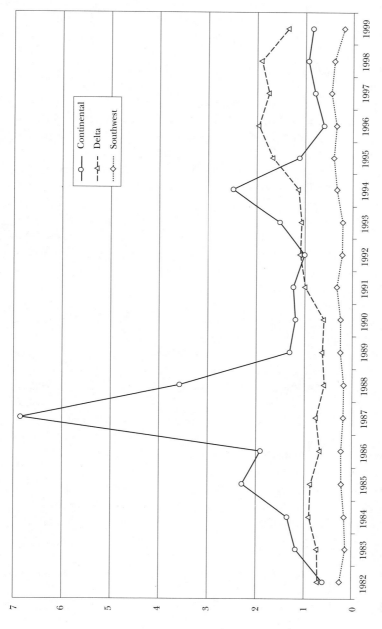

Figure 6.1. Customer complaint index for selected U.S. legacy airlines, 1982–1999. Complaints per 1,000 passengers for specific airline divided by industry median complaints per 1,000 passengers (1.0 indicates that airline experiences same rate of complaints as the industry median).

Source: Department of Transportation, Air Travel Consumer Report.

Continental, into bankruptcy. Eastern never made it out of bankruptcy, liquidating in 1990. Finally, Lorenzo's behavior eventually led not only to the bankruptcy court ousting him from his company but also to the Department of Transportation effectively banning him from forming another company in the airline industry.

Although Lorenzo successfully ousted unions at Continental and drastically reduced labor costs via wage cuts at many of his acquired airlines, eventually his whole empire collapsed into bankruptcy. This collapse was due in no small part to severe conflicts with unions, particularly at Eastern. In all, Lorenzo's airlines were the target of seven of the industry's thirteen strikes between 1982 and 1991. Not only did Lorenzo's highly adversarial approach adversely affect the efficiency and service quality of his airlines, but it may even have compromised its safety. Following up on employee revelations, the Department of Transportation indicted and penalized Eastern for falsifying maintenance records. Although Lorenzo's aggressive control/ suppression approach helped fuel some of the labor-management conflict in the first decade of deregulation, it ultimately proved to be unsustainable.

Low-Cost Operations

Rather than challenging union legitimacy or seeking across-the-board wage concessions, incumbents have more frequently tried to reduce wages (and other labor costs) on the peripheries of their organization. In chapter 2 we discussed the two-tier wage scales that spread in the 1980s and petered out in the early 1990s. While dealing with the industry downturn and subsequent financial crises of the early 1990s, some legacy airlines tried an alternative approach to having a two-tier wage system: setting up a low-cost operation for *short-haul* routes, where the cost disadvantages of the incumbents are most pronounced.

These low-cost operations (LCOs)—sometimes called the *carrier-within-a-carrier* model—adopted some of the operational features of the new-entrant model and also adopted employment terms different from the mainline labor contract, especially lower wages and fewer work rules to allow more cross-functional work.

As noted earlier, Lorenzo's New York Air was the first example of this model in 1980. New York Air was reasonably successful through the early 1980s but was then merged with several other airlines owned by Texas Air (including Continental).[4] The LCO next appeared in the wake of the industry down cycle of 1990–94. Continental launched CALite in 1993, United launched Shuttle-by-United in 1994, Delta launched Delta Express in 1996, and US Airways launched Metrojet in 1998. In each case, one of the key sources of lower costs was lower wage rates and fewer work rules. In contrast to the New York Air example, these efforts resulted from negotiations with unions who accepted the lower rates, however grudgingly. In United's case, for example, the LCO labor agreements were one of the terms that management negotiated in exchange for employees' acquisition of a majority of the company.

There is little publicly available information regarding the financial performance of these LCOs as the airlines have not divulged their independent results. Thus, evaluations of the effectiveness of LCOs must be based on their persistence and growth as well as on media reports. By these metrics, there is little evidence that the LCOs of the U.S. legacy airlines have been financially successful. Most inferences are that the operations lost money, with reports that CALite lost hundreds of millions in its less-than-two-year history[5] and that Delta Express's results deteriorated significantly over time.[6] Perhaps more tellingly, these LCOs were all discontinued, which tends to confirm the inferences. CALite was shut down in 1995, Shuttle in 2002 as United entered bankruptcy, Metrojet in 2001, and Delta Express in 2003.

Surprisingly, in view of the history of LCOs in the 1990s, both United and Delta tried again in 2003, with Ted and Song, respectively. However, Delta discontinued Song in 2005, in conjunction with its bankruptcy filing, leaving Ted as the only remaining U.S. LCO. Two reasons are usually cited for the lack of success of such LCOs. First, the initially lower wage rates were negotiated away as improving industry conditions increased union bargaining power in later contract negotiations. At United and Delta, for example, the wage differentials were all but eliminated by 2000.[7] Second, the LCOs may have been too tightly connected to the mainline business, which imposed various costs on the LCOs, including direct overhead costs and also indirect costs of the bureaucracy of the main line, as well as the subordination of the LCO's operations to the main line's interests. When Delta launched its second LCO attempt, Song, in 2003, it sought to avoid this flaw by making Song more independent. But Song's abrupt discontinuance in 2005, as part of the restructuring that attended Delta's bankruptcy filing, precluded finding out whether this was the missing ingredient for a successful U.S. LCO.

Outside the United States, however, there are some LCO success stories. Qantas's Jetstar has been successful (Qantas has published its stand-alone results), and will be discussed in more detail later in this chapter. In addition, Lufthansa's and BMI's LCOs (Germanwings and Bmibaby, respectively) apparently have also been successful. It remains to be seen whether this survival of LCOs outside of the United States is analogous to the early success of some of the U.S. LCOs—and is thus only temporary—or whether it results from different conditions or strategies. However, in several cases the LCOs are considerably more independent than has been the case in the United States. Germanwings, for example, was founded by a regional airline that was only affiliated with Lufthansa, rather than being founded directly by Lufthansa managers. Jetstar, too, was founded as an independent company (Impulse), which was then acquired by Qantas. It operates independently on a day-to-day basis, though the Qantas Group is still involved in business planning and financing (for example, funding all aircraft purchases). Thus, while the experience of LCOs in the United States suggests that it is difficult to sustain the model, it may be that the independence of an LCO is an important factor in its long-term viability.

Shared Governance via Employee Ownership and Board Representation

Employee ownership in the form of employee stock ownership plans (ESOPs) represents another important variation on the traditional employment relationship. The distinctive characteristic of airline ESOPs is the combination of collective employee ownership of a significant share of the airline's equity with the right to collectively nominate some members of the airline's board of directors. In this way, employees, usually via their unions, have a formal voice in corporate decision making. Referring back to our analytic framework in figure 1.2, we can place the ESOP model in the "Partner" column, but we should note that this represents a more *formal* version of partnership— marked by structural elements of corporate governance—in contrast to the less formal mode discussed in chapter 5 (particularly in the context of Southwest), which features processes and norms of interaction, but no formal structural elements. United (from 1994 to 2002) is perhaps the most famous case of employee ownership of an airline, but there have been several other examples among legacy airlines since deregulation, including Western (1984), Eastern (1984), TWA (1992), and Northwest (1993).

What are the potential benefits of an ESOP, as an ownership-based part-nership approach? One benefit might be greater employee motivation both because employees have a stake in the firm's performance and because being an owner may engender greater commitment. Greater motivation could lead to higher productivity and/or friendlier service, leading to higher firm profit-ability. A second benefit might be less conflict and volatility between labor and management. Involvement of employee representatives on the board of direc-tors could lead to better discussions and sharing of information, mitigating the asymmetries of information in bargaining. And an ownership stake ties em-ployee compensation more closely to the firm's fortunes, reducing the need for constant renegotiations of wages as industry and firm-level conditions change.

However, few of these benefits have accrued to U.S. airlines with ESOPs. Our earlier quantitative research has shown that ESOP airlines were associ-ated with more reliable service. But they were no more profitable and no more productive than those without ESOPs—with some slight evidence that the ESOPs were less profitable and less productive.[8] These unimpressive re-sults are less surprising when we look at the cases more closely. In all the cases noted above, employee equity and board representation were essen-tially a quid pro quo for large wage concessions. Furthermore, without the concessions, in four of the five cases the airline was facing an impending bankruptcy. Thus, ESOPs have generally been adopted by struggling airlines and have been viewed by both management and unions as a financial trans-action and a necessary evil, rather than an opportunity for partnership. This helps explain two additional findings from that research. First, ESOPs are associated with lower relative wages (the result of concession agreements). Second, although ESOP airlines were not more profitable than other air-lines, they were more profitable in their ESOP years than before their ESOP. Thus, the financial benefits of the ESOP stem largely from the wage conces-sions that purchased the ownership stake in the first place—and despite this wage advantage, ESOP airlines still did not outperform rival airlines.

Nor have the ESOPs led to sustained improvements in the labor-management relationship. Interestingly, despite the less-than-ideal starting conditions, each of the airlines that adopted an ESOP experienced an initial burst of cooperation and improved labor relations.[9] For example, after adopt-ing its ESOP, Eastern was being heralded as a national example of how em-ployee involvement at the workplace, more cooperative labor relations, and employee voice in strategic decision making could transform a failing com-pany into one with a bright future.[10] But in each case, the newfound goodwill, which had fueled joint productivity improvements, was dissipated as the parties came back to the negotiating table. Contract negotiations were as contentious and drawn out as ever—perhaps more so. This is most vividly illustrated by Northwest and United, the two airlines that survived long enough to negotiate a post-ESOP contract.

At Northwest, the ESOP began in 1993 and the accompanying concessionary labor contracts became amendable in 1996. By 1998, two years after negotiations began, talks had progressed so well that the pilots went on strike for fourteen days! But at least that contract was settled shortly afterward. Flight attendants did not settle for two more years (four years past the amendable date) and mechanics not for another three years (five years past the amendable date). At United, too, negotiations on contracts that opened in 1998 were long and were accompanied by job actions. United did not settle with its pilots until two years later, and only after pilots began refusing overtime assignments, which caused United to cancel five thousand flights per month between May and August 2000.[11] After the pilots settled, the mechanics launched a set of slowdowns.[12] After two more years, not only did the mechanics contract go to a Presidential Emergency Board (see chapter two, "Negotiating in the U.S. Airline Industry"), but the board's recommended settlement was rejected by the rank and file before the parties eventually settled in 2002 (four years after talks began). So much for the idea that ESOPs would catalyze more cooperative, less volatile labor-management relationships.

ESOPs in the airline industry have been short lived, by and large. Within two years of establishing their ESOPs, Western and Eastern were both acquired (by Delta and Texas Air, respectively) and the acquisition ended the employee ownership and board representation. TWA's also ended when it was acquired by American. The ESOPs at United and Northwest ended when those airlines entered bankruptcy. The longest-lived was Northwest's, from 1993 to 2005. So the ESOPs did not deliver demonstrable advantages and they have also not survived for long.

Our examination of ESOP experiences at U.S. airlines supports the view expressed by those who have examined these arrangements in other settings, namely that a one-time change in the formal governance structure cannot, by itself, sustain a long-term improvement in firm performance.[13] In fact, without an accompanying improvement in the underlying relationship between employees and management, an ESOP can lead to a worsening of the labor-management relationship because of disappointed expectations. Unions also have to transform their roles to make an ESOP work, shifting from a traditional arm's-length relationship to a partnership strategy in which they promote employee involvement and improvements in the workplace culture and add value to board-level deliberations by linking employee and human resource issues directly to other strategic decisions. Unions in the United States have had a difficult time making this strategic shift in behavior and roles. This was all too visible in the United case where conflicts between union representatives on the board and other board members were often widely publicized, as when some union board members publicly opposed United's bid to purchase US Airways.

Commitment-Based Workplace Relationships: Continental's Transformation

As chapter 5 has shown, a number of new-entrant airlines feature commitment-based relationships in the day-to-day workplace interaction between employees and managers. However, the high-commitment approach has been rarer among legacy airlines, which have usually operated with more control-based workplace relationships. One noteworthy exception is Continental. Yes, that Continental—the one just detailed above in the context of Lorenzo's union busting.

As part of Texas Air, Continental entered bankruptcy for a second time in 1990. The bankruptcy court ultimately ordered Lorenzo to cease any affiliation with Continental and the airline exited bankruptcy in 1993. But the airline was still in sorry shape. By 1994 it had been profitable in only two of the previous sixteen years and its service quality routinely ranked last among major U.S. airlines. Worse still, by the end of 1994 Continental was already running low on cash again and faced an imminent third bankruptcy. At this point, yet another new management team took over, with Gordon Bethune as chief executive officer, Greg Brenneman as chief operating officer, and shortly thereafter, Michael Campbell as the head of human resources (a different Michael Campbell than the person with the same name at easyJet). But under this management team, Continental achieved a remarkable and sustained turnaround.

Superior Performance

Continental not only became profitable in 1995 but has posted above-average profits relative to the other legacies ever since. From 2001 to 2005, Continental had the best or second-best operating profitability among the major

U.S. airlines (excluding Southwest). Continental's service quality improved markedly as well, culminating in a no. 1 ranking for customer satisfaction from JD Power and Associates in 2000. In 2003, *Fortune* ranked Continental the second–most-admired airline both in the United States and globally, second only to Southwest in the United States and second only to Singapore Airlines globally.

At the same time, Continental experienced an equally impressive transformation in its relationship with employees. By the end of Lorenzo's adversarial regime, absenteeism was rampant and morale was low.[14] Since 1994, Continental's relationship with employees has generally been regarded as among the best in the industry. Employees consistently express high levels of pride in the airline. The airline has been ranked in *Fortune*'s "100 Best Companies to Work For" every year since 1999.

Additionally, collective bargaining at Continental during the past decade was marked by shorter negotiations with less residual acrimony. In the early 1990s, the main employee groups reunionized. Since 1994, Continental has reached agreements on labor contracts, on average, within five months after the amendable date of the old contract, in contrast to an average of sixteen months for its major rivals.[15] Even in its recent post-9/11 restructuring, Continental and its unions reached negotiated agreements without recourse to bankruptcy and in a much shorter time than its rivals—three months for all contracts except the flight attendants' contract, which took just under a year. This more effective, less volatile bargaining is another of the beneficial spillovers of the underlying commitment-based relationship. Michael Campbell, vice president of human resources during those years, said that "collective bargaining is an extension of the corporate culture, of the way supervisors and employees interact." The relationship seems marked by more trust and respect than is often seen at other airlines. A leader of the flight attendants union remarked: "We are able to solve a lot of problems. . . . We've achieved a level of trust that sometimes is hard at other companies. . . . I feel they are very fair. In the way they do business they try to be very fair."

This improved relationship appears to be an essential factor in the financial and operational turnaround. Certainly senior management has said as much.[16] Our research indicated that Continental features a high-commitment culture, with similarities to that of Southwest Airlines, and that such cultures are associated with superior performance.[17] By contrast, some industry participants we interviewed have attributed Continental's turnaround largely to its relatively low wages and work rules (hence higher productivity), and to the industry upturn from 1994 through 2000. But the company had the wage and work rule advantages for ten years before 1994, yet still achieved inferior results. And the industry upturn explains neither Continental's relative performance improvement nor the improvement in its customer service. Moreover, Continental's more recent superior performance has occurred with wage rates much closer to competitors. Like Continental, TWA also exited bankruptcy in the early 1990s with low wage rates, but that did not prevent TWA from posting negative margins throughout the industry's boom years. Taking the evidence together, we conclude that the actions of Continental's new management team were critical to the turnaround.

What is the source of Continental's superior relationship with employees? There are three key dimensions on which Continental's employment relationship is distinct from its own pre-1995 relationship and from those at rival airlines: (1) the exercise of authority; (2) the underlying management philosophy; and (3) performance-based compensation.

The Exercise of Authority: Communication and Discretion

The exercise of authority at Continental is distinguished by *communication* and *discretion*. Extensive communication was far and away the distinctive feature most frequently cited by managers and employees at Continental. Three aspects of this communication are noteworthy: frequency, substance, and voice. In terms of *frequency*, management constantly broadcasts information, through a range of media, including daily e-mails, a weekly voice mail from the chief executive officer, top management visits to stations throughout the country, as well as daily meetings between managers and employees. While these practices seem straightforward, they still require effort that not all management teams are willing or able to exert, as noted by a Continental public relations manager who had worked at two previous airlines:

> All the other airlines I've worked at, they've talked about, "Oh, communications is important," but here it really is important. . . . Other CEOs I've worked with don't feel comfortable with people and so it's a lot bigger of a challenge to get them out to do employee meetings and stuff like that. But this place, they really actually follow through on what they say.

In terms of *substance*, management seeks to explain the rationale for decision making. This approach is best summed up as "here's why"—a phrase used by numerous personnel at Continental. This is manifested in broadcasts from senior management explaining strategy and recent performance as well as in daily conversations between managers and employees. The "here's why" philosophy was often contrasted with pre-1995 practice, where managers would simply issue terse commands with no explanation, as illustrated by these comments:

It was "I said do it, so do it." (baggage agent)

It was communication [of] basically "do this," with no explanation why. Now, you've got direction, but you're told why we're doing it. (vice president of maintenance)

They [hourly employees] respect the fact that we're honest enough to say "no" when the answer is no. But it's not just "no" with a closed door, it's "no, and here's why." (human resource manager and former mechanic)

I don't always agree with them at all. But they give us respect by sharing with us the rationale for decision making. (flight attendant union leader)

In terms of *voice*, employees feel that they have avenues to express their concerns and suggestions and that their input is acknowledged and responded to. This is manifested in formal channels for employee feedback as well as in a general "open door policy," in which employees feel comfortable having productive conversations with managers, as opposed to simply receiving orders or reprimands:

We don't have a little wooden suggestion box sitting on the table, which years ago we did have. You dropped it in this black hole and you never heard from anybody. [Now] when you call the 800 number, at any time there's a person on the other end [and] you get some response. The creation of that line allowed us to vent. Instead of "nyeh nyeh nyeh nyeh" among your fellow flight attendants, you had a way to say to somebody "this is what happened." (customer service representative)

[Before 1994] we had a lot of lousy equipment. They'd tell you to just use it and don't say anything. They'd say "go use it anyway, or we'll get someone else." Now, it's friendlier. You can talk to your supervisor about problems—

technical problems and personal problems. They'll help you out, even when they don't have to help out. (mechanic)

I don't have any gripes that I feel I can't take to management, at any level, and it wouldn't be addressed. Management wants to hear "How can we make this better?" What they've allowed us to do is say, "Hey, a lightbulb just went off, how 'bout let's do this?'" And they'll say, "Mmm, okay." They listen. (customer service representative)

Employees also felt greater *discretion* in their daily work. Employees felt trusted to make decisions and take actions in response to local situations:

There is, in my position, flexibility in what I do, if I need to do something. There's not necessarily "this is the way you do it." It's treating you as an adult, as a responsible adult. There's no micromanagement. (public relations manager)

An essential aspect of feeling trusted in this way was a reduction in the fear of being blamed for any operational deviations, because management sought to understand and correct, not just reprimand:

In the past [employees] wouldn't do anything without being told because of the reprisals [if] they didn't do it the way their bosses wanted 'em to. If something goes wrong—an airplane's not up, cancelled flight—obviously at the other carriers someone's gonna get in trouble for it, and it's usually the lowest man on the totem pole. The way we look at it is, "Hey, we're not interested in finding fault. We're interested in finding the corrections so this never happens again." There's no fear of reprisal or being the scapegoat, like at other airlines. (vice president of maintenance)

Before Gordon [Bethune], if something came back on you, let's say a letter came in and the customer said, "[She] was rude to me," there were [managers] that would say, "Look, Mr. Jones said you were rude to him, therefore you were rude to him, therefore you now have an instance against you." The difference now would be that we have an opportunity to say, "I did say that to him. I did hang up. But I gave him fair warning: 'I'm going to disconnect the call if you're being abusive.'" I feel that my group of managers gives me the benefit of the doubt now. They listen a whole lot more than what we used to get. (baggage agent)

Underlying Management Philosophy

The involvement-based authority described above is supported by a management philosophy that entails commitment to key principles regarding their relationships to employees. One principle is captured in a phrase often repeated by managers and employees alike: "dignity and respect." This essentially means taking each employee seriously as a valuable team member, which entails that management listen to, trust the judgment of, give the benefit of the doubt to, care about, and show appreciation to employees. Involvement-based authority is intimately tied to the "dignity and respect" principle since explaining decisions, listening to employees, and trusting them to make decisions contributes to them feeling like valuable team members. In addition, Continental's management seeks to make employees feel cared about and appreciated, as the human resource director explained: "We care about how employees are treated, materially and emotionally. We recognize that employee outcomes aren't just about money but also about feeling cared about, about being respected and treated fairly." Many of the stories that employees tell about "Gordon" (former chief executive officer Gordon Bethune)—e.g., how he knew everyone's name, visited the frontlines—reflect feeling cared about or appreciated.

The second key principle is *consistency*, whereby managers make efforts to be consistent in the application of rules and policies. First, policies are applied, where possible, to all functions equally. Second, the firm strives to enforce policies consistently, making sure that some people are not exempted from following the rules. This requires a certain "toughness" that stands in contrast to the idea that a high-commitment system and involvement-based authority are "soft" or "touchy feely":

> There's some rules that are set in stone. And you have to be fair. And you have to enforce them the same way with everyone. You want to be compassionate. However, what you do for one employee you have to do for another employee. There's certain rules, like attendance, that some people tend to abuse. And there's no giving there, 'cause the rules are set forth and people know what they are. (vice president of maintenance)

> We are not afraid to have "tough love" conversations. It's not all kumbaya. (human resource director)

Performance-Based Compensation

A third element of Continental's employment system, more visible to outside observers, is a set of performance-based compensation programs for employees. This includes a well-known monthly on-time bonus, originally $65 to every employee at the end of each month when an on-time performance target was hit;[18] a lottery for a sports utility vehicle for employees with six months' perfect attendance; and a profit-sharing program. But it would be a mistake to view these programs as the essence of Continental's commitment strategy. In the first place, interviewees all mentioned the day-to-day communication and discretion first as Continental's distinguishing feature. Second, the bonuses are not large amounts of money and two are based on firmwide results, which should pose huge "free-rider" issues, so they are unlikely to generate effort by themselves.[19] Instead, the contingent-compensation mechanisms seem to function in symbolic support of the underlying management philosophy, signaling that each employee is a valued team member. Third, these programs have been imitated to a large extent by rival airlines yet Continental has remained a superior performer. The management philosophy and involvement-based authority, which are diffused through the airline and thus much harder to imitate, are the more likely source of advantage.

Facilitating the Transformation

How did the Bethune management team effect this transformation? Several factors probably contributed: both deliberate actions by the new management as well as conditions they inherited. Most notably, *extensive communication* was adopted from the outset. Bethune and Brenneman were highly visible; the strategic plans were communicated in detail; news of layoffs was delivered in face-to-face meetings. This extensive communication likely contributed to employees' sense of being team members and the in-person nature of it may have signaled a higher level of caring by management.

The *on-time bonus* also seemed to contribute to the turnaround. In arguing that Continental's improved on-time performance can be attributed in part to the on-time bonus, one study acknowledges that the bonus was accompanied by a host of other human-resource-related actions, but interprets these additional actions as increasing the effectiveness of the bonus.[20] As just discussed, we suggest a reverse interpretation: that the bonus plan was one of a number of actions that functioned to establish the new involvement-based authority and a broader level of improved effort in general. As a mechanics union executive said about the bonus: "It was enough to get your attention. It signaled a change in philosophy."

The third action was a drastic and rapid pruning of the management ranks. This process was used to diffuse the involvement-based behavior, as managers were evaluated by superiors and subordinates for their "team play" as well as their functional competence.[21] This pruning was another signal of sincere change, and demonstrated commitment to enforcing the involvement-based authority.

What the new management team did was simple, at one level: they "walked the talk." They behaved differently than the previous regime and in harmony with the new style of authority. At another level, it was also difficult, in that displaying and enforcing the new behavior required investments of personal effort and attention that could have been allocated instead to restructuring routes, finances, and so forth.

However, the efforts of the new team were likely aided by the condition of the employment system already in place by 1994. The union busting of 1983 left Continental with lower wages and fewer work rules than its rivals. So the new management did not have to seek significant economic concessions to regain competitiveness. Continental managers were also able to take swift action without much consultation with or opposition by unions and without constraints from a "legacy-style" labor contract, since Continental had thrown out such contracts a decade earlier. Hence Continental had more scope than other legacies to innovate in terms of its employment system. In addition, several interviewees suggested that the turmoil and strife that plagued Continental from 1981 through 1994 left employees with low expectations for wages and working conditions, relative to employees at other legacies: they had "hit rock bottom" and were "ready to change." These conditions will be revisited later in the chapter, in comparing recent efforts by American Airlines to implement a commitment-based relationship.

The reborn Continental suggests three lessons. First, superior performance, in terms of employee productivity and service levels as well as the collective bargaining process, may be more likely to result from the quality of the underlying workplace relationship—from the firm's culture—than from a set of formal practices or structures alone. Second, the advantages of a commitment strategy are not limited to the new entrants. And third, a successful commitment strategy can be achieved even by legacy airlines, which have a history of a control/accommodation strategy.

Bearing in mind that Continental achieved a high-commitment relationship as a unionized legacy airline with a history of labor-management conflict, such a model may be possible for other legacy airlines. In the restructuring of the legacy airlines after 9/11, have any other legacies started down this promising path?

U.S. Legacies since September 11, 2001

After 9/11, the legacy airlines faced an urgent need for major restructuring. The attacks themselves led to a sudden drop in demand but the economic environment had already been deteriorating for about a year, with air travel demand already slumping. At the same time, the competition from new-entrant airlines was surging to more than a 26 percent market share and encroaching on many more routes, leaving the legacies with fewer "protected" routes with which to cover their higher costs. At the end of 2001, the major U.S. airlines posted combined operating losses of $9 billion. Despite drastic and wrenching cost-cutting efforts, the legacy airlines would continue to suffer massive losses for several more years. Industry observers generally described the magnitude of the crisis as unprecedented and asserted that the survival of the legacy airlines would require major changes to their business model and their employment relationships.

The legacy airlines faced two cost-cutting imperatives: substantially reducing capacity to match the suddenly lower demand and reducing marginal costs to stem the tide of low-cost competition. Legacies responded to the first imperative immediately after 9/11 with massive capacity cuts of around 20 percent for each airline that included eliminating routes, grounding aircraft, and laying off up to 20 percent of the workforce.[22] These capacity cuts continued on a smaller scale for the next four years for most of the large U.S. legacies.

The legacies next embarked on restructuring their unit costs. Two steps were taken. One was overhauling their operational model. The legacy airlines began to emulate certain aspects of the archetypal new-entrant model. Fleets were simplified by reducing the number of types of aircraft (although the new-entrant paradigm of a single aircraft type was not feasible). Prices were not only lowered but simplified to fewer types of fares. And frills were reduced: e.g., meals were no longer free in economy class, the quality of first-class meals declined, and fees were added to formerly free services. While saving costs, these reductions in service quality have exposed the U.S. legacies to the loss of high-paying corporate passengers, as noted below.

The Dangers of "De-frilling"

As part of their restructuring to meet the threat of low-cost competition, the U.S. legacies have cut a range of amenities. For example, frequent flyer awards have become harder to achieve, and harder still to redeem as the number of seats devoted to these programs has been reduced. Penalties for changing tickets and for exceeding baggage limits have increased. Perhaps most notably to customers, meals have largely been discontinued in economy class (replaced by boxes of packaged snacks sold for around $5) and the quality of meals has been reduced in business and first classes. One of the authors, for example, bemoans American Airlines' replacement of Häagen Dazs ice cream sundaes with "some generic ice-coated substitute."

Although they reduce costs, these reductions in service quality may be weakening U.S. legacy airlines in the competition for high-margin, frequent-flying corporate passengers who are much less sensitive to price and more sensitive to comfort and convenience.

· One threat comes from non-U.S. airlines on international routes, some of whom are adding more frills while the U.S. legacies reduce frills. Emirates Airlines has been growing rapidly with its "high frills" model.

Several business-class-only new entrants have entered the transatlantic market with lower prices than the legacies. Certain European legacies have responded by offering selected business-class-only flights as well as upscale airport lounges.[23] By contrast, U.S. legacies have been cutting services. Nevertheless, at the time of writing, all but one of the business-class-only new entrants have discontinued operations in this competitive market.

When we asked a passenger who frequently traveled for business between Australia and the United States to compare his experience on U.S. and non-U.S. airlines, the best thing he could say was the U.S. airline treatment was "utilitarian," while the rest of his comments are not repeatable in print.

Another threat even domestically comes from the recent rise of fractionally owned corporate jets. In the mid-1990s, several firms pioneered the concept of fractional jet ownership—in other words, time-shares for corporate jets, in which customers (usually corporations) purchase a partial ownership in a jet and buy the right to schedule its use given a roughly half-day advance reservation. The fractional jet firms manage fleets of jets such that customers do not own a particular jet but can instead use whichever jet in the fleet is most readily available. In the last few years, these firms have been growing rapidly and have become profitable, as they attract high-end corporate travelers with much greater convenience at a much lower cost than the traditional model of owning a jet individually.

Although losing price-sensitive passengers to low-cost airlines hurts the legacy airlines, so would the loss of price-insensitive passengers whose high fares may cross-subsidize many of the low fares offered on the same aircraft.

The second aspect of unit cost reduction involved negotiations with various suppliers—aircraft lessors, airports, unions—to reduce both fixed cost obligations as well as input rates such as prices for planes and wages. We focus here on the restructuring of employment relations: namely, negotiations with unions for concessions on wages, benefits, work rules, and outsourcing allowances.

Bankruptcy

Given the suddenness and magnitude of the post-9/11 crisis, it was not so surprising that major U.S. airlines would enter bankruptcy, especially since several had done so in previous industry downturns. What was more surprising was, first, how many went bankrupt, and second, why a few did not. Four of the big six legacy airlines—US Airways, United, Northwest, and Delta—achieved their restructuring only by recourse to the bankruptcy process. Several other large U.S. airlines also went bankrupt, including ATA, Aloha, and Hawaiian.

However, two of the big six—American and Continental—restructured while avoiding bankruptcy. Interestingly, whether a major airline filed for bankruptcy was not determined primarily by its financial condition after 9/11. Although US Airways and United were in very precarious financial positions, Delta and Northwest were in relatively strong positions with substantial cash reserves and less exposure to low-cost competition. One factor in avoiding bankruptcy that seems to have been at least as important as their financial condition was the ability of the airline and its unions to reach agreement on concessions. For example, American, whose post-9/11 financial position was weaker than that of Delta and Northwest, reached restructuring agreements with its unions in the spring of 2003, two and a half years before Delta and Northwest finally entered bankruptcy in the fall of 2005. Continental reached concession agreements in just three months of negotiating with pilots and mechanics and after one year with flight attendants, after a rank-and-file rejection of the agreement reached in the first three months. By contrast, United was unable to reach an agreement with its mechanics not only before but during bankruptcy. And Northwest's bankruptcy followed immediately when negotiations with mechanics collapsed in a strike. In both of these cases, a new union, the Airline Mechanics Fraternal Association (AMFA), had been voted in to represent the mechanics, reflecting the memberships' frustrations with continued concessions. At Northwest the strike proved to be especially devastating to the union and its members. Northwest contracted out a substantial portion of its maintenance work to other firms, resulting in the permanent layoff of most of its mechanics.

One of the most drastic restructurings via bankruptcy was that of US Airways. A brief history of US Airways offers a useful illustration of the magnitude of legacy restructuring in the United States.

From High Cost to Low Cost: US Airways in Chapter 11

US Airways was founded in 1939 as All-American Airlines, ultimately changing its name to Alleghany Air in the 1950s and then USAir shortly after deregulation. At the time of deregulation, USAir was a large airline but had a regional focus. To establish itself as a national airline, USAir acquired two other large airlines, PSA and Piedmont, in 1987, but a difficult merger integration process left the airline with a cultural legacy of internal conflict.

Through the 1990s, US Airways was roughly the sixth largest airline in the United States. Its route network, though, was still more regionally concentrated than its large rivals. In particular, US Airways' network included many short-haul flights around the central eastern part of the country. These shorter routes contributed to one of US Airways' key disadvantages through the 1990s: the highest unit costs in the industry. This unit cost position was also the result of a combination of high wage rates, work rules, and the adversarial workplace culture, which yielded the industry's highest unit labor costs as well. The airline nonetheless survived because many of its routes not only had a large percentage of corporate passengers but also faced minimal competition, allowing US Airways to charge a price premium. The cost disadvantage generally outweighed the price advantage, however, and US Airways' financial performance as a result was generally poor relative to its rivals (see figure 6.2).

Post 9/11, US Airways was hit particularly hard. One of its hub airports, Reagan National Airport in Washington, D.C., was closed for security reasons for a month after the attacks. In addition, new-entrant competition began encroaching into much of its territory, especially Southwest Airlines in Baltimore and Philadelphia. Not surprisingly, US Airways was an early candidate for bankruptcy, filing in the fall of 2002.

The airline reached a concession agreement with its unions by late 2002. However, subsequent operating results were not positive and made worse by an increase in fuel prices. The airline had to ask the unions for a second

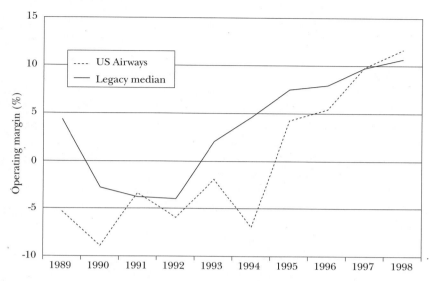

Figure 6.2. Operating margin of US Airways versus median operating margin of major airlines, 1989–1998.

Source: U.S. Department of Transportation, Form 41.

round of wage and benefit cuts. After the majority owner made an explicit threat of liquidation, a second set of concessions was agreed to. The airline exited bankruptcy in March 2003 but its operating results remained poor and the environment—namely jet fuel prices—worsened. In the fall of 2004, US Airways went back into bankruptcy and asked the unions for yet a third round of cuts. In addition to the threat of liquidation, the other source of bargaining leverage for the airline was the possibility of asking the bankruptcy judge to void the labor contracts if no agreement could be reached after good faith efforts. Although the pilots and flight attendants eventually agreed to this third round of cuts, the mechanics did not and eventually had their contract voided by the presiding judge. However, rather than impose its own terms, US Airways proposed the last terms offered in negotiations, which the mechanics accepted.

Over three rounds of concessions, employee wages were cut by about 40 percent in some instances. All the defined-benefit pensions were terminated and turned over to the government agency that backs up private pensions, the Pension Benefit Guaranty Corporation (PBGC). This meant that existing employees would still receive some pension benefits, paid by the

PBGC, but only up to a certain amount. In the case of the pilots, for example, the payouts would likely be one third of what the original plans would have provided. The concessions also included significant changes to work rules, leading to employees working more hours per day and per month and allowing US Airways much more operational flexibility. The airline also won the right to outsource significantly more maintenance work and to use more regional jet aircraft, which tended to go with lower pay rates for pilots and other staff.

The agreements included some quid pro quos that offered employees participation in the firm's governance and financial performance. Unions were given the right to nominate four of the members of the board of directors. And employees had three mechanisms for financial participation: a grant of stock options, a profit-sharing program, and bonuses based on meeting various operational performance targets.

Then, shortly after reaching these final concession agreements, US Airways exited this second bankruptcy by working out a merger agreement with America West, one of the few surviving new-entrant airlines from the first wave of new entry in the early 1980s. Although America West was the acquirer, it adopted the US Airways name because of its greater brand recognition. The merger with America West ended employee representation on the board of directors.

In essence, US Airways, via two bankruptcy trips, had gone from having the industry's highest unit costs to having unit costs lower than all of its legacy rivals, to the point of being attractive to and compatible with a new-entrant airline. Although keeping US Airways alive and reaching the concession agreements was no small feat for the airline's management and its unions, employees gave up a considerable amount in terms of expected future compensation and quality of work life in the process. The new merged airline has unit costs lower than other legacy airlines and has billed itself as the "world's largest low fare airline." In 2006, US Airways even launched a bid to acquire Delta out of bankruptcy, but was rebuffed. For now, we infer that a legacy airline can, via bankruptcy, successfully reduce its costs to match the new-entrant airlines. But whether it can sustain that position through subsequent contract negotiations is yet to be seen. Given the magnitude of concessions and the strife of multiple negotiating rounds during bankruptcy, it is an open question as to whether it will be even harder to build improved relationships with employees and unions and move in the direction of a commitment strategy. Even bigger challenges may lie ahead: in 2008 the com-

Table 6.1. Comparison of labor contract restructuring outcomes, as of the end of 2006

Airline	Bankrupt	Wage Cut (%)	Pensions	Variable Pay	Board Seats	Amendable Date
American	No	16–23	Preserved	Stock options, profit-share, performance bonus	No	Apr 2008
Continental	No	9 (pilots)	Frozen / converted	Stock options, profit-share, performance bonus	No	Dec 2008
Delta (pilots only)	Yes	30–50	Terminated	Equity, profit-share, performance bonus, raises tied to profits	Nonvoting seat for pilots	Dec 2009
United	Yes	30–50	Terminated	Equity, profit-share, performance bonus	No	Dec 2009
US Airways	Twice	30–50	Terminated	Equity, profit-share, performance bonus (pre-merger)	No (eliminated in merger)	Dec 2009
Qantas	No	3 gain	Preserved		No	N/A
Aer Lingus	No	Freeze	Preserved	ESOP increased from 4% to 15%, profit-share	No	N/A

pany discussed but abandoned another merger with United Airlines. Should such a merger occur, it would bring together two airlines with rather adversarial labor relations.

Restructuring Outcomes

In due course all of the legacy airlines achieved some kind of restructuring that included substantial labor contract concessions. Key aspects of the labor agreements reached at the major legacy airlines are summarized in table 6.1. By and large, however, the airlines that restructured via bankruptcy achieved larger cost reductions. The most notable difference is that the bankrupt airlines were able to reduce their obligations to their retired and soon-to-be retired employees. In particular, this meant the termination of defined-benefit pensions, which were turned over to the PBGC. The levels of some benefits, such as the pilot pensions, were substantially reduced by this transfer. In addition, medical insurance costs for retirees were eliminated or reduced. Thus, the "legacy" aspects of these airlines—the long-term cost obligations resulting from a long-operating employment system—were vastly reduced. By contrast, the airlines that avoided bankruptcy retain the financial obligations to fund these pension and health care costs. Recent legislation has reduced the burden of pension funding for these airlines. But it remains to be seen whether this discrepancy will play a significant role in the relative success and competitiveness of the legacy airlines.

Another interesting outcome is that contingent pay, in multiple forms, has become standard. Employees of all the major legacy airlines have stock options or stock grants, a profit-sharing plan that pays out a percentage of profits above a threshold level, and bonuses related to operational performance benchmarks. However, the idea of employee representation on the board of directors has not been preserved.

At first look, these contingent compensation mechanisms might seem like a way to reduce the historical volatility of the industry's labor relations, by ensuring that employees will be rewarded when airline performance improves and by generally tying compensation to industry conditions, rather than negotiating fixed wages that prove hard to adjust when the business cycle inevitably repeats. However, the amounts of compensation involved do not match the future wages that employees gave up in concessions. Pilots at the major legacy airlines, for example, are projected to receive between $5,000 and $15,000 each, depending on the airline, from profit-sharing programs in 2008, which may be a peak year of profitability in the current cycle—that is, from 2000 until the next downturn (see figure 6.3). If we assume that the average pilot earned about $120,000 in 2001 before all the restructuring and eventually agreed to wage concessions averaging about 30 percent, this means he or she gave up some $36,000 per year. In addition, many had their pension benefits significantly reduced. Not surprisingly, in anticipation of the renegotiation of labor contracts in the next few years, unions have been talking of regaining lost wages and benefits as *the* way to share in the airlines' recovery, with no mention of any of the contingent pay mechanisms.

Despite all the rhetoric about how the legacy airlines' business model is no longer viable and despite all the wrenching restructuring of the conditions of employment, relationships at the workplace have not changed fundamentally, except for a decline in morale. Neither the legacy airlines nor the unions at these airlines have taken this recent crisis as an opportunity to

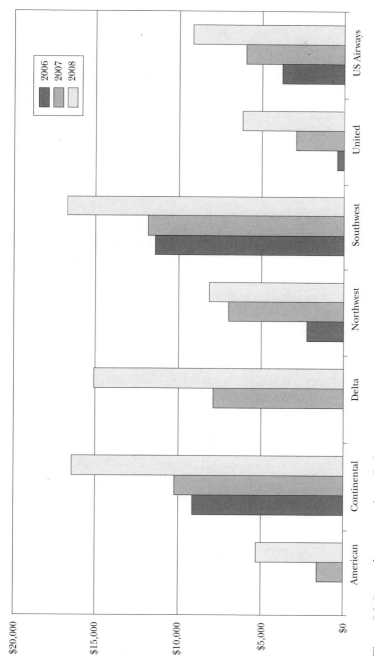

Figure 6.3. Projected per capita pilot profit-sharing payouts, 2006–2008.

Source: ALPA Economic and Financial Analysis.

reinvent the workplace relationship—with the partial exception of American Airlines.

Attempting a Commitment-based Relationship: American Airlines

Since deregulation in 1978, American Airlines has been either the largest or second largest airline in the United States. Since at least the 1970s, American has also been one of the most innovative airlines, initiating several of the industry's major competitive developments, including computer reservations systems, frequent flyer loyalty programs, revenue management practices, and two-tier wage scales.

In terms of its employment model, American has been a typical control/accommodation legacy airline. The relationship between management and unions has been characterized by arm's-length interactions and an adversarial attitude. The senior vice president of human resources described its organizational culture as "very hierarchical," with little input from or discretion extended to subordinates and little cross-departmental coordination, and clearly in the control mode: "There was a general kind of approach that said, 'Come to work, do your job, go home, we don't want to hear from you.'"

In 2003, American and its unions agreed on concessions—at the brink of bankruptcy—that cut labor costs 21 percent, via wage cuts of 16 to 23 percent, benefits cuts, changes to work rules, and more layoffs (see table 6.1).[24] The agreement included some major drama. Just before the unions agreed, a regulatory filing revealed that American had implemented an executive-retention plan that included bonuses and secured pensions for senior executives, a plan that the unions only became aware of via a *Wall Street Journal* article. When the unions called off the agreements, it took the resignation of chief executive officer Don Carty, some contract improvements, and board approval for a bankruptcy filing to get the unions back to an agreement.

But on the heels of this restructuring, American's new chief executive officer, Gerard Arpey, launched an effort to build and sustain a more collaborative relationship between management and unions—that is, to change to a partnership approach to unions:

There is something very different happening today. When we did the restructuring agreements, we used that experience to change the relationships with our unions and immediately following that we have undertaken a collaborative approach with respect to the unions, and I think that is changing a lot of things. (vice president of employee relations)

The cornerstone of this initiative involves changing the relationship at the workplace. And the key change is in the nature of authority, as it was at Continental. The change involves listening to employees and involving them more in decision making:

There is a lot of work going on with both the independent employees and the union-represented employees to find ways to involve people in decision making. I think the other focus that we have to come to is we have to push that decision making down as far as we can in the organization. (senior vice president of human resources)

It's kind of a simple model . . . change what people see in the workplace. Behave differently, treat them differently, involve them more, educate them more than [we] ever have in the past. They'll feel part of it and part of the decision-making process, which will improve overall results. (managing director of employee relations)

The desired principles are neatly summed up on laminated business cards that the chief executive officer, Gerard Arpey, distributed to his senior executives, which read:

Involve before Deciding
Discuss before Implementing
Share before Announcing

In other words, American was not only attempting to shift to a partnership model with unions but was attempting to do so by shifting to a commitment-based relationship with employees, based on involvement-based authority. And the airline intended for this new relationship to be a source of competitive advantage, by generating both more ideas and more cooperation from employees:

It is fueled by a belief that the only way we are going to be competitive in the future with low-cost carriers and with legacy carriers is by creating a competitive advantage through our employees. And the way to do that is through involvement. (vice president of employee relations)

At the start of 2008, the success of American's relationship transformation efforts had yet to be determined. On the one hand, there had been promising signs through 2005, such as the strength of management's support for the effort, initial reactions from union leaders, and early productivity improvements. On the other hand, since early 2006 a conflict over executive pay and a new round of contract negotiations seem to have put the effort significantly at risk, particularly with the pilots and flight attendants.

Promising Signs

In early 2004, there were several promising signs regarding American's relationship transformation plan. First, senior management was both strongly supportive of the effort—chief executive officer Gerard Arpey is the effort's foremost champion—and also had a comprehensive vision of what they were trying to achieve, including the recognition that it involved changing the way that managers throughout the airline exercised authority:

> My theory is that the type of manager in the company will change because we will have a very different expectation as to what success means as a manager. It's not someone who simply makes their numbers. It's someone who has an engaged workforce. I hate to use the term, but that's what it is. (senior vice president of human resources)

American's vision also includes a desire to build "structure" around the new relationship—to establish organizational processes that institutionalize the desired actions and interactions, rather than depending on the personalities and interpersonal relationships of specific managers and union leaders. This structure includes an interconnected series of joint teams of management and union personnel—at different levels of the organization and across functional boundaries—that work on productivity improvements as well as resolve other issues. It also includes changes to the managerial evaluation process to increase the importance of the "people side of the business," relative to just "making the numbers."

> There [is] essentially an equal degree of emphasis on the people side of the business as well as "the business" side of the business, the financial side of business. . . . So there is a structure there as opposed to an ad hoc, "Well, Joe does a great job, he made his numbers for the last three quarters, let's pro-

mote Joe." Well, Joe may have made his numbers for the last three quarters, but his department is a disaster. They don't make their objectives and they don't do the people stuff, and so Joe may not be the right guy for that area. We are building that into the formal performance management structure. (senior vice president of human resources)

Second, union leaders were supportive of the effort and agreed that the atmosphere at the airline felt different. They were pleased with an unprecedented sharing of information that began during the concession negotiation, but continued thereafter via monthly consultation meetings. And they felt involved in and consulted on important decisions, in contrast to the old norm of unilateral management decisions made without much input and announced to the unions after the fact.

We are far more involved [as] part of the process. Our access now to information and to sharing is unlike any exposure I've ever seen. In my view we are more involved now in almost every aspect of the managing of the company. (Transport Workers Union representative)

Third, there were signs that the effort was yielding visible outcomes on the ground. In 2004, an article in the *Fort Worth Star-Telegram* (the local paper in American's hometown) detailed instances of joint productivity improvements among frontline maintenance personnel and included comments from employees acknowledging a "profound cultural shift" at American.[25] Furthermore, in late 2005, the pilots union, after commissioning a study of the airline's pilot productivity vis-à-vis competitors, voluntarily initiated negotiations with American on changes to work rules that would allow pilots to fly more hours (per day and per month), thus increasing pilot productivity.

Worrisome Signs

Despite the initial positive signs, there are still critical obstacles to overcome. The biggest threat has been a dispute over management bonuses that erupted in 2006. In January 2006, American informed employees that because of a substantial increase in American's stock price, about one thousand managers would be paid bonuses in April 2006 totaling more than $75 million, based on a compensation plan agreed to in 2003. (At the same time,

American also noted that employees' stock options, which would vest in April, were worth a collective $500 million). Unions and employees objected vehemently to the idea of management bonuses when the airline was still losing money each quarter. The unions jointly filed a grievance claiming that the bonus plan violated a clause in their own contracts that prohibited cash bonuses that did not also apply to union employees.

In addition, and perhaps more alarmingly, the pilot and flight attendant unions announced they were halting any cooperation in joint productivity-saving programs, including the negotiations over pilot productivity improvements. However, they did not pull out of the joint consultation teams. Two months later, American revised the bonus plan to pay out in stock, rather than cash, which resolved the formal grievance. However, public signals from the two unions in 2006 and 2007 indicated that the issue had not been resolved emotionally or politically. The airline, though, continued to tout the ability to use collaborative processes to resolve the conflict and maintained that the new relationship was working.[26] Furthermore, collaborative efforts continued with the mechanics union (the Transport Workers Union, or TWU), which had facilitated not only the retention of heavy maintenance activity in-house but also its growth through providing services to other airlines.

Another looming threat, though, is contract negotiations with the unions, whose contracts are all amendable in 2008. These are beginning to reveal significant discrepancies between employees' and management's expectations. In 2004, American's employees already appeared to be expecting to reclaim many of the concessions made in 2003 at the next contract negotiations. For example:

> That's what our pilots are thinking: "We made it a year, we only have four more years to go before our contract's up. . . . I can come back for [industry leading] pay rates. I get to come back to the golden goose." (Allied Pilots Association president)

On the other hand, management spoke of a desire to rely more heavily on variable forms of compensation to share the airline's future profitability, primarily the stock options, profit sharing, and operational bonuses adopted in 2003 (see table 6.1). Furthermore, since American did not reduce its "legacy" costs nearly as much as did its rivals that went through bankruptcy, its unit labor costs were higher than all but one of its rivals in 2005. So the airline may be in no position to offer improved wages and benefits. A contentious round of contract negotiations could be very hazardous to the culture change effort.

Table 6.2 Average contract negotiation duration, in months, by union, 1982–2000

Union	Mean	Standard Deviation	Number of Contracts
IAM-AMFA^	39.0***	24.1	2
APFA	27.4*	11.7	3
IPA	21.8	7.2	2
IBT^	20.6***	14.8	26
APA	19.0	11.9	3
IAM^	15.2	12.4	55
AFA^	13.6	13.6	30
ALPA^	10.1**	12.2	55
TWU^	8.2	6.1	11
SWAPA	7.3	1.3	3
ALEA^	8.7	12.3	3
IUFA	5.4	3.8	2
All	*13.9*		*194*

^=unions representing workers at more than one airline.

Statistical probability that a given mean is different from the overall mean: *=p<.10;**=p<.05;***=p<.01.

Note: Negotiation duration is measured as the number of months between the amendable date of the previous contract and the ratification date of the next contract. "IAM-AMFA" indicates contract negotiations that were begun by the IAM but subsequently concluded by the AMFA, which successfully won the right to replace the IAM.

AFA=Association of Flight Attendants; ALEA=Airline Employees Association; ALPA=Air Line Pilots Association; APA=Allied Pilots Association (American Airlines); APFA=Association of Professional Flight Attendants (American Airlines); AMFA=Airline Mechanics Fraternal Association; IBT=International Brotherhood of Teamsters; IAM=International Association of Machinists; IPA=Independent Pilots Association (UPS); IUFA=Independent Union of Flight Attendants (PanAm); SWAPA=Southwest Airlines Pilots Association; TWU=Transport Workers Union.

Source: Andrew von Nordenflycht and Thomas A. Kochan, "Labor Contract Negotiations in the Airline Industry," *Monthly Labor Review* (July 2003); with data courtesy of Airline Industrial Relations Conference.

Recent relations with the pilots provide an inauspicious example. In 2006, American applied to the U.S. government for authority for a new route to China, in competition with most of its rivals. The route involved a flight time that violated flight time restrictions in the pilots' contract, but the pilots union refused to grant an exception unless American agreed to discuss an immediate wage increase. So the company submitted an application for a one-stop trip, in contrast to the nonstops proposed by all the other airlines, which essentially killed American's chances from the outset. Furthermore, public statements from the pilots union indicate an expectation not only of recovering all of the conceded wages but getting an increase beyond that as well, and have mentioned expectations of a strike.[27] These sentiments seem in violation of the spirit of the new relationship.

American vs. Continental

It is useful to compare the experiences of American and Continental. One key difference between Continental's transformation and American's effort is the strength of the existing employment paradigm and employees' expectations about what is fair. Continental's transformation seems to have been facilitated by the earlier "unrestrained forcing"[28] of the Lorenzo era, which greatly reduced union bargaining power and over time dampened employee expectations regarding wages and employment security. Furthermore, the union suppression and massive wage cuts occurred a decade before the new management team launched its transformation effort. In contrast, American's effort was launched immediately after employees agreed to huge concessions. Additionally, the strength of American's incumbent unions as well as employee wage expectations may prevent a similar transformation or at least require larger, more sustained signals from management regarding the credibility of its intentions. Whether the opposition of unions and employees to the establishment of a new system can be accomplished via persuasion and negotiation, rather than aggressive, unilateral forcing is an outstanding question.

It Takes Two to Tango: Union Strategies

Our research has shown that unions are compatible with airline financial success. Levels of unionization are not systematically correlated with levels of productivity or financial performance, and the examples of Southwest and Continental show that some of the industry's performance leaders are substantially unionized.[29] However, this does not mean that unions are passive players in the dynamic of labor and employment relations, nor are their actions and responses determined by those of airline managements. Rather, unions also face strategic choices about how to accomplish their goals.

For example, our data on contract negotiation durations can also be looked at from a union point of view. There were differences across unions in the average negotiation duration in the 1982–2000 period (see table 6.2). Unions whose average negotiation times are statistically significantly different from the industry average of 13.9 months are marked with asterisks in table 6.2. The Association of Professional Flight Attendants (APFA, the independent union for flight attendants at American) and the Teamsters (IBT, which represents a range of occupations, including pilots, flight attendants, and mechanics, at a number of airlines) have average times that are almost or more than double the industry average. Conversely, the Air Line Pilots Association (ALPA, which represents pilots at a majority of U.S. airlines) is below the average, at ten months.

In terms of different options that unions might pursue, there are some issues that are analogous to the lessons conveyed by airlines themselves. In particular, highly aggressive and adversarial approaches by unions are unlikely to be any more sustainable or successful in the long run than they have been for airlines. Demands for large wage increases, backed up by threats of strikes or other job actions early in the negotiating process, are likely to fuel the volatile boom/bust cycle. They also may risk further delays in reaching agreements if the National Mediation Board decides either to hold the parties in negotiations (i.e., in technical terms to not "release" the parties to engage in a legal strike or lockout) or to recommend that the president invoke the Presidential Emergency Board process. Even if unions are successful in negotiating large "catch-up" wage increases, this may ultimately make future wage *reductions* more likely, especially if, as was often the case in the past, those demands come as industry conditions are deteriorating.

For example, in 2000, the ALPA unit at United (despite being a majority owner of the airline) took a hard-line stance for large wage increases. The negotiations were accompanied by a job action in the summer of 2000—refusals of voluntary overtime—that led to thousands of flight cancellations. Ultimately, the airline agreed to wage increases of about 30 percent. Not surprisingly, United was among the highest cost airlines when the downturn and 9/11 hit and was an early entrant into bankruptcy—where pilots not only saw their wages cut substantially but also saw their pensions terminated. Similarly, in 2002, as United was on the verge of bankruptcy after the crises of 2001, the International Association of Machinists (IAM) unit representing mechanics demanded wage increases, and its refusal to join other unions in agreeing to concessions triggered the airline's bankruptcy filing. The mechanics union at Northwest, AMFA, conducted a strike—the one post-9/11 strike—rather than reaching a concession agreement, which prompted Northwest's bankruptcy filing.

By contrast, more conservative approaches (to wage, benefit, and work rule demands) may yield more steady, long-term progress in employment levels and compensation. For example, such an approach by the Transport Workers Union (TWU) at Southwest, which represents customer service agents, has facilitated steady employment growth and resulted in the highest wage rates in the industry. In the 1990s, Continental's turnaround—and ultimately employees' relatively smaller recent concessions—were facilitated by the unions' acceptance, however grudgingly, of incremental but steady wage increases, rather than demanding immediate leaps to industry-leading pay with the threats of job actions. By contrast, regarding wage levels, a pilot at United told us "what's fair is as much as you can bargain for." This attitude fails to leave much room for smoother negotiations that preserve long-term goodwill—and seems no more useful than an airline attitude of "what's fair is as little as we can pay an employee without them leaving or striking."

Unions also have choices regarding how much to support or oppose alternative employment paradigms. ESOPs, for example, have typically been initially proposed by unions, showing that unions may support, not just oppose, alternative approaches. However, similar to airline managements, unions have typically viewed ESOPs more as a financial quid pro quo and less as an opportunity to forge an improved relationship either at the union-management level or the workplace level. Unions, too, seem to have failed to recognize that the equity and board seats of an ESOP by themselves will not improve relationships.

Contingent compensation is another "innovation" (relative to traditional airline employment practices) whose benefits will depend in part on union attitudes. The spread of multiple forms of contingent compensation across many legacies could in the end provide a mechanism whereby the cyclicality of the industry's fortunes does not have to translate into conflictual negotiations over wage cuts and gains—that is, it is an automatic way to share an airline's economic success broadly. However, union attitudes toward such compensation mechanisms—whether to disregard them and discuss any gain sharing only in the form of fixed wages or instead to embrace them and tout them as valued sources of employee compensation—may affect their eventual effectiveness.

A particularly counterproductive union strategy is holding alternative employment approaches hostage to collective bargaining negotiations or disputes over strategic decisions at the board level. For example, after United's ESOP, the airline and its unions created joint teams to identify and implement productivity improvements. However, the pilots pulled out of the joint teams when bargaining bogged down and when the dispute over the potential purchase of US Airways erupted.

In an example of constructive support for an alternative approach, the APFA, APA, and TWU at American not only preserved their members' pension plans by agreeing to concessions that averted bankruptcy but they also cooperated with the airline in launching the relationship improvement effort noted above. This included jointly selecting a consultant and participating constructively in a range of joint committees to identify productivity improvements and to develop joint communications to employees. However, after the conflict over executive bonuses, the APFA and APA suspended their participation in many of these joint efforts. And, worse still, the APA then linked a contract variance for the China route to an immediate wage raise. For partnership strategies to be sustained long enough to generate significant benefits to both the company and the workforce, union and management leaders will need to find ways to work through disagreements and other crises that will continue to occur without holding workplace cooperation and employee involvement hostage. This is a challenge that has long been recognized as critical to the success and sustainability of labor-management partnerships in other industries. The airline industry is no exception.

Another challenge unions in the airline industry face is the need to overcome the long history of separate craft (occupation) bargaining. Separate bargaining units and rules for each craft are built into the Railway Labor Act and have therefore a long tradition in the U.S. airline industry. Individual unions guard their autonomy and often have experienced difficulty in working with one another in a coordinated fashion within airline companies. Yet the reality is that the unions and workers in these companies are "all in it together." Each group, from pilots to flight attendants to mechanics and customer service agents, have taken deep wage cuts and all expect that whatever one of them gains back will be extended to the others. Moreover, as the American case illustrates, employees and their union leaders are scrutinizing movements in management and executive salaries and related compensation. In essence the bargaining structure has shifted in a de facto sense, if not in a legal or formal way.

Several efforts have been made to bring the various airline industry unions together to coordinate their strategies. At the national level the secretary treasurer of the AFL-CIO hosted several meetings of its member unions in the industry, but was unable to generate support for a coordinated approach. Examples of coordination across unions within specific firms have also occurred and there is more informal communication occurring. But these are only tentative steps. It remains to be seen whether they will generate a process that achieves companywide agreement on compensation principles that will both help support a return to sustained profitability and an equitable sharing of whatever gains are achieved, whenever they are achieved.

Comparisons Outside the United States

Low-cost competition has been growing rapidly outside the United States. Non-U.S. legacy airlines have also had to adjust strategies and restructure to meet the threat. However, partly because the demand shock of 9/11 was less profound outside the United States, these other legacy airlines have generally not experienced quite the same level of financial losses and the substantial concession negotiations as have those in the United States. Nonetheless, it is useful to look at whether the patterns are similar or different. The following discussions of Qantas and Aer Lingus are based on studies by Sarah Oxenbridge and Russell Lansbury (Qantas) and Joe Wallace, Siobhan Tiernan, and Lorraine White (Aer Lingus).[30]

Qantas

Qantas is the dominant airline in Australia. Qantas was privatized in the 1990s and since then has posted strong results. At the beginning of the twenty-first century, Qantas experienced increased competition, especially in its domestic markets from Virgin Blue and in some of its international markets from new entrants such as Emirates. However, such competitive threats were offset by the collapse of the other domestic legacy airline, Ansett, in 2001. Qantas maintained strong profitability after 9/11. Consequently, relative to U.S. legacies, it has faced less immediate pressure for radical restructuring.

Qantas's primary response to the successful threat by Virgin Blue has been the launch of its own low-cost operation, Jetstar. In contrast to the LCOs at U.S. legacies, Jetstar was originally an independent new entrant, Impulse, which Qantas bought. Jetstar's unit costs were approximately 40 percent lower than those at Qantas. Part of this cost advantage stemmed from the adoption of operational aspects of the low-cost airline model: some secondary airports or terminals, point-to-point routes, no frills. And part came from lower labor costs, which were achieved through lower wages, a less senior workforce, more flexible work rules (hence, longer hours), and more outsourcing.

Jetstar has been more successful than the U.S. LCO attempts. It has posted profits in recent years. Qantas has been transferring increasing numbers of routes from the main line to Jetstar, including some international routes to compete with Asian airlines. Jetstar is different from the U.S. LCOs in its greater independence from the Qantas main line. It was founded independently of Qantas in the first place; has been operated more separately; its labor contracts are separate from those at Qantas; and Qantas has even considered selling it as an independent entity. There are still key dimensions on which it is not independent, particularly financing aircraft purchases and route planning. Nevertheless, our hypothesis is that Jetstar's greater independence (relative to LCOs in the United States) underlies its greater success.

Although the launch of Jetstar and the arrangements of its labor contracts were negotiated with some of the same unions that negotiate at Qantas, Qantas has subsequently used Jetstar as a benchmark for "competitive" wage rates in negotiations on restructuring at the mainline operations—that is, highlighting the significant wage gap and the "uncompetitive" wage rates at the main line. However, restructuring at the main line has been more modest than that in the typical U.S. legacies. In terms of wages, Qantas has generally limited wage *increases* to only 3 percent per year. Layoffs were achieved primarily via voluntary leaves. And outsourcing has increased. However, this legacy airline was unable to effect significant changes in work rules. To cut costs, it has established bases in Asia and London, but has failed in some of its other attempts to outsource offshore (e.g., maintenance) because of public disapproval and political opposition.

Nonetheless, Qantas may be heading toward a more fundamental restructuring of its employment paradigm. New legislation in Australia in 2006 allowed companies to offer employees individual employment contracts, even if existing employees are unionized. Qantas's management began using such individual contracts at Jetstar, particularly with its international staff, and has publicly stated that it might begin experimenting with such individual contracts at Qantas main line. However, in 2007 there was a change of federal government in Australia, which precipitated a partial repeal of the legislation mentioned above. Nevertheless, although its labor contracts have generally called for management consultation with unions on changes to workplace organization, Qantas management has been attempting to assert more unilateral control. Thus, Qantas may be moving toward an even stronger control model at the workplace but also toward some level of an "avoid" strategy in regard to unions. In this case, we see a move toward less employee involvement, either via unions or individually, even where the competitive threats have been less pronounced and mitigated by the launch of an LCO.

Aer Lingus

Aer Lingus has experienced low-cost competition increasingly since the early 1990s. Ryanair was launched in 1985 and the Irish government slowly opened up routes to competition. But it was not until Ryanair's reinvention in 1991—to become a no-frills, cut-costs-to-the-bone airline—that Aer Lingus faced a significant threat. By 2001, Aer Lingus suffered a large loss, had yielded significant share to Ryanair, and faced the need for restructuring.

As Wallace, Tiernan, and White report, Aer Lingus's response to the events of 2001 involved two key elements. First, this legacy airline sought to transform itself into a low-fare airline on all its short-haul routes, rather than creating an LCO for certain more competitive routes. This necessitated substantial cost cutting. Second, Aer Lingus's plan was also predicated on significant expansion to routes throughout Europe and across the Atlantic. This raised the need for substantial capital investment for the refurbishment and expansion of its fleet.

In terms of strategy, Aer Lingus has positioned itself as a "some frills" airline—a hybrid between the legacy full service and the new-entrant no-frills model, with particular differences between short-haul and long-haul routes. While adopting some new-entrant features such as more point-to-point routes and fleet rationalization, Aer Lingus maintains service to primary airports, and offers seat assignments and meals (on long-haul routes)—a package that they tout as "low fares, way better" compared with Ryanair.

This reinvention required union concessions. Aer Lingus completed two rounds of negotiated concessions in 2001 and 2004. And while the process has been described as "bruising" and as a "non-existent bargaining relationship"[31] with threats of work stoppages, there were no work stoppages, in contrast to the negotiations during the late 1990s. In the face of a competitive threat from a common enemy, Ryanair, there appeared to be a general consensus between Aer Lingus and the unions on the need to lower costs and to reinvent Aer Lingus.

The concessions at Aer Lingus included a wage freeze to be lifted by 2003; thirty-eight hundred voluntary redundancies (i.e., job cuts through voluntary retirements) with no forced layoffs; and changes to work rules to allow increased productivity. Again, relative to U.S. legacies, these concessions seem mild. Furthermore, Aer Lingus was not able to gain agreement to allow more outsourcing. And the airline provided a quid pro quo in the form of an increase in employees' ESOP stake.

With these concessions, Aer Lingus rebounded quickly, posting profits in 2002, 2003, and 2005 with a small loss in 2004. With this turnaround, Aer Lingus then faced the need for capital investment. But the Irish government, its owner and source of investment, was unwilling to invest in it further, because one of the coalition government's minority parties wanted to sell the airline. So Aer Lingus planned a partial privatization in 2006, selling a large percentage of the government's stake, but still leaving 28 percent state ownership (reduced to 25 percent shortly after the privatization) and 14.9 percent employee ownership.

To win approval from unions and employees for the privatization, which seemed essential to get the state's approval, Aer Lingus had to offer some reverse concessions, sweetening employment conditions. Employees received a 4 percent raise, a commitment to no outsourcing, funding for underfunded pensions, additional employment protections, and a profit-sharing program. The only primary change to the employment system was increased productivity from reduced work rules and leaner staffing (hence more hours worked) as well as an increased employee ownership stake. This seems to have been sufficient to make Aer Lingus competitive, even in the face of competition from one of the world's largest and most profitable new entrants, Ryanair.

In late 2006, Aer Lingus's plans and employment system were suddenly subjected to considerable uncertainty when Ryanair surprised Aer Lingus, as well as the Irish government, with a hostile takeover offer for the newly privatized airline. Ryanair's motive was probably to limit its competition from Aer Lingus. In mid-2008, Ryanair's bid was still being resisted. This reflected opposition to it by the employees, unions, and the government, which was the largest shareholder, as well as a ruling by the EU competition authority that the bid was anticompetitive for the Irish and wider European markets. However, Ryanair retained a 29 percent stake in Aer Lingus and there is still uncertainty about whether Aer Lingus will be able to remain independent, in view of its small scale and the increasingly tough competition.

What's Changed? Lower Wages, More Contingent Pay—But Too Little Commitment

Despite apocalyptic rhetoric from industry insiders and journalists about the potential demise of the legacies and notwithstanding massive financial losses after 9/11, by 2007 U.S. legacy airlines were returning to modest levels of profitability and regaining some competitiveness against new entrants. In spite of the bankruptcies, no legacies had ceased operations and there had been only one merger. In other countries, many legacy airlines had stayed profitable even after 9/11. Thus, the legacies remain a dominant force in the worldwide industry, accounting for some 75 percent of domestic traffic in the United States and much more internationally.

The survival of the legacies in the United States has been facilitated by massive layoffs and huge concessions from employees. Employees have agreed to these concessions without recourse to strikes or other job actions, with isolated exceptions such as the mechanics at Northwest, perhaps recognizing that the alternative would have been liquidation. Thus, in terms of the question "What has changed in the employment relationship in the face of increasing price competition?" one of the major changes in the United States has been a large reduction in the level of wages and benefits for legacy employees. In the main, adjusting to price competition has come at the expense of "good jobs."

Another change has been the more widespread use of contingent compensation. As table 6.1 indicates, many of the major U.S. legacy airlines offer at least three types of contingent payment mechanisms: stock options, profit sharing, and operational performance bonuses. Such mechanisms used to be more the exception than the rule. Southwest's stock options plans from the 1990s were exceptional as was Continental's on-time bonus program from 1994. Earlier instances of employee participation in an airline's financial performance were in the form of ESOPs.

Employees do not appear to view these mechanisms as important or substantial elements of their compensation. Therefore, if the formulas governing these mechanisms produce increases that are only small fractions of the amount employees conceded in recent years, they may not reduce the volatility of wage negotiations and the seesaw battles that follow the industry's cycles. Already the rhetoric from some union representatives echoes the familiar refrain of "now that the airline is profitable, it's our turn to share in the gains and get back what we lost," with no mention of the built-in gain-sharing mechanisms. To an important degree this is probably because the potential upside does not match what was given up. However, it is not clear whether contingent compensation plans that would pay out larger percentages of salary would ultimately reduce employees' focus on wage gains in future negotiations—or would reduce the need for concession demands from airlines in future downturns. It may be that there also needs to be a cultural shift in how contingent pay is perceived and valued.

Aside from these changes to compensation levels and mechanisms, however, there has been relatively little change in the basic employment paradigm among legacy airlines. Although alternative approaches have been tried, in many cases they have not persisted. The most prominent union-suppression attempt ultimately collapsed. Despite Qantas's rhetoric in that direction, it is not likely to move to an avoidance strategy, especially since a Labor government was elected in Australia in 2007. In the other direction, attempts to involve unions in governance via ownership and board seats have also not persisted; they have usually ended either with mergers or bankruptcy. An ESOP arrangement continues at Aer Lingus, but if Ryanair takes it over, this might end or reduce the ESOP.

Mergers tend to be one of the homogenizing forces in the industry, frequently ending attempts at more significant employee involvement. As noted, several of the shared governance initiatives ended after mergers—at Western, Eastern, and TWA—and the recent merger of US Airways and America West eliminated labor's board-level representation. In addition, US Air's acquisition of Piedmont and PSA in 1987 meant the end of the exceptional approaches to a commitment-based workplace culture at those two airlines. It remains to be seen what forms of employee and labor relations emerge if the industry continues to consolidate. The Delta-Northwest merger that is pending at the time of writing will be especially challenging since it brings together a largely nonunion airline (Delta) with an airline with a long history of adversarial labor-management relations (Northwest). If history is a guide, this does not bode well for this merger, unless, before the merger is consummated, the unions and the companies involved negotiate how representation issues will be decided, seniority lists will be merged, and initial wage and benefit differences and future wage adjustments will be handled. This is not likely to happen; therefore, employee and labor relations issues may severely impact the performance of the merged organization in its formative years.

Turning to the workplace level, the commitment strategy is more promising, given the benefits that accrue to airlines that successfully pursue that model. Southwest, JetBlue, Virgin Blue, and easyJet achieve higher levels of productivity partly on the basis of a committed workforce that engages in relational coordination. Perhaps more important, the commitment strategy at Continental indicates that such an approach is possible for unionized legacy airlines. Not only has Continental posted superior financial performances relative to its legacy rivals since 1995, but it has experienced less volatility in its labor contracting, reaching contracts quickly, with less rancor, and was able to pursue smaller concessions. Therefore, we were pleased to see Conti-

nental state in April 2008 that it would not participate in any merger, specifically noting its "significant cultural, operational, and financial strengths
compared to the rest of the industry . . . which would be placed at risk in a
merger."[32]

Nevertheless, this commitment route may be harder to implement in
practice than in concept. American's experience indicates that it can be
hard to maintain a successful commitment strategy. Efforts to reduce the
volatility of the industry and to improve outcomes for all the industry's
stakeholders might focus on working out how movements toward such
commitment-based approaches might be facilitated and sustained, either at
the enterprise level or via public policy.

Despite the upheavals and restructuring that gripped the U.S. legacy
airlines after 9/11, the industry's employment system has not been redesigned. Unfortunately, if this means more of the same, we can expect to see
yet more conflictual contract negotiations when contracts become amendable. And given the large scale of recent concessions as well as the apparently increasing magnitude of the industry's volatility, future conflicts could
be more serious and damaging than ever.

CHAPTER 7

Building a More Balanced Airline Industry

The global airline industry is undergoing a transformation driven by increased price competition that has arisen from three interrelated forces: deregulation of product markets, the growth of new lower-cost entrants, and increasing customer price sensitivity. Older legacy carriers have responded by dramatically cutting labor costs in an effort to close the cost and price gap with new entrants. Although these trends emerged first in the United States, they have spread to other countries, albeit in somewhat more varied fashion.

For the most part these changes have been a boon to customers as air travel is more affordable and accessible than ever—which also facilitates economic activity in general. But this benefit has come at a high cost to the industry's workforce and its levels of service quality. It has also produced a growing volatility that increases risks for investors, employees, and customers, and perhaps even for the general public that depends on a stable and sustainable airline *industry* for safe and reliable transportation and the jobs and economic growth that it generates.

For the workforce in particular, a look at the industry's recent developments might suggest that this increasing price competition spells the end of good jobs. In the legacy sector, a primary thrust of airlines' response to the low-cost advantage of the new entrants has been a dramatic cutting of labor costs via cuts to employment levels, wages, and benefits, especially in the

United States. And in the new-entrant sector, the growing new airlines are often assumed to have nonunion workforces working long hours at wage and benefit levels significantly lower than those at the legacies. Indeed, Ryanair, one of the most successful of the new entrants—and the most profitable airline in the world in some recent years—is renowned for its aggressive union-avoidance strategy and for the long hours and high turnover of its employees.

Hence one of our primary questions was "Do low fares inevitably mean low-quality jobs?" Does intensifying price competition necessitate low wages, no unions, and an employment strategy to avoid unions and control employees? Our investigation into the industry, reported in the preceding chapters, indicates that the answer is "no." A number of airlines, both legacy and new entrant, have been successful with a commitment-based paradigm, an accommodation or partnership approach to unions, and industry average wages. Not only have these airlines delivered superior returns to investors and provided high-quality jobs for employees, but they have also provided high levels of service quality and have negotiated labor contracts in a timely fashion, which reduces volatility in wages and benefits. In other words, they are not only viable but perhaps also more sustainable than other airlines. Thus, we see the potential for a stronger industry in the improvement of relations between airlines and their unions and employees, particularly in the moves toward commitment-based relationships in the workplace. However, there is a lot of hard work to be done if these examples are to become the norm rather than the exception in the airline industry.

In this chapter we first summarize the quantitative and case study evidence that supports our answer. We recap the variation in employment strategies observed among legacy and new-entrant firms in the United States and other countries as well as the evidence on the effects of these variations on key stakeholder outcomes. Then we discuss how to capitalize on these conclusions to achieve stronger, more sustainable airlines.

Low Cost Doesn't Mean Low Wages and No Unions

In chapter 4, our analyses offered important insights on the source of low costs across airlines. First, although labor unit costs are one source of cost advantage for new entrants, they are not the only or even the primary source—new entrants also enjoy substantial cost advantages from a range of other components, including higher aircraft utilization, lower fuel unit costs, and lower transport-related costs. Second, low unit *labor* costs do not always translate into low *total* unit costs. For example, the airlines in the United States with the *highest* unit labor costs in each segment in 2006 (Southwest and American) also had the *lowest or second-lowest* total unit costs. Third, low unit labor costs are not solely the result of low *wage* rates. Southwest had among the lowest unit labor costs in the industry until the wave of legacy bankruptcies produced large wage and benefit cuts. Labor unit costs are also determined by labor productivity. So to the extent that higher wages can be translated into greater employee effort in identifying and cooperating with productivity improvements, they can be offset by productivity gains. Both our quantitative and case study research, for example, show that the combination of higher wages and a commitment-based strategy are associated with higher service reliability, aircraft productivity, labor productivity, and operating margins—while the combination of higher wages and a more conflictual union relationship are associated with lower service reliability, aircraft productivity, and operating margins.[1] Thus, although low wage rates may contribute to a total unit cost advantage, they are by no means a necessity. To the extent that an airline can translate higher quality jobs into greater employee cooperation, commitment, and coordination, it can achieve competitive (or even lower) total unit costs by achieving superior productivity (as well as superior service, in terms of reliability and "friendliness"). These results also suggest that legacy airlines that reduce costs largely via wage and benefit cuts may not necessarily see those cuts translate into lower total unit costs.

In addition, our analyses have shown that the greater presence of unions at an airline, although it is associated with higher wage rates, is not at all associated with lower profitability—and in fact, may be associated with slightly greater profitability.[2] Furthermore, the case studies in chapter 5 indicate that a number of new entrants that are unionized are successful (including Southwest, Virgin Blue, easyJet, and AirTran). In fact, the best-performing airline in the United States, Southwest, is also the most unionized.

These data indicate that a focus on wage rates and unions per se as the sources of airline advantage or disadvantage (and success or failure) is too simplistic. They also point to the importance of the quality of the underlying relationships between airlines and their unions and employees.

Employment-Relations Strategies: The Power of Improved Relationships

The airlines from our case studies are arrayed in figure 7.1 in the employment-relations-strategy matrix, with legacy airlines in *bold* and new-entrant airlines in *italics*. For legacy airlines, the control/accommodation paradigm dominates. It was well established before deregulation among most of the legacies around the world (with airlines from coordinated market economies [CMEs] marked by elements of formal partnership, based on national-level labor market institutions). To the extent that this paradigm remains dominant, it is hard to foresee anything but "business as usual" in terms of the industry's volatility (at least in the legacy segment). However, there are and have been alternative approaches, as we summarize below.

For new entrants, there is not one dominant paradigm. Rather, there are two polar opposites represented by two of the most successful new entrants: Ryanair, which adheres to a control model and engages in union avoidance of the suppression variety; and Southwest, which adheres to a commitment model and engages informally (but authentically) with unions as partners. Many other new entrants have looked to these two as models and have debated about which to adopt. For example, at Jetstar there have been debates about the relative merits of Ryanair and Southwest. The argument was posed

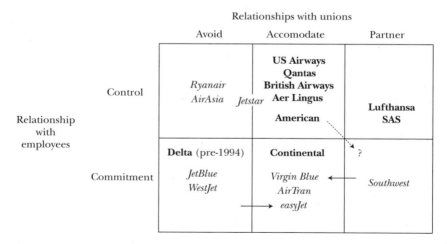

Figure 7.1. Employment-relations strategies of selected airlines. Legacy airlines are in bold, new-entrant airlines in italics.

in terms of "just getting the job done" at Ryanair rather than "all that touchy-feely relationship stuff" at Southwest. Perhaps because several key members of Jetstar's top management team had come from Ireland, the Ryanair employment-relations model seemed to be winning. At Virgin Blue and easyJet, there were more signs of an aim to pursue a Southwest-type employment-relations strategy, but Ryanair was still in the background as a model that directors could point to and attempt to impose on the management team. For instance, Virgin Blue's original head of people aimed to follow the Southwest strategy and to engage the unions to identify mutual-gains solutions for Virgin Blue's workers. However, in 2005 Chris Corrigan's Patrick Corporation took over Virgin Blue. Corrigan (who had challenged the role of unions on the Australian waterfront in the mid-1990s) then became Virgin Blue's nonexecutive chairman. He questioned why the managers were dealing with unions on behalf of Virgin Blue's staff and why managers would wish to communicate with union leaders any more than was strictly necessary. In effect his preference was to move the airline away from the Southwest model toward the Ryanair one. In our observations, many new entrants have implemented hybrid approaches, drawing selectively from both models.

The greater diversity of employment strategies among new entrants is not surprising, as they have begun from scratch with models based on the values of the founders.[3] Does this diversity persist as these airlines mature? For example, to what extent can airline maintain a union-avoidance strategy?

Avoid, Accommodate, or Partner with Unions

As noted in chapter 1, *avoidance* means to actively discourage employees from unionization either by offering conditions that will make employees feel unionization is unnecessary (substitution) or by suppressing efforts through fear of retribution (suppression). *Accommodation* means to put up with unions and negotiate with them as required, maintaining an arm's-length relationship. *Partnering* refers to a range of approaches that increase union-management interaction beyond the minimum specified in the collective bargaining framework that we see in the United States and other liberal market economies. In most instances, *partnering* refers to sharing more information more often than required and seeking mutual-gains solutions. But it can take a range of forms, some relatively informal, some based on formal structures, such as ESOPs, or legal rules such as codetermination (in Germany and Scandinavia).

Legacies

Accommodation has been the dominant strategy for legacy airlines around the world. This is particularly true for airlines in the United States and other liberal market economies. Legacy airlines in coordinated market economies, operating in national contexts that require greater consultation with the workforce and its unions, have necessarily engaged in relationships that look more like partnering.

The dominance of accommodation has persisted despite a number of attempts to change the nature of the relationships with unions, toward either the avoidance or partnering direction. Lorenzo's efforts to suppress existing unions at Continental and Eastern met with such conflict that it drove both legacies into bankruptcy and destroyed Eastern. Delta has been a long-standing exception, using a substitution approach that has kept all but the pilots and dispatchers nonunion. But once Delta's distinctive commitment-based workplace culture eroded in the mid-1990s, Delta no longer achieved superior results on service levels or profitability. For legacy airlines, imagining a nonunion future is usually a nonstarter in the liberal market economies as well as in coordinated market economies.

Legacy attempts at partnership have usually been short lived. In the United States, ESOP arrangements that traded wage cuts for collective stock ownership and employee/union representation on the board of directors have produced, at best, only short run, unsustainable mutual gains and, at worst, further alienation and distrust when the workers did not experience an improvement in the workplace culture (i.e., a transformation to a commitment-based relationship). American Airlines' twenty-first-century attempt at more informal partnership continues to deliver some productivity and employment expansion gains in conjunction with its mechanics, but has stalled with pilots and flight attendants. Outside the United States, British Airways and Aer Lingus also have had only limited success with partnering. Even some of the airlines in coordinated market economies (e.g., SAS and Germanwings) have sometimes compromised their partnerships with unions and also behaved as if they were only accommodating unions.

New Entrants

New-entrant airlines are by no means all nonunion. Not only are there unionized and nonunion new entrants, but there is variation within those categories. Some nonunion airlines have adopted suppression (Ryanair, AirAsia) while others pursue substitution (JetBlue). Most unionized new entrants are characterized by accommodation (AirTran, Virgin Blue, easyJet), while Southwest stands out as a relatively rare new entrant in the partnership category, based on its informal but substantial interaction with its unions to find sources of mutual gains.

The chief difference between the legacy and new-entrant airlines in terms of union relationships, of course, is the presence of nonunion airlines among new entrants. Since most of the new entrants start up without union representation, perhaps the surprising point is that many *become* unionized. This raises the question of whether or how long the nonunion new entrants will remain that way. New entrants from earlier waves have at least one organized group (typically pilots). A key question that we raise in the following discussion of control vs. commitment is whether attempts to avoid or suppress unions preclude an airline's ability to pursue a commitment approach, especially if unionization takes place nonetheless.

In the United States, we have found only one long-term case of a partnership approach: Southwest. Like organizational change efforts in other firms we have studied in other industries, efforts to build partnership inevitably encounter conflicts or "pivotal events" that can often undermine such efforts. Often partnership attempts are born of the desire to gain union support for cost reduction efforts, which has proven to be a difficult path to negotiate. Successful partnership requires a willingness to partner by employees and their unions, which often requires overcoming a memory of distrust. The key to this may be at the workplace, in the nature of the relationship with employees.

Control vs. Commitment

Control is a traditional approach to managing people, where managers specify what needs to be done, with little input from employees, and managers direct employees to comply with these instructions. *Commitment* is an alternative approach in which managers engage employees to understand the interests of the organization and its customers and act accordingly, in return for a greater commitment by the firm to the employees' long-term financial and social welfare.

Our case studies suggest that the traditional control approach to managing employees is still more common than the commitment approach in this industry, for legacies *and* for low-cost airlines. But there are also examples of legacy and new-entrant airlines that are following the commitment approach. Among the new-entrant airlines, Southwest, JetBlue, and Virgin Blue are employing various features of a commitment strategy, with easyJet and Air-Tran showing signs of also having moved in that direction. Among the legacy airlines, Continental has employed a commitment model since its 1994 leadership change, Delta did so until about 1997, and American Airlines has been trying to adopt such a strategy.

Yet these examples offer evidence that a commitment-based model, while potentially hard to implement and sustain, may offer superior outcomes, not only for investors but also for employees and customers, as well as lower volatility. We noted earlier that a commitment-based workplace culture could be associated with high wages, high service quality, high productivity, and high operating margins.

Let us recap the two primary examples in each segment, Southwest and Continental. For investors, Southwest has been the most profitable U.S. airline for many years. For customers, it has also won the "triple crown" of service quality (highest on-time rating, lowest baggage loss rate, and lowest complaint rate) over a number of years. For employees, it has routinely been ranked among *Fortune*'s 100 Best Companies to Work For, has never laid off employees, has delivered steady wage gains, and has created millionaires out of some of its rank-and-file pilots based on stock option compensation. Continental has also been one of the most profitable U.S. legacy airlines since 1995. It routinely wins awards from customers for its service quality. It also has been ranked among *Fortune*'s 100 Best Companies to Work For. It restructured outside of bankruptcy, preserving employee pensions, and requested lower concessions than all its legacy rivals. In terms of volatility, Southwest and Continental feature the shortest labor contract negotiation times in the U.S. industry.

A commitment approach is most compatible with a partnership with unions, where unions are present. However, it also may be possible to sustain where union relations fall into the accommodate category, provided they are predictable and not deteriorating toward either an avoidance or more adversarial accommodate approach to negotiations and union-management relations. Delta and JetBlue also have shown that commitment strategies can be sustained over time when following a union substitution strategy. A commitment approach, then, does not appear contingent on a particular approach to unions. We do not have strong evidence from the airline industry regarding whether one type of strategy toward unions makes a commitment approach more easily achieved or sustained than another. However, in conjunction with a union substitution approach (as at Delta and JetBlue), the approach can be tested severely if there is a union organizing drive. This is particularly true since there are no examples of a commitment model in conjunction with a union-suppression strategy in the airline industry. Southwest has combined commitment and partnership with unions since 1971, evidence that it can be a sustainable strategy. But the numbers of cases in the airline industry are too limited to draw definitive conclusions.

Although commitment may be feasible under a variety of approaches to unions, it may be that the partnering approach to unions is feasible only in conjunction with a commitment-based workplace strategy. Apart from Southwest, the many attempts at some form of partnership relationship with unions in the United States have all been of limited and short-term success at best, in part because the partnership efforts were not complemented with commitment-based strategies for frontline workers or middle managers.

Improved Relationships Lead to More Sustainable Airlines

Financial success in the airline industry does not depend on one particular type of employment-relations strategy. Ryanair became the most profitable airline in the world by implementing a tough control/suppression strategy for minimizing labor and total costs. By contrast, Southwest has had more than four decades of superior financial results based on a contrasting employment-relations strategy.

However, our research shows that improved relationships between airlines and their employees and unions—that is, commitment and partnership models—are a path to superior results for the three main stakeholders as well as lower volatility of outcomes. Ryanair's opposite approach appears to have the potential for financial success, but creates a strong trade-off between the interests of investors and employees (as well as a trade-off in terms of good service for customers), thus failing to maintain a balance. There are well-documented positive relationships between employee satisfaction and customer satisfaction observed in other service industries. Further, our research shows that positive labor and employee relations are associated with better service quality; commitment-based approaches appear to serve customers better than strategies that demoralize and frustrate employees.

What, then, are the prospects for improved relationships at the workplace and with unions—and what might make those prospects brighter?

Lessons for the United States

Our analysis of the airline industry and variations in practices observed in the United States and other countries leads us to suggest three possible scenarios for the future of the industry in the United States. The first is a default scenario—the likely future, if the past predicts future trends. The second and third scenarios are less deterministic, but depend on the ability and willingness of parties in the industry to *learn* from each other's experiences, from the industry's history, and from airlines in other countries, and for leaders to serve as catalysts for innovation and improvement at the organizational and industry levels.

Scenario 1: The Future Is an Acceleration of Past Trends

Scenario 1 is the default option. If no catalyst for improvement is forthcoming, the oscillating boom-bust cycle of the past two decades not only will be repeated but the oscillations will continue to intensify in magnitude. Among the legacies, the potential for more episodes of labor-management conflict is high, rising, and may peak soon as earlier concession agreements come up for renewal. Unlike earlier periods, such as 1998–2000, when similar pressures were building, contracts for different groups within and across firms are due for renegotiation in close proximity, thereby increasing the potential scope and impact of bargaining impasses. Under this scenario, the day of reckoning for legacy airlines is drawing nigh.

There does not appear to be as clear a default path for airlines in the new-entrant segment. Although labor costs are rising and in some cases getting close to converging with legacies, competitive success depends eventually on *total* costs, which most new entrants have controlled more successfully than the legacy airlines. However, it is likely that such efforts to hold the line or reduce total costs will intensify. Those pressures will likely require at least marginal if not major efforts to shift business strategies to attract more higher- revenue customers (e.g., business travelers), further increase productivity through more commitment and partnership strategies, or press for lower labor costs through intensified control/union suppression policies. The key question for the parties (airlines and unions) in this segment is whether they will learn from the history of the legacy carriers or repeat their mistakes.

The default scenario is not in anyone's interest. The return to profitability is likely to be at best limited in the short run and unsustainable in the longer run; employee morale will continue at its low levels or fall further in those airlines that intensify efforts to hold down or reduce wages; customers will experience threats of or actual service disruptions; and the stresses on the air transportation system will intensify. Over the longer run, more of the legacies will probably face either bankruptcy, acquisition by an unsolicited bidder (e.g., another airline or a private equity fund), or even liquidation with all its resulting costs to its employees, customers, suppliers, and the communities that depend on them.

The default scenario includes the ingredients for a potential "perfect storm,"[4] where the stresses on the air transportation system reach or surpass their limits. As we write this in April 2008, the U.S. industry is experiencing the most delayed flights on record; air traffic controller staffing is down, as retirements outpace recruitment and training; and airline executives and Congress debate who should pay for upgrading traffic control technologies (from reliance on radar to global positioning systems). One airline (Northwest) was forced to cancel four hundred flights in July 2007, because pilots reached their legal limit of work hours before the end of the month. Weather and congestion in the busy Northeast U.S. corridor mean that it is unusual when a flight leaves on time; overbooked flights make for irritable customers and stressed employees, while employee morale is at or near historic low levels, just as airlines are making profits (at least up until 2008, when the price of oil went over $100 a barrel). Low employee morale is exacerbated by airlines paying certain executives multimillion dollar bonuses. (In some cases, this is despite their airline performing poorly in financial terms.)

Such stresses are not unique to the United States. London Heathrow is the world's busiest international airport. It has descended into chaos several times in recent years. This has been precipitated by various factors including bad weather, computer problems, labor disputes, environmental protests, threats of terrorist attacks to planes or to the airport itself, more rigorous security checks, and mismanagement of the baggage handling system when it opened its much trumpeted Terminal 5.[5] One commentator observed that passengers confronted by Heathrow's chaos can experience more stress than if they were engaged in bungee jumping. However, a key difference is that bungee jumping lasts only a few moments, but the stress of trying to navigate a chaotic airport might last for hours or even days.

Waiting for "the perfect storm" or some other system meltdown is unwise and irresponsible.

A second scenario is that individual airlines and unions might learn from their own experiences and those of others and initiate efforts to improve their relationships and achieve results that better balance the interests of employees, shareholders, and customers. We outline a strategy for doing so that draws on the evidence presented in earlier chapters. Although the steps to be taken are fairly clear, success is likely to be as difficult to achieve on an airline-by-airline or union-by-union basis in the future as it has been in the past. Moreover, this approach does little to address the interdependence among airlines, the "culture" of the industry, or interdependencies (e.g., security challenges, airport efficiency, air traffic capacity constraints, and technology upgrades) with other aspects of the air transportation system that affect the operations and performance of individual airlines.

While recognizing the difficulties of taking an airline-by-airline and union-by-union approach to innovation, it is an appropriate initial approach. It is usually worth trying to start small before expecting a broader approach to succeed. What can we infer from our research and the experiences of deregulation about a path to sustained recovery that achieves a better balance among stakeholder interests?

The clearest lesson we draw from the ups and downs of the industry since deregulation and particularly since the beginning of the 2000 downturn is that labor cost reductions may have been necessary from time to time and particularly in the post 9/11 markets, but by themselves they have never proved to be sufficient for achieving a sustainable recovery. Moreover, as the data in chapter 4 showed, employees have borne a disproportionate share of cost reductions so far among the U.S. legacy airlines. The effects of this are already being felt in calls for catch-up increases that, if delayed until the concession agreements are due for renegotiations, will stress individual airlines, unions and their leaders, and increase the risk of further service disruptions. The result is likely to be intensified conflicts and a return to the growing magnitude of the oscillations observed over the past two decades. Even worse, the "boom" side of the cycle may get attenuated before it reaches its full potential.

These cases, along with the broader quantitative data, document what industry and labor representatives in this and other service industries know: success in most markets is more likely if there is a committed, engaged, well-trained, and well-managed workforce and successful labor-management processes for working through and sharing equitably in good and bad times. A key question is how to do this given the conditions facing airlines and their employees in the industry.

The basic elements of such a recovery path below draw on the lessons we infer from the evidence in the preceding chapters.

Positive Workplace Culture

High levels of productivity and customer service in airlines, like other service industries, require a workplace culture that promotes trust and employment practices that promote coordination and productivity among employees. The first step in building a positive workplace culture is to ask employees themselves for their ideas. Firms such as Continental that have had successful employment relationships in the past and those that are making progress have actively communicated with their employees honestly, openly, and consistently about the state of the business and discussed options for the future with employees.

To yield high levels of productivity and customer satisfaction, a positive workplace culture has to be translated into practices that achieve high levels of coordination and teamwork among the different employee groups involved in airline operations. Southwest Airlines, more so than most other airlines, has achieved high levels of relational coordination between employee groups—the ability to coordinate work through frequent, timely, problem-solving communication, based on shared goals, shared knowledge, and mutual respect. Relational coordination has enabled greater aircraft productivity, greater employee productivity, fewer customer complaints, fewer lost bags, and fewer flight delays.[6]

This high level of coordination among employees at Southwest has been supported over the years by a distinctive set of employment practices, starting with credibility and caring by senior executives and an active coaching and feedback role for frontline supervisors. In addition, hiring, training, and performance measurement have been designed to develop team players rather than individual performance. Jobs have been designed with flexible boundaries, such that each employee has core responsibilities but is also encouraged to "do whatever is needed to ensure a successful operation." Conflicts between employees are treated proactively as occasions for strengthening work relationships. Employees are encouraged to maintain strong family and community ties along with their workplace relationships. Further, Southwest's management has worked with its employees' union representatives to achieve shared goals since it was founded. Given the high levels of unionization at Southwest Airlines, this informal partnership approach has been critical to Southwest's success. Southwest's partnership with its unions and its more conservative financial management (lower debt levels) made it possible for Southwest to avoid layoffs after 9/11.[7] This sustained record of performance is why so many of the airlines outside the United States, such as easyJet and Virgin Blue, that have started operations in recent years turn to Southwest as their model and attempt to follow similar commitment-oriented human resource practices.

Since 2003, American Airlines has attempted to implement a Southwest-style partnership as it negotiated wage and benefit reductions with its unions and employees. Its experience demonstrates that efforts to build trust with frontline employees and their union representatives are highly sensitive to perceptions of whether all stakeholders—employees, executives, and others—are sharing the risks and rewards. The shock that a fund was set aside to protect the financial interests of top executives while employees were voting on their concession agreement cost the chief executive officer at American his job. The momentum built up over a year of working together following this episode was again broken when the stock appreciation plan generated significant gains for executives, well before any gains would be realized by employees.

These events demonstrate how fragile the trust essential to recovery efforts can be and why an all-encompassing organizational strategy and commitment to it is needed from management and from the unions involved if such innovations are to be sustained. Experience in building partnerships in other industries tell us that conflicts over policy issues or actions such as those that derailed the change efforts at American inevitably arise from time to time. They should be expected, addressed, and resolved directly so the change effort can proceed, rather than be held hostage by opponents of innovation in either the union or management.

Negotiations and Conflict Resolution

U.S. airline industry contract negotiation processes and procedures have been subject to increased criticism. It has been taking an average of seventeen months to negotiate an agreement, and even longer if one party or the other sees tactical advantages to delay. Going slow exacerbates the magnitude of the oscillations in performance and trust. The conflicts associated with these delays tend to be associated with significantly lower productivity and service quality. This need not be the case, as again evidenced by firms such as Southwest and Continental that have managed to reach agreements in less than half the industry average.

The industry, labor, and government working group our research team assembled in 2004 to explore options for reaching agreements in a more timely fashion outlined a variety of steps (summarized below) that negotiating parties and the National Mediation Board (NMB) could take to do so.

Working Group Recommendations for Improving Negotiations

- Negotiation of voluntary protocols for negotiating labor agreements in a timely and effective fashion.
- Development of joint implementation and contract administration teams to resolve issues and problems that arise due to circumstances that negotiators cannot anticipate or as conditions change during the term of the agreement.
- Increased use by the NMB of different tools and techniques for resolving disputes and continued expansion of the array of services offered the parties for improving labor-management relations during the term of their agreements.
- Collection of feedback data on the services and administrative changes introduced by the NMB, and consideration of options for providing joint industry and labor input in the appointment of NMB Board members.
- Development of an on-going education and training program in state-of-the-art techniques and NMB procedures for labor and management negotiating teams.[8]

Adopting these recommendations is the easy part. Committing to use them to reach fair agreements that reinforce the trust of workers and top management and investors who look over the shoulder of negotiations is much more challenging. But this is only a first, necessary, but not sufficient step for updating the negotiation and conflict resolution processes in the industry.

It is generally no longer practicable for negotiations by pilots, flight attendants, mechanics, or other groups to take place separately or even privately. Consistent with the craft principles built into the U.S. Railway Labor Act, pilots, flight attendants, mechanics, passenger service employees, and other groups are typically represented by different unions. Although in the past informal pattern bargaining has sometimes characterized relationships across occupational groups within and across companies, crises tend to increase the interdependence in wage and benefit adjustments within firms. This is the environment in which the parties are interacting. The key players therefore need to adapt their negotiation processes in ways that recognize such realities.

Regardless of the formal craft-based negotiating rules and traditions inherited from the past, the parties will need to move to a more coordinated enterprise-wide approach. There are several ways of doing this, from formal processes in which all parties negotiate jointly to less formal private consultations among labor representatives and their management counterparts inside each airline. The latter is likely to be a more realistic and less risky process. Moving successfully in this direction will require more coordination among the unions within individual companies at an industry level than has been characteristic of interunion relations in the past.

Several efforts have been made to bring the various airline industry unions together to coordinate their strategies. At the national level the secretary treasurer of the AFL-CIO hosted several meetings of its member unions in the industry, but was not able to generate support for a coordinated approach. In early 2008 the unions of flight attendants held an industrywide "summit" meeting to discuss ways to coordinate their efforts. There have also been examples of coordination across unions within airlines and there is more informal communication occurring. But these are only tentative steps. It remains to be seen whether they will generate a process that achieves companywide, much less industrywide, agreement on compensation principles that will both help support a return to sustained profitability and an equitable sharing of whatever gains are achieved, whenever they are achieved. Thus, some efforts to improve interunion communication and coordination are under way. More will be needed.

Compensation Equity

Employees want assurances that in return for absorbing a share of the sacrifices, they will share equitably in the gains from recovery, if and when it occurs. Because employees are sensitive to how any wage or benefit improvements are distributed between managerial and nonmanagerial groups and across occupational and craft lines, the compensation principles guiding these adjustments should be transparent and clear to all concerned. Consensus on the principles and timing of compensation adjustments for all employees is critical for building and maintaining the cohesion and trust needed to sustain recovery once it begins. This means the principles need to be designed in ways that mitigate rather than contribute to the oscillations and volatility in wages and benefits that continue to plague this industry. The various contingent compensation provisions in most bargaining agreements are a starting point for the design of such principles and for better aligning the interests and motivation of employees, managers, and investors. But they need to be combined with principles for adjusting base salaries and benefits that, taken together, produce a compensation program and structure that attracts and retains the talent needed in the industry and helps to rebuild workforce morale and confidence in management from the current low levels in the industry.

The thorny issue of executive compensation should also be considered. This is not as simple an issue as it first appears. It is easy to call for equal sacrifices from executives and middle managers and equity argues for this principle. Yet the competition for managers and executives is also a concern. Airline chief executive officers are, on average, paid less than their counterparts in other industries in the United States. This, however, is not a new issue. Compensation strategies have always had to balance internal equity and external market pressures. The key issues are transparency, predictability, and moderation. Transparency is almost a given in the twenty-first century. Executive compensation plans are increasingly open to public, shareholder, and employee scrutiny and comment. So transparency has to be a key feature of compensation policy—for executives down through the ranks of management to frontline employees, unless, of course, companies want a repeat of the experiences at American Airlines when undisclosed executive bonuses, discovered in the immediate aftermath of major concessions by employees, cost the chief executive officer his job and set back the cooperative efforts of the unions and the company.

Predictability is a second key principle. If employees and managers all know what factors will drive their compensation and have some ability to influence those factors, motivation is enhanced and the results generated have a greater chance of being accepted as fair.

Third, there is no substitute for moderation in the compensation of high-level executives. Although this is a national problem in the United States (and increasingly in other liberal market economies), the airline industry could lead the way in reversing the long pattern of growing inequality between top executive salaries and frontline workers. This will only happen, however, if there is some force on the "other side of the table" in setting executive compensation levels, which is lacking in the way compensation consultants, chief executives, human resource professional staff, and board compensation committees are intertwined. Should employees and their unions continue to negotiate for principles of common risk and rewards and hold corporate boards and top executives accountable for reversing the large gaps that have grown up between chief executive officers and all others in the industry? The strength of unions in the airline industry and the need to rebuild trust and confidence in management make this industry a good place to begin what needs to become a national and international campaign. Perhaps the Dutch unions and society have something to teach the industry in this regard, as the case of KLM executive bonuses shows, summarized below. SAS provided another example from Sweden. When rank and file employees agreed to 3 percent pay cuts executive pay was reduced by 10 percent.

Aborted Bonuses at KLM

In 2004 KLM Royal Dutch Airline announced a generous executive "synergy bonus" scheme. Top executives were to receive bonuses of as much as 50 percent of their annual salaries in the years after KLM merged with Air France. But unions were concerned the bonuses would give managers an incentive to make more job cuts on top of the forty-five hundred layoffs that KLM had already announced. Dutch unions threatened to stop wage talks and to consider wildcat strikes if the bonus plan was not dropped. They asked the Dutch government to intervene. After its finance minister publicly denounced the bonuses as "excessive," KLM decided to "withdraw the proposed synergy bonuses."[9]

Sustainable Business Models

Changing employment relations in the ways outlined here is necessary, but not sufficient, as a strategy for generating a sustainable recovery for individual airlines or the industry as a whole. Passenger traffic and load factors have returned to pre-9/11 levels. Labor costs have declined and employee productivity has increased significantly.

Further gains in employee productivity will be necessary. But we infer from our research that employees play a critical role not only in improving employee productivity but also in improving the productivity of other key assets such as aircraft and gates, and in improving customer service. The lessons from Toyota and other companies that have embraced the principles of total quality management by using continuous improvement and employee engagement deserve more careful attention in this industry. So too do the strategies of companies in both the legacy segment, such as Continental, and international airlines, such as Lufthansa, Singapore Airlines, and even Emirates and Virgin Atlantic, two of the youngest full-service airlines. These international competitors have all set higher benchmarks for service on international routes than do their U.S. counterparts.

In the new-entrant segment, JetBlue and Southwest in the United States and Germanwings, Virgin Blue, and easyJet from other countries have been able to maintain (albeit with occasional bumps) reputations for good service. The comparison is Ryanair—an airline that has been successful financially, but at the cost of harsh employee relations, low pay, and "no frills" service levels. Low costs need not inevitably mean minimalist wages and harsh employee relations. It depends on whether we see Southwest or Ryanair as the benchmark. Engaging employees to achieve these broader improvements will help in achieving business models with lower unit costs across the board, not just low labor costs, and with higher levels of customer satisfaction.

There are, however, limits to reliance on employee-driven productivity improvements. Southwest appears to recognize that it is close to this limit and needs to adapt its business model to attract higher revenue customers or serve higher revenue markets. It is reported to be exploring a variety of strategies, from limited international routes to adding amenities to its flights to changing the way it boards planes and assigns seats. Given that its labor costs are now at or near the top of the industry it may also need to negotiate compensation policies that further link salaries to improvements in individual, facility, or organizational performance, or a combination of these.

The key point here is that employee and labor relations strategies need to be complemented and supported by business strategies that generate sufficient revenue and market share to sustain both profitability and positive employee relations.

It would be naïve to expect all firms to embrace a service orientation and employee-centered strategy for achieving high productivity in either the new-entrant or legacy segments of the industry. In these settings, achieving minimally acceptable labor standards and conditions of employment will continue to be subject to hard bargaining from unions. The need for fair rules governing how unions can recruit members and gain collective bargaining rights and for resolving labor-management disputes must continue to be part of an enlightened strategy for improving public policy.

Longer Term Structural Issues

There have been only tentative moves toward international strategic alliances; for instance, two of the world's largest airlines, American Airlines and British Airways, have tried to form an international alliance to share codes and some revenues on operations between the United States, Britain, and other markets. Regulatory authorities are suspicious and are reluctant to approve such strong alliances, which they tend to see as anticompetitive. Nonetheless, in 2004 the European Union did approve the merger between Air France and KLM, which seems to have been successful. Lufthansa owns almost 30 percent of BMI (or British Midland International, the second largest airline at London Heathrow). In 2008 Lufthansa announced an aim to take over BMI. Nonetheless, such international mergers confront great challenges in linking computer networks, employees, and national and organizational cultures. Hence it is unlikely that there will be many more international mergers in the foreseeable future.

By contrast, it is likely that the consolidations, mergers, and restructuring processes that have been so prominent in the U.S. airline industry will continue. Evidence from other industries, as well as experience in the airline industry, suggests that the success of mergers and consolidations rests heavily on the process of integrating the diverse cultures, practices, workforces, and union organizations. The vice president of culture at US Airways stated his challenge clearly in the early months following the airline's merger with America West:

Cultural integration is one of the more challenging things we have to do. US Airways is an East Coast company, built over time as a much more serious company with uniform standards for employees. We're [America West] much more laid back.[10]

When a company with a longstanding reputation for high-quality service such as Midwest Airlines is threatened with being taken over—or actually is taken over—by a management associated with lower quality carriers, the challenge is even more profound. As a quote from a flight attendant from Midwest—"they take away the chocolate chip cookies and I'm out of here!"—suggests, changing business strategies in a merger would probably cause more cultural challenges than those experienced in merging firms that had in the past followed similar strategies. These issues, however, tend to be underplayed in the financial and network modeling that firms, consultants, and investment bankers use in estimating and, therefore, exaggerating, the benefits of a merger.

Another challenge is the complex process of integrating seniority lists and labor contracts when airlines merge or consolidate. The parties have learned a series of principles for doing so from experience with this process. Seth Rosen, a veteran of working on these issues with pilots affected by mergers, summarized the issues that need to be attended to as follows:[11]

- A process to maintain proportionality during the transition period
- A seniority integration process with a real timeline
- A timely contract amalgamation process
- A process for resolving union representation issues
- A process for addressing the adverse impact of job abolishment or dislocation of employees
- Integration of different corporate cultures that affect labor relations and human resource practices
- Labor-management consultation throughout the merger process
- Communications with rank and file

The airline industry developed in an era when most employees could expect to work for the same company over the full course of their careers. This led to a firm-centric employment model in which pensions and (in the United States) health insurance were tied to individual employers, high returns to seniority were built into compensation structures and career paths, and steep costs were experienced in moving across firms. Employees tended to be loyal to the industry (not least since it usually offered better economic rewards than most other industries, particularly before deregulation). These conditions have changed significantly, both because of current and likely future restructuring and changes in the expectations and aspirations of younger workers. Thus one of the most difficult and complex issues that warrants discussion by industry and labor leaders involves how to transform the seniority rules and progression ladders, pensions and health benefits, and other contract provisions from ones that assume employees will work for the same firm throughout their career to ones that lower the costs of mobility between firms. This cannot be done instantly. It will require a gradual change to a more mobile employment system.

In summary, there is a path to sustainable recovery that individual firms, employees, and their unions can take. The path is neither smooth nor clear of obstacles and risks but new entrants to the industry and legacy airlines have examples in Southwest and Continental to look to for guidance and assurance. Others should not try merely to copy such examples but rather to learn from their experiences and adapt them to fit different organizational settings.

Scenario 3: Efforts to Build a Stronger Airline Industry

> This is simply not an industry where the market will produce a solution. Leadership needs to come from the government. We need a coherent national transportation policy, new labor law, new bankruptcy law . . . some part of which [has] the objective of preserving reasonable competition and an acceptable standard of service and taking the needed steps to assure U.S. airlines are competitive on the world stage. If the Germans and the French can do it, we can do it. There is a national interest involved here.
>
> Robert Crandall, retired chief executive officer, American Airlines

Robert Crandall's clarion call is akin to the mythical child who points out that the emperor has no clothes. He puts valuable suggestions on the table for discussion, something others are reluctant to discuss for fear of reverting back to the regulated industry of the past. But perhaps his suggestions could be used to reframe the issue to one that asks: What type of air transport system is in the nation's interest and what leadership is needed from federal transportation, labor, and other policymakers to achieve it? Our third potential scenario assumes government leaders break out of their present passive state and begin working with industry and labor leaders in ways that link labor and employment policies and practices to a national air transportation policy that works for investors, employees, customers, and the national interest.

The starting point for an industry-level effort is a clear articulation of the problem and interests at stake, most of which have been noted at various points in this book. The air transportation system is highly interdependent, involving not only individual airlines but all parties at airports—airport authorities, federal airport screeners, air traffic controllers, contracting firms providing a variety of services, and so forth. Each of these parties has a stake in and influences the performance of the others.

Pressures build within the system as traffic congestion increases, air traffic control technology ages faster than budgets allow for upgrading, and controllers retire faster than replacements are being trained. As particular airlines cut capacity, retire aircraft, adopt leaner staffing levels, and add hours to flight crew schedules, the system becomes more stressed and vulnerable to delays and cancelled flights, which add further stress to the system. As employee morale declines, motivation to "run the extra mile" for the company and customers similarly declines. This leads to higher levels of absenteeism and turnover and retirement rates that exceed the level of recruitment and training, causing further delays, cancellations, and operational problems. The buildup of these stresses in a highly interdependent and tightly constrained system should be worrisome to all who share a stake in air transportation. Systems theories predict that the probability of a breakdown increases exponentially as these components reach their maximum stresses. JetBlue experienced this in midwinter 2007 in the aftermath of a storm that disrupted its schedule and stranded crews. Northwest experienced a smaller version of this in midsummer 2007 as pilots reached the end of their monthly schedules and an insufficient number reported to cover the company's flights, resulting in four hundred cancellations. British Airways was in chaos in the spring of 2008 because of mismanagement of the baggage handling system when it opened Heathrow's new Terminal 5. These examples should be warning signals that the potential for worse system "meltdowns" is high and rising. A "perfect storm" may be coming.

Even apart from these growing pressures, nations have a direct economic stake in the performance of their airline industries. The industry supports multiple jobs beyond those employed directly by airlines; good airline transportation is vital to the economic development and health of local economies, and, not least, governments have to pick up the pieces as insurer of last resort when company pension plans fail.

The boom-and-bust nature of the industry also imposes costs that divert scarce resources from improving service and providing a return to the key stakeholders. The multiple bankruptcy proceedings experienced in this industry in the United States alone (at least ten among the major legacy carriers since deregulation) have diverted hundreds of millions of dollars to law firms, expert witnesses, consultants, and financial institutions and away from suppliers, creditors, shareholders, and employees. One large airline had to set aside nearly $400 million to cover the anticipated costs of filing for bankruptcy and then managing the various costs associated with that process. Assuming the other large airlines had to do likewise, this adds up to over $4 billion that was diverted away from the industry's primary stakeholders.

Taking an industry perspective would also highlight the employee and labor relations issues that are essential to achieving a sustainable recovery. The evidence presented in this book leads to a clear conclusion: reducing labor costs was necessary given the fundamental changes in market conditions since 2000. But there are sustainable and nonsustainable ways of reducing labor costs. Furthermore, the reduction of labor costs in itself is not a sufficient condition or strategy for recovery or sustaining profitability and high levels of customer service in the industry. Employee and labor relations issues, therefore, should be addressed in tandem with other efforts to build a strong and high-performing airline industry.

How can an industrywide effort be initiated? Perhaps we can learn from our own efforts to initiate an industrywide dialogue. In 2000 our research group hosted a small meeting of management and labor leaders to discuss ways they might begin working together. Plans for a larger follow-up conference were then put on hold by the 9/11 tragedy. In 2003 the follow-up meeting was held in which labor and management leaders discussed lessons learned from their experiences in dealing with the first rounds of concessions following the dramatic turn in industry fortunes. The consensus of that meeting is presented here:

Lessons Learned through Industry-Level Dialogue

On June 26, 2003, more than sixty industry, labor, and government leaders met to discuss lessons learned from recent experiences in airline industry negotiations and from longer term efforts to build a culture of trust in day-to-day relations at the workplace. Some of the lessons these leaders took away from these experiences include the following:

- Open, honest communications and information sharing were critical to successfully concluding recent crisis negotiations. The same will be true going forward in future negotiations.
- Agreement on a methodology for estimating the costs of labor agreement provisions facilitated negotiations where it was present and held up negotiations where it was not. Prenegotiation agreements on a common approach to costing proposals and options should become a standard bargaining practice.
- Reaching agreement with any single employee group was contingent on negotiating or implementing agreements that called for shared sacrifices from other employee groups, including nonrepresented employees, managers, and executives. Where this principle was violated, agreements were either held up or rejected by employees. This suggests that any future compensation adjustments will likely receive the same cross-occupation–within-company scrutiny and have to meet the same test of fairness. One effect of this crisis therefore is to heighten the importance of within-company–cross-occupation and cross-level comparisons. Since many of the negotiated agreements will be amendable at about the same time, thought needs to be given to how the structure of negotiations accommodates this new reality.
- In times of extreme crisis it is important for a firm to have a clear and single target for what reductions in costs are needed while being flexible and responsive to input from union representatives in how different elements of cost reductions are arranged. Having to return for more than one round of cuts because the initial target is not sufficient reduces the credibility of the management and labor leaders involved and makes acceptance/ratification extremely difficult.
- Bargaining in the age of the Internet is an open and public process with information, false or accurate, often communicated to employees almost immediately. Future bargaining processes will need to have an agreed-upon strategy for how to communicate with constituents and other interested parties to keep them accurately informed.
- Improving labor relations requires a consistent approach to how people are treated on a day-to-day basis and in the negotiations process. Effective and timely negotiations will not be realized unless a culture of high trust has been achieved at the workplace.

The 2003 meeting led to formation of a working group charged with the task of drafting a blueprint for improving the process of negotiating new labor agreements. Several months of meetings and use of a "single text" drafting strategy produced the consensus document on ways to improve the negotiations process (summarized earlier in "Working Group Recommendations for Improving Negotiations"). To our knowledge this was the first time since the passage of the Railway Labor Act in 1926 that a consensus on how to improve the provisions of the law governing negotiations had been reached. If nothing else, this experience demonstrated that a facilitated dialogue among the parties can sometimes generate a shared sense of how to improve industry operations and performance.

There are at least two lessons from these efforts. First, if brought together, industry and labor leaders are capable of using their considerable experience and expertise to generate ideas and strategies for improvement. Second, research groups like ours are not influential or powerful enough to bring all the stakeholders to the table and motivate them to work toward solutions to problems that go beyond labor and employee-relations strategies and practices to encompass the broad transportation and labor policy questions that need to be addressed in an integrated fashion. To make progress on these issues requires governmental leadership. Perhaps it will take another abrupt shock—a financial crisis or recession, a terrorist attack, or a system failure that reverberates through the industry—to stimulate this type of governmental leadership. A shock similar in magnitude to 9/11 would intensify the pressure for change and perhaps highlight the national interests at stake in this industry and might even revive calls for an industry-labor-government cooperative response.

Governmental leadership could bring some new ideas to the table that neither labor nor management representatives are likely to raise on their own. For example, one approach to breaking the boom-and-bust cycle of wages and labor conflict would be to propose that companies and unions negotiate long-term (say, ten year) labor agreements with scheduled periodic wage increases tied to some overall industry or national metric and some wage adjustments that would be contingent on performance improvements. The metrics might include average growth in private sector compensation, increases in cost of living, or average growth in industry revenue. Contingent compensation provisions linked to some combination of individual or group, location or domicile, and/or company performance could be included as part of a compensation program that meets the standards outlined in scenario 2 for predictability, the alignment of incentives, and equity across occupational groups and among workers, managers, and executives. In return, the long-term contracts would provide the industry with guarantees of labor peace for a period of time needed to achieve sustained profitability.

This approach would have another virtue. It would avoid the need for long-drawn-out and tired debates over whether or not to reform the Railway Labor Act or the procedures of the National Mediation Board, or both. In essence the parties would be voluntarily agreeing to modify their established bargaining procedures de facto rather than wait for the government to act in ways that might add more divisiveness to management and union relations.

With a long-term agreement in hand, the individual companies and unions could then go to work on rebuilding trust, commitment, and coordination at their workplaces. They could also maintain the types of discussions with workers and their union representatives needed to foster continuous improvements in customer service and productivity.

With bold leadership, top-level government officials could jump-start this type of process. It remains to be seen whether we will have to await the next crisis to motivate action or whether leadership will emerge to act before a crisis or perfect storm is imminent

Learning across Borders: Lessons for the Global Airline Industry

Too often U.S. researchers find themselves in the dubious position of being more critical of practices and policies of their country than do scholars (and particularly practitioners) from other countries. This receptivity to American practices leads some to believe that the spread of U.S.-based policies and practices around the world is inevitable. But as we have seen, the picture is more complex and varied than this tendency toward convergence might suggest.

On the one hand, Southwest has been a model for nearly all new-entrant airlines in other countries. But each seems to have adopted only *selected* parts of Southwest's business and employment-relations model and then adapted them to fit their particular preferences and institutional settings. Southwest's business model has been replicated or adapted to work in many other parts of the world including Ireland, Britain, continental Europe, Australia, Latin America, Africa, India, and Asia. So too have many of the features of its human resource system with its emphasis on coordination, performance management incentives, and high levels of employee motivation and commitment. Southwest's partnership approach to labor relations has been adapted by some to fit different national institutional and legal contexts. In Europe and Australia stronger labor legislation and a stronger union presence make it less likely that large employers will try to avoid unions. The role of unions in the newer firms such as easyJet, Jetstar, and Virgin Blue seems to be more limited, however, than the European interpretation of "social partnership" would imply. Paradoxically, new-entrant airlines in other countries have learned more from Southwest than most of the legacy airlines in the United States.

In contrast, Ryanair rejected the Southwest employment-relations model and opted for a control strategy rather than a commitment one. In addition, Ryanair has followed a classic union-suppression strategy. It provides an alternative benchmark for airlines that are not prepared to engage employees in a similar way to Southwest, or to partner with their union representatives.

The implicit contest between these two alternative models will continue to play out in future new-entrant airlines around the world. Although it may still be unclear which model produces the greatest return to investors, the consequences of adopting each one are profound for the employees involved. Countries committed to achieving a balanced return to multiple stakeholders will, therefore, need to be vigilant in setting minimum standards and enforcing workers' rights in order to counteract excesses that may accompany the use of Ryanair as the benchmark model.

The trends across the globe are in the direction of greater openness to the entry of new airlines and to more international competition. The open skies agreements reached between the United States and the European Union are just one example of the increasing globalization of the airline industry. This need not, however, mean that a single model of competition and management practices—the "U.S. model"—will inevitably spread across the globe. There were vigorous debates in Australia about the (failed) efforts of a private equity group to take over Qantas and leverage it to the brink in 2007. These provided an important reminder that even conservative governments, such as the one then in power in Australia, have to consider their national interests alongside their ideological views. Such debates are healthy. Even in the United States some doubts are emerging about the risks associated with high leverage and the short-term orientation that often accompany private equity or other takeover bids. This is not to say that all current ownership arrangements are better than any potential bids of others. As already noted, more restructuring is likely. The key lesson should be to consider the interests and likely consequences to all the stakeholders involved and make decisions accordingly.

Tentative Conclusions: More Change to Come?

Offering "conclusions" about the state and future of the global airline industry is like shooting at a moving target. Cutting through the complexity, however, there is one undeniable fact that characterizes the prevalent employment situation in U.S. airlines. Wages, benefits, working conditions, and labor standards have been ratcheted down. Most airline employees are working harder, longer, and for relatively less pay and benefits than did their counterparts in an earlier generation. They have borne the brunt of the radical transformation occurring in this industry. Customers who seek low prices have been the big beneficiaries in this transition period. Some shareholders have also fared well as the share prices of some new entrants have taken off and analysts have bid up legacy carrier share prices largely on speculation over which firms might be taken over and which will survive the current turbulence. But those who held stock in or worked for airlines that went bankrupt have suffered along with their suppliers and creditors. Attorneys and investment bankers who thrive on bankruptcy and merger business have also prospered. Whether there will be an employee backlash that seeks to recapture some of their lost ground remains to be seen. Whether employees can do so even if they try is also open to question.

The dynamic precipitated by the emergence and growth of new competitors that began with lower costs will continue around the world. However, by laying out alternative scenarios and pointing out the nondeterministic paths available to different firms and nations concerned about the sustainability of their airlines, we suggest that the future directions of the industry can be improved by thoughtful leaders. It remains to be seen whether the required leadership will be forthcoming. In its absence in the United States, pressures toward a perfect storm continue to build that if unattended may have consequences well beyond U.S. shores.

Postscript: Developments in the Industry in 2008

As this book goes to press in mid-2008, the latest developments in the airline industry appear to be accelerating toward a "perfect storm."

The International Air Transport Association (IATA) observed in September 2008: "More airlines (approximately 30) have gone bust in 2008 than in the aftermath of 9/11. . . . While some regions will show small profits, the negative impact of the industry crisis is universal."[12] North American airlines are expected to post losses of $5.0 billion in 2008 making them the hardest hit by this industry crisis. Twelve U.S. airlines have declared bankruptcy and seven of those have discontinued operations.

Perhaps the most significant issue is the dramatic rise in oil prices that resulted in an 80 percent increase in the price of jet fuel between July 2007 and July 2008. Large legacies have responded by again cutting back capacity and announcing layoffs, including British Airways, Qantas, and most of the U.S. legacies. Even Continental Airlines announced plans for 3,000 layoffs. Additionally, several airlines have announced new charges for once-free services, including charges for *any* checked bags and even for soft drinks and water (US Airways). Thus, some full-service legacies have cut service quality amenities below the level offered by some of the new-entrants, further blurring the distinctions between the two sectors.

One major development through the first half of 2008, mentioned in chapter 6, was the merger agreement between Delta and Northwest. While the two airlines have agreed to terms, the deal still needs government approval (from both the Department of Transportation and the Department of Justice). However, despite the widespread assumption among industry analysts that this deal would trigger other mergers, no others have yet come to fruition. United looked for a merger partner of its own but was rebuffed by Continental and failed to reach an agreement with US Airways. As noted in chapter 6, Continental decided that the advantages it derives from its organizational and cultural model would be put at risk by any merger. We see this as further indication that Continental derives competitive advantage from its commitment-based approach to the employment relationship.

The lack of enthusiasm for other merger activity perhaps indicates that industry participants *have* learned from history and have come to realize that the benefits of airline mergers are uncertain at best, while the costs, in terms of lengthy and difficult integration processes and potentially on-going internal conflict, are high. Delta and Northwest are likely to have an especially difficult time since it will be a merger of a largely non-union carrier (except for the pilots) with a highly unionized carrier that has a particularly contentious relationship with its unions. If the parties do nothing to address their labor and employee relations differences, they will likely face a prolonged period of conflict over representation issues (i.e., Will employees be unionized and if so, which unions will represent them?) and in negotiating their initial labor agreements. If that scenario plays out, the merged organization will likely experience low productivity, low service quality, and poor profitability. Yet the merger could serve as an opportunity to head off these disastrous results. The pilots have shown the way to do this. Delta and Northwest pilot unions negotiated with management a single integrated labor agreement that restores some of their lost wages and benefits and agreed on a process for integrating their seniority lists, with the commitment to arbitrate any differences that cannot be resolved. A similar proactive approach to work out the many other complicated labor issues in a timely and less-conflictual way would clearly improve the chances of this merger's success.

There appears to be renewed interest in mergers in Europe. For example, Lufthansa was considering takeovers of SAS as well as of UK airline BMI. There were continuing talks about a merger of Lufthansa's Germanwings with another German new entrant peer TUIfly. Air-France KLM and Lufthansa drew back from bidding for loss-making Italian carrier Alitalia. However, British Airways was proposing to take over Spanish rival Iberia and to form a stronger alliance with American Airlines. This was the third time in a dozen years that American and British Airways have sought antitrust immunity from the regulators on both sides of the Atlantic if they combine their codes on flights between the United States and London Heathrow. Virgin Atlantic has challenged the proposed alliance with the regulators. It re-launched a critical publicity campaign, painting some of its planes with the slogan "No Way, AA/BA."

While the industry continues to change, our prognosis still applies. Without more bold and open-minded leadership, the airline industry will, at best, continue on with "business as usual": increasingly volatile financial outcomes—with periods of substantial losses for investors, employees, and customers—and contentious labor relations. If this happens, it increases the risk of experiencing the worst-case scenario in which the downward spiral of financial losses, demoralized employees, congested skies, and over-burdened infrastructure leads to a major breakdown in air transport service. Yet, as pointed out in this book, there are also exceptions to "business as usual" that offer a potential path to a more sustainable industry that, by better balancing the interests of all stakeholders, thereby better serves them all.

Notes

Low-Cost Competition in the Airline Industry

1. Jeff Bailey, "Fliers Fed Up? The Employees Feel the Same," *New York Times*, December 22, 2007, 1.

2. The analogy to a "perfect storm" was used in reference to airlines by Alexander Marks on U.S. National Public Radio program *On Point* on August 2, 2007. Michael O'Leary, the chief executive officer of Ryanair, one of Europe's biggest airlines, warned of the possibility of a "perfect storm" of higher oil prices, poor consumer demand, weaker currency exchange rates, and higher costs at unchecked monopoly airports: Cathy Buyck, "Ryanair Profit Dips in Third Quarter as 'Perfect Storm' Threatens," *Air Transport World Daily News*, February 5, 2008, www.atwonline.com/news/story.html?storyID= 11625. The phrase *perfect storm* was first used in 1991 with regard to a storm stronger than any in recorded history that hit the coast of Massachusetts. It was called a "perfect storm" because it was three storms combined into one. See http://perfectstorm.warner bros.com/cmp/flash-thestorm-fr.html. The term has subsequently been used to refer to the simultaneous occurrence of events that, taken individually, would be far less powerful than the result of their combination.

3. Interview with Robert Crandall, September 4, 2007.

4. Peter A. Hall and David Soskice, eds., *Varieties of Capitalism: The Institutional Foundations of Comparative Advantage* (New York: Oxford University Press, 2001).

5. Robert Reich reminds us of this point in *Supercapitalism: The Transformation of Business, Democracy, and Everyday Life* (New York: Knopf, 2007).

6. John Budd, *Employment with a Human Face* (Ithaca: Cornell University Press, 2004).

7. Paul Osterman, Thomas Kochan, Richard Locke, and Michael Piore, *Working in America* (Cambridge: MIT Press, 2001).

8. For data on trends in average wages and chief executive officer compensation, see Lawrence Mishel, Jared Bernstein, and Sylvia Allegretto, *The State of Working America, 2006–2007* (Ithaca: Cornell University Press, 2007).

9. Air Transport Action Group, *The Economic and Social Benefits of Air Transport* (2004), available at http://www.atag.org.

10. Campbell-Hill Aviation Group and Steven G. Craig, "Economic Impact Study: Houston Airport System," in *The Economic and Social Benefits of Air Transport*, Air Transport Action Group (2004); available at http://www.atag.org.

11. We draw on these studies, several of which will be published in a special issue of the *International Human Resource Management Journal* in 2009, and on the journal's website. See www.tandf.co.uk/journals/routledge/09585192.html.

12. See, for example, Thomas A. Kochan, Robert B. McKersie, and Peter Cappelli, "Strategic Choice and Industrial Relations Theory and Practice," *Industrial Relations* 27 (Winter 1984), 16–39; Thomas A. Kochan, Harry C. Katz, and Robert B. McKersie, *The Transformation of American Industrial Relations* (New York: Basic Books, 1986).

13. Richard E. Walton, "From Control to Commitment in the Workplace," *Harvard Business Review* 63, no. 2 (1985): 77–84.

14. Richard E. Walton, Joel Cutcher-Gershenfeld, and Robert B. McKersie, *Strategic Negotiations* (Boston: Harvard Business School Press, 1994).

15. Harry C. Katz, Thomas A. Kochan, and Alexander J. S. Colvin, *An Introduction to Collective Bargaining and Industrial Relations*, 4th ed. (Homewood, Ill.: Richard D. Irwin, 2007), 114.

16. Jeffrey Pfeffer, *Competitive Advantage through People: Unleashing the Power of the Workforce* (Boston: Harvard Business School Press, 1996); Jeffrey Pfeffer, *The Human Equation: Building Profits by Putting People First* (Boston: Harvard Business School Press, 1998); Peter Cheese, Robert J. Thomas, and Elizabeth Craig, *The Talent Powered Organization: Strategies for Globalization, Talent Management and High Performance* (Philadelphia: Kogan Page, 2007).

17. Peter Boxall and John Purcell, *Strategy and Human Resource Management* (New York: Palgrave Macmillan, 2003).

Developments in the U.S. Airline Industry

1. A thorough review of labor relations in the airline industry is contained in Nancy Brown Johnson, "Airlines: Can Collective Bargaining Weather the Storm?" in *Collective Bargaining: Current Developments and Future Challenges*, ed. Paul Clark, John T. Delaney, and Ann Frost (Urbana-Champaign, Ill.: Industrial Relations Research Association, 2002).

2. Testimony of Alfred E. Kahn to the U.S. House of Representatives Aviation Subcommittee, *Congressional Digest* (1978), 184–85.

3. Dan Reed, "You Can Thank This Guy for Low Airfares," *USA Today*, July 24, 2007, 8B.

4. Dan Reed, "You Can Thank This Guy."

5. Thomas O. Gorin, "Assessing Low-Fare Entry in Airline Markets: Impacts of Revenue Management and Network Flows," PhD diss., MIT Department of Aeronautics and Astronautics, 2004.

6. Thomas Petzinger Jr., *Hard Landing* (New York: Random House, 1996), 131.

7. Peter Cappelli, "Competitive Pressures and Labor Relations in the Airline Industry," *Industrial Relations* 24, no. 3 (1985): 316–38.

8. Michael E. Levine, "Airline Competition in Deregulated Markets: Theory, Firm Strategy, and Public Policy," *Yale Journal on Regulation* 4 (1987): 393–494.

9. Jody Hoffer Gittell, "JetBlue Airways: Starting from Scratch," Harvard Business School Case #9-801-354 (2001).

10. Johnson, "Airlines: Can Collective Bargaining Weather the Storm?"

11. Thomas A. Kochan, Andrew von Nordenflyht, Robert McKersie, and Jody Hoffer Gittell, "Airborne Distress: How Can Labor Recover in the Airline Industry?" *New Labor Forum* 14, no. 2 (2005): 39–50.

12. Gorin, "Assessing Low-Fare Entry," 294.

13. See David Card, "Deregulation and Labor Earnings in the Airline Industry," in *Regulatory Reform and Labor Markets*, ed. James Peoples (Norwell, Mass.: Kluwer Academic, 1998); Pierre-Yves Cremieux, "The Effect of Deregulation on Employee Earnings: Pilots, Flight Attendants, and Mechanics, 1959–1992," *Industrial and Labor Relations Review* 49, no. 2 (1996): 223–42; Barry T. Hirsch and David A. Macpherson, "Earnings, Rents, and Competition in the Airline Labor Market," *Journal of Labor Economics* 18, no. 1 (2000): 125–55.

Developments in the Airline Industry in Other Countries

1. Andrew Herdman, *Full Service Airlines: Adopting New Business Strategies in the Crowded Sky* (2007), http://www.aapairlines.org/resource_centre/SP_AAPA-Herdman LCACongressSingapore-24Jan2007.pdf. This source draws on market research data from Boeing and Airbus.

2. Rigas Doganis, *The Airline Business* (London: Routledge, 2006), 223.

3. See Peter A. Hall and David Soskice, "Varieties of Capitalism: An Introduction to the Varieties of Capitalism," in *Varieties of Capitalism: The Institutional Foundations of Comparative Advantage*, ed. Peter A. Hall and David Soskice (New York: Oxford University Press, 2001), 1–68; Kathleen Thelen, "Varieties of Labor Politics in the Developed Democracies," in Hall and Soskice, *Varieties of Capitalism*, 71–103.

4. "Foundation of the International Civil Aviation Organization (ICAO)" ICAO website, Montreal, www.icao.int/cgi/goto_m.pl?icao/en/hist/history02.htm; Rigas Doganis, *Flying Off Course: The Economics of International Airlines* (London: Routledge, 2002), 26.

5. In 2007, agencies in the United States, the European Union, the United Kingdom, Australia, and other countries were conducting investigations into anticompetitive behavior by a dozen airlines around the world, including Qantas. In 2007, for example, British Airways was fined $300 million for price fixing by the U.S. Department of Justice and $245 million by the U.K. Office of Fair Trading. James Hall and Vesna Poljak, "Qantas Takes $47m Hit in Cartel Case," *Australian Financial Review*, August 14, 2007.

6. Doganis, *Flying Off Course*, 5; ICAO Digest of Statistics, Series F, Financial Forecast. This May 2008 forecast proved to be optimistic. The IATA later forecasted significant losses continuing in 2009.

7. See International Transport Workers' Federation, www.itfglobal.org; International Federation of Air Line Pilots' Association, www.ifalpa.org.

8. In the interests of simplicity, we generally use the term European Union (EU). In 2007 this included twenty-seven member states. However, before the 1990s, predecessors

to the EU were known under other names, including, initially, the European Coal and Steel Community, the European Economic Community (EEC), or the Common Market, which began in 1957 with only six countries, but after the 1960s it was enlarged in several stages. On the history, policies, and structure of the EU, see "The EU at a Glance," Europa, http://europa.eu/abc/history/index_en.htm.

9. Joe Wallace, Siobhan Tiernan, and Lorraine White, "Industrial Adaptation in Aer Lingus: The Path from Legacy to Low Fares Airline," unpublished case study, 2007.

10. Peter Morrell, "Air Transport Liberalization in Europe: The Progress So Far," *Journal of Air Transportation World Wide* 3, no. 1 (1998): 42–61; European Commission, *Europe at a Crossroads: The Need for Sustainable Transport* (Luxembourg: Office for Official Publications of the European Communities, 2003); European Commission, *Air Transport Portal of the European Commission* (2007), http://ec.europa.eu/transport/air_portal/internal_market/competition_en.htm.

11. For a British perspective on liberalization and airline competition, see Civil Aviation Authority, *Liberalisation and Competition*, http://www.caa.co.uk/default.aspx?catid=589&pagetype=90&pageid=2388.

12. Another possible explanation was that the "social charges," such as the nationally mandated social insurance and vacation pay components of labor costs, were lower in the United Kingdom and Ireland compared with most other EU countries; see Doganis, *Airline Business*, 123.

13. On the British context, see Mick Marchington, John Goodman, and John Berridge, "Employment Relations in Britain," in *International and Comparative Employment Relations: Globalisation and the Developed Market Economies*, ed. Greg J. Bamber, Russell D. Lansbury, and Nick Wailes (London: Sage, 2004), 36–66.

14. IPA, *Definition of Partnership*, http://www.ipa-involve.com/60/61/64/71/index.php.

15. For more information on the airline companies that preceded the current BA, see Thomson Reuters, *British Airways Fact Book 2006*, http://media.corporate-ir.net/media_files/irol/69/69499/bafactbook/Fact_Book_2006.pdf.

16. British Airways' chief executive officer Colin Marshal, *Financial Times*, May 28, 1984, cited in Trevor Colling, "Experiencing Turbulence: Competition, Strategic Choice and the Management of Human Resources in British Airways," *Human Resource Management Journal* 5 (1995): 18–32.

17. James Arrowsmith, Tony Edwards, and Keith Sisson, "Industrial Relations at British Airways—Setting a New Course?" European Industrial Relations Observatory (2000), http://www.eurofound.europa.eu/eiro/2000/04/feature/uk0004168f.htm.

18. Veena Josh, *Gate Gourmet Row Rumbles On* (2005), British Broadcasting Corporation News, http://news.bbc.co.uk/1/hi/business/4478346.stm.

19. Adapted with permission from Greg Pitcher, "Who Will Take on British Airways Director for People Vacancy?" *Personnel Today*, February 13, 2007, http://www.personneltoday.com/articles/2007/02/13/39235/who-will-take-on-british-airways-director-for-people.html.

20. Andrew Clark, "British Airways Warns Staff of Further Job Cuts," *Guardian*, March 10, 2006, http://www.guardian.co.uk/business/2006/mar/10/britishairways.theairlineindustry.

21. Geraint Harvey, *Management in the Airline Industry* (London: Rutledge, 2007), 115.

22. "The BA Way in the Workplace" (2006), British Airways, http://www.britishairways.com/cms/global/pdfs/corporate_responsibility_report_2006/the_BA_way_in_the_workplace.pdf.

23. Cathy Buyck, "Interview: British Airways Chief Executive Rod Eddington," *Air Transport World*, August 2005, 24, www.atwonline.com/channels/airlineFocus/topic.html?topicID=19.

24. Robert Peston, "BA: Heavy Turbulence," *Peston's Picks*, British Broadcasting Corporation News, January 30, 2007, http://www.bbc.co.uk/blogs/thereporters/robertpeston/2007/01/british_airways_heavy_turbulen.html.

25. Pitcher, "Who Will Take on British Airways?" Also on British Airways, see Irena Grugulis and Adrian Wilkinson, "British Airways: Hype, Hope and Reality," *Long Range Planning* 35, no. 2 (2002), 179–94; Paul Blyton and Peter Turnbull, *The Dynamics of Employee Relations* (London: Palgrave Macmillan, 2004).

26. *That Was Then: Sir Freddie Laker* (2006), British Broadcasting Corporation News, http://news.bbc.co.uk/1/hi/uk/2283244.stm.

27. Richard Branson, *Losing My Virginity: The Autobiography* (London: Virgin Books, 1999; New York: Random House [rev. ed.], 2002).

28. Sir Richard Branson's letter to staff. For the full text of the letter, sent to the homes of forty-eight hundred Virgin Atlantic cabin crew members, see *Times Online*, December 31, 2007, http://business.timesonline.co.uk/tol/business/industry_sectors/transport/article3114968.ece.

29. Marcus Leroux, "Sir Richard Branson Tells Virgin Atlantic Strikers to Resign," *Times Online*, December 31, 2007; http://business.timesonline.co.uk/tol/business/industry_sectors/transport/article3114534.ece.

30. "Pay Deal Averts Virgin Air Strikes," *Guardian*, January 7, 2008; http://www.guardian.co.uk/uk/2008/jan/07/world.transport.

31. Cathy Buyck, "Fuel, GB Integration Sink easyJet to Heavy First-Half Loss," *ATW Daily News*, Air Transport World, May 8, 2008, www.atwonline.com/news/story.html?storyID=12652.

32. Harvey, *Management in the Airline Industry.*

33. This section draws on Hashi Syedain, "Plane Speakers," *People Management* 13 (2007): 26–29; http://www.peoplemanagement.co.uk/pm/articles/planespeakers.htm?name=analysis++features++opinion&type=section.

34. This section draws on various sources, including advice from Joe Wallace, mass media reports and corporate websites (e.g. www.aerlingus.com/Corporate/AL%20Fact%20Sheet%20October%2023%202006.pdf), as well as Joe Wallace, Siobhan Tiernan, and Lorraine White, "Industrial Adaptation in Aer Lingus: The Path from Legacy to Low Fares Airline," case study presented at the annual meeting of the Airline Industry Council, Labor and Employment Relations Association, Chicago (2007); Sarah Oxenbridge, Joseph Wallace, Lorraine White, Siobhan Tiernan, and Russell Lansbury, "A Comparative Analysis of Restructuring Employment Relationships in Qantas and Aer Lingus: Different Routes, Similar Destinations," *International Journal of Human Resource Management* (forthcoming).

35. Siobhan Creaton, *Ryanair: How a Small Irish Airline Conquered Europe* (London: Aurum Press, 2004), 24.

36. Michelle O'Sullivan and Patrick Gunnigle, "'Bearing All the Hallmarks of Oppression': Union Avoidance in Europe's Largest Low-Cost Airline," *Labor Studies Journal* (forthcoming).

37. *Ryanair Workers Mobilised to Strike*, International Transport Workers' Federation, Ryan-be-Fair: www.ryan-be-fair.org, http://www.itfglobal.org/campaigns/mobilised.cfm.

38. *Ryanair Tops IATA International Passenger Ranking*, Centre for Asia Pacific Aviation; Peanuts! Online: The Low-Cost Airline News website, http://peanuts.aero/low_cost_airline_news/index.php?option=com_content&task=view&id=3465&Itemid=59.

39. "Virgin Blue Holdings Limited Share Offer," *Virgin Blue*, 74; Prospectus, corporate website, www.virginblue.com.au/AboutUs/Virginbluecorporateinformation/Investorinformation/Financials/index.htm.

40. On the Australian context, see Russell D. Lansbury and Nick Wailes, "Employment Relations in Australia," in *International and Comparative Employment Relations: Globalisation and the Developed Market Economies*, ed. Greg J. Bamber, Russell D. Lansbury, and Nick Wailes (London: Sage, 2004), 119–145.

41. Mark Bray and Nick Wailes, "Reinterpreting the 1989 Pilots' Dispute: The Role of Managerial Control and Labour Productivity," *Labour & Industry* 10 (1999): 79–105.

42. Lufthansa IR Portal, Lufthansa Investor Relations, http://www.lufthansa-financials.de/servlet/PB/menu/1014558_l2/index.html.

43. This section draws on M. Barry and W. Nienhueser, "Coordinated Market Economy/Liberal Employment Relations: Low-Cost Competition in the German Aviation Industry," *International Journal of Human Resource Management* (forthcoming).

44. On the German context, see Berndt Keller, "Employment Relations in Germany," in *International and Comparative Employment Relations: Globalisation and the Developed Market Economies*, ed. Greg J. Bamber, Russell D. Lansbury, and Nick Wailes (London: Sage, 2004), 211–253.

45. Peter Turnbull, Paul Blyton, and Geraint Harvey, "Cleared for Take-off? Management-Labour Partnership in the European Civil Aviation Industry," *European Journal of Industrial Relations* 10, no. 3 (2004): 287–307.

46. Geraint Harvey and Peter Turnbull, *Contesting the Crisis: Aviation Industrial Relations and Trade Union Strategies after 11 September*, report prepared for the International Transport Workers' Federation, Cardiff University, Cardiff, 2002: www.itfglobal.org/files/seealsodocs/726/contesting%5Fthe%5Fcrisis.pdf; Holger Hätty and Sebastian Hollmeier, "Airline Strategy in the 2001/2002 Crisis—the Lufthansa Example," *Journal of Air Transport Management* 9, no. 1 (January 2003): 51–55.

47. We acknowledge with many thanks that this section draws on discussions with former SAS staff.

48. On the Swedish context, see Olle Hammarstrom, Tony Huzzard, and Tommy Nilsson, "Employment Relations in Sweden," in Bamber, Lansbury, and Wailes, *International and Comparative Employment Relations*, 254–76.

49. On such Asian institutions, see Greg J. Bamber, "How Is the Asia-Pacific Economic Cooperation (APEC) Forum Developing? Comparative Comments on APEC and Employment Relations," *Comparative Labor Law & Policy Journal* 26 (2005): 423–44.

50. Doganis, *Flying Off Course*, 21.

51. Andrew Herdman, *Full Service Airlines: Adopting New Business Strategies in the Crowded Sky* (2007), http://www.aapairlines.org/resource_centre/SP_AAPA-Herdman-LCACongressSingapore-24Jan2007.pdf. This source draws on market research data from Boeing and Airbus.

52. Pierre Condom, "Low-Profit Carriers," *Interavia Business and Technology* 676 (Summer 2004): 4.

53. Centre for Asia Pacific Aviation, *Aviation Market Research—Low-Cost Airline Directory* (2006); http://www.centreforaviation.com/aviation/blogcategory/Low_Cost_Airline_Director; and C. Baker, D. Field, and N. Ionides, "Global Reach," *Airline Business* (May 21, 2005): 60–65. *Etihad* is Arabic for united.

54. Joan Enric Ricart and Daxue Wang, "Now Everybody Can Fly: AirAsia," *Asian Journal of Management* 2, no. 2 (2005): 231–53. Online journal at http://ajc.sagepub.com.ezproxy.library.uq.edu.au/content/vol2/issue2/.

. 55. Airports Council International, *Global Traffic Forecast 2006–2025* (2007), http:// www.airports.org/aci/aci/file/Press%20Releases/2007_PRs/ACI_Forecast_Executive_ Summary.pdf.

56. This section draws from Byoung-Hoon Lee and Seong-Jae Cho, "Employment Relations of the Korean Airline Industry: Comparison of Korean Air and Asiana Airlines" (2007), unpublished case study.

57. Lee and Cho, "Employment Relations of the Korean Airline Industry."

58. Korean Labor Institute, cited in Lee and Cho, "Employment Relations of the Korean Airline Industry."

59. Lee and Cho, "Employment Relations of the Korean Airline Industry."

60. On the South Korean context, see Young-bum Park and Chris Leggett, "Employment Relations in the Republic of Korea," in Bamber, Lansbury, and Wailes, *International Journal of Human Resource Management* (forthcoming).

61. Teresa Poon and Peter Waring, "The Lowest of Low-Cost Carriers: The Case of AirAsia," unpublished case study, 2008.

62. AirAsia Profile, http://peanuts.aero/low_cost_airline_news/index.php?option=com_ whoswho&task=viewwhoswho&id=21.

63. "Air Asia X Launch Delayed," http://www.airfinancejournal.com/includes/news/ PRINT.asp?SID=680438&ISS=23546; Jeff Chu, "The $3 Flight," Condé Nast Portfolio, November 2007, http://www.portfolio.com/business-travel/features/2007/10/15/Air-Asia -Airlines.

64. Poon and Waring,; "Web Forum Gives Employees at Low-Cost Malaysian Airline a 'Safe Space'," *ITF News Online*, April 18, 2007; http://www.itfglobal.org/news-online/ index.cfm/newsdetail/1266/region/1/section/.

65. Poon and Waring, "The Lowest of Low-Cost Carriers."

66. *The MAS Way: Business Turnaround Plan* (2007), Malaysian Airlines, http://cms. malaysiaairlines.com/mys/eng/about_us/investor_relations/MASWay_F.pdf.

67. *The MAS Way: Business Turnaround Plan* (2007).

68. "Audra Atkinson v. Malaysia Airlines System Berhad," blog, September 5, 2007, http://muststopthis.blogspot.com/2007/09/sept-5th-2007-audra-atkinson-v-<->malaysia. html.

69. *The Business Turnaround Plan (BTP) in a Nutshell* (2008), Malaysian Airlines, http://www.malaysiaairlines.com/getdoc/e14d592c-61a3-442d-91fc-16ef706a69fd/ 300507-2007-BTP-Updates.aspx.

70. "Discriminatory Practices at MAS," February 24, 2005, International Transport Workers' Federation, http://www.itfglobal.org/solidarity/itflettertomas.cfm.

71. "United Arab Emirates," Central Intelligence Agency, https://www.cia.gov/library/ publications/the-world-factbook/geos/ae.html#Intro.

72. "Aviation Analyst," Centre for Asia Pacific Aviation, November 12, 2007, http:// www.centreforaviation.com/aviation/News_&_Intelligence/Perspectives/Emirates_ makes_history_(again)._Up_to_143_new_aircrft_takes_order_book_to_246_worth_ USD60_billion/.

73. "Aviation Analyst," Centre for Asia Pacific Aviation, March 20, 2008, http://mid-dleeastaviation.aero/news/airline/8214/59/Emirates%20to%20launch%20a%20low %20cost%20carrier%20-%201,000%20seat%20A380s%20coming%20to%20an%20air-port%20near%20you?; also see Leslie Wayne, "A Flight Plan for the Long Haul," *New York Times*, July 6, 2007; Emirates Group Careers Centre, http://www.emiratesgroupca-reers.com/index.asp?cid=EKGCREF_INT_NA_EKGROUP_LINK_MENU_EN.

74. Doganis, *Airline Business*, 132.

75. There has been some controversy surrounding this claim, as many suggest that the Emirates close ties to the government has helped it to minimize its costs; *The Emirates Story*, Emirates, (2007), http://emirates.com/english/about/the_emirates_story.aspx.

76. "Business: Easy Oz; Emirates Airlines," *Economist*, October 29, 2005, 82.

77. *Employee Benefits* (2007), Emirates, http://emiratesgroupcareers.com/WorkHere/Benifits/EmployeeBenifits.asp.

78. The Emirates Group Careers Centre (2007), Emirates, http://www.emiratesgroupcareers.com/index.asp?cid=EKGCREF_INT_NA_EKGROUP_LINK_MENU_EN.

79. K. Griffiths, "A Strategic Review of the Multicultural Considerations during the Recruitment and Selection of Expatriate Flight Crew for Emirates Airlines" (2005), Virtual Scholars, http://64.233.179.104/scholar?hl=en&lr=&q=cache:Je4NETujRi4J:virtualscholars.brad.ac.uk:8080/handle/10004/1563+Emirates+airline.

80. Terry O'Connell, interview at Australian Federation of Air Pilots, Melbourne, October 8, 2007.

81. *Trade Unions Set to Be Legalised* (2007), United Arab Emirates (UAE) Interact, March 8, 2006, http://uaeinteract.com/docs/Trade_unions_set_to_be_legalised_/19972.htm.

82. Meena Jenardhan (2006), International Labour Day: *Trade Unions to Transform UAE Labour Climate*, Dubai, May 2, Inter Press Service (IPS), http://ipsnews.net/news.asp?idnews=33077.

83. *UAE to Allow Construction Unions* (2007), British Broadcasting Corporation News, http://news.bbc.co.uk/2/hi/business/4861540.stm.

84. *UAE: Workers Abused in Construction Boom*, Human Rights Watch, Human Rights News, http://hrw.org/english/docs/2006/11/12/uae14547.htm.

85. "Business: Easy Oz; Emirates Airlines," *Economist*, October 29, 2005, 82.

86. "Rise of the Emirates Empire," *CNN Money*, http://money.cnn.com/magazines/business2/business2_archive/2005/10/01/8359251/index.htm.

87. "Will a Merger between Air France and KLM Really Work?" *Yield: The Interactor Investor Journal*, http://www.yeald.com/Yeald/a/11821/will_a_merger_between_air_france_and_klm_really_work.html;jsessionid=83ECE60AE31F0CB442D0523507B-C7C0C.

88. "Air France/KLM Merger: Perilous Flight Ahead," *Universia Knowledge Wharton*, http://www.wharton.universia.net/index.cfm?fa=viewArticle&id=673&language=english&specialId=.

89. "Can Air France–KLM Rescue Alitalia?" *Business Week*, December 11, 2007, http://www.businessweek.com/globalbiz/content/dec2007/gb20071211_487483.htm.

90. "2007–08 Q3 Results," Air France KLM, http://www.airfranceklm-finance.com/index.php.

91. We are grateful to Pete Turnbull for reminding us of this point and for much other good advice while writing this book. The other major international alliance is SkyTeam, which includes Air France–KLM, Korean Air, Delta, Continental, Northwest, and other airlines.

92. Interview, February 16, 2008, with a captain who asked to remain anonymous.

93. "1st Interim Report January–March 2008," Lufthansa website, www.lufthansa-financials.de/servlet/PB/show/1026055/DLH_E_ES_ZB1.pdf.

Industry Trends in Costs, Productivity, Quality, and Morale

1. We thank Peter Belobaba, William Swelbar, Gerry Tsoukalis, and James Lee of the MIT Global Airline Industry Program for assistance with data analysis. Analyses are based on publicly available data from the International Civil Aviation Organization (ICAO) and U.S. Department of Transportation's Form 41. Because many data are missing from the ICAO dataset for European and Asian airlines, analyses were conducted using only airlines with complete or near-complete data for the seven-year period of interest. All costs are presented in U.S. dollars per available seat mile. Averages that are presented across airlines in the new-entrant·and legacy sectors are nonweighted averages to reflect the typical airline in each sector rather than giving additional weight to the larger airlines in each sector.

2. Jody Hoffer Gittell, Kim Cameron, Sandy Lim, and Victor Rivas, "Relationships, Layoffs, and Organizational Resilience: Airline Industry Responses to September 11th," *Journal of Applied Behavioral Science* 42, no. 3 (2006): 300–29.

3. *IATA Jet Fuel Monitor,* May 8, 2008, http://www.iata.org/whatwedo/economics/fuel_monitor/index.htm.

4. See, for example, Kyle Peterson, "Cost Advantage of Low-Cost Airlines Seen Eroding," Reuters, April 12, 2006. For a thorough analysis, see Gerassimos Tsoukalas, *Convergence in the U.S. Airline Industry: A Unit Cost and Productivity Analysis* (Cambridge: MIT Press, 2007). The Tsoukalas analysis removes transport-related costs from total unit costs, and then shows some degree of convergence between U.S. legacy and new-entrant airlines on this measure.

5. Data analyses were based on publicly available *Air Travel Consumer Reports,* published monthly since 1987 by the U.S. Department of Transportation.

6. See J. Edward Deming, *Out of the Crisis* (Cambridge: MIT Press, 1986). For a specific application to the airline industry, see Jody Hoffer Gittell, "Cost/Quality Tradeoffs in the Departure Process? Evidence from the Major U.S. Airlines," *Transportation Research Record* 1480 (1995): 25–36, which shows that higher quality outcomes in the airline industry over a fifteen-year period are associated with lower rather than higher costs.

7. For more information on the Toyota production system, see James Womack, Daniel Jones, and Daniel Roos, *The Machine That Changed the World: The Story of Lean Production* (New York: Scribner, 1994). See also John Paul MacDuffie and John Krafcik, "Integrating Technology and Human Resources for High-Performance Manufacturing: Evidence from the International Auto Industry," in *Transforming Organizations,* ed. Thomas Kochan and Michael Useem (Oxford: Oxford University Press, 1992).

8. Chris Isidore, "Airline Performance Hits Bottom: On-Time Arrival Rate of 72.46 Percent for January–April Period Is Lowest in 13 Years of Government Reports," *CNN Money,* June 5, 2006.

9. Associated Press, "Flight Delays at Worst Level in at Least 13 Years," *CNN.com,* August 6, 2007.

10. Phil Comstock, "Work-Related Views of Pilots and Flight Attendants since 9/11," paper presented to the Airline Industry Council, Washington, D.C., June 16, 2005.

11. Andrew von Nordenflycht and Thomas Kochan, "Contract Negotiations in the Airline Industry," *Monthly Labor Review,* August 2003.

12. Jody Hoffer Gittell, Andrew von Nordenflycht, and Thomas Kochan, "Mutual Gains or Zero Sum? Labor Relations and Firm Performance in the Airline Industry," *Industrial and Labor Relations Review* 57, no. 2 (2004): 163–79.

13. Gittell, Nordenflycht, and Kochan, "Mutual Gains or Zero Sum?"

Alternative Strategies for New Entrants: Southwest vs. Ryanair

1. U.S. Department of Transportation, *Update on the Airline Industry* (1993).

2. See Jody Hoffer Gittell, "A Theory of Relational Coordination," in *Positive Organizational Scholarship: Foundations of a New Discipline*, ed. Kim S. Cameron, Jane E. Dutton, and Robert E. Quinn (San Francisco: Berrett-Koehler Publishing, 2003). See also Jody Hoffer Gittell, "Relational Coordination: Coordinating Work through Relationships of Shared Goals, Shared Knowledge, and Mutual Respect," in *Relational Perspectives in Organizational Studies: A Research Companion*, ed. O. Kyriakidou and M. Ozbilgin (London: Edward Elgar, 2006).

3. For more details about Southwest's human resource management practices, see Jody Hoffer Gittell, *The Southwest Airlines Way: Using the Power of Relationships to Achieve High Performance* (New York: McGraw-Hill, 2003).

4. Jody Hoffer Gittell, Andrew von Nordenflycht, and Thomas A. Kochan, "Mutual Gains or Zero Sum? Labor Relations and Performance in the U.S. Airline Industry," *Industrial and Labor Relations Review* 57, no. 2 (2004): 163–80.

5. Susan Warren, "Keeping Ahead of the Pack: As Low-Fare Imitators Nip at Southwest's Heels, CEO Kelly Plans New Growth," *Wall Street Journal*, December 19, 2005, B1.

6. Siobhan Creaton, *Ryanair: How a Small Irish Airline Conquered Europe* (London: Aurum Press, 2004), 51.

7. Creaton, *Ryanair*, 56.

8. Creaton, *Ryanair*, 27.

9. Creaton, *Ryanair*, 28.

10. Interview with a former member of Ryanair Engineering Department, February 22, 2005.

11. Creaton, *Ryanair*, 28.

12. Interview with former member of Ryanair Engineering Department, February 22, 2005.

13. Creaton, *Ryanair*, 96.

14. Interview with former member of Ryanair Engineering Department, February 22, 2005.

15. Joe Wallace, Siobhan Tiernan, and Lorraine White, "Industrial Adaptation in Aer Lingus: The Path from Legacy to Low Fares Carrier," unpublished case study (2007), citing B. Sheahan, "Ryanair and Union on 'War Footing' as Legal Battles Heat Up," *Industrial Relations News* (2005): 21.

16. Wallace, Tiernan, and White, "Industrial Adaptation in Aer Lingus," citing M. Raftery, "Something Rotten in Ryanair," *Irish Times*, October 12, 2006.

17. Interview with IALPA representative, November 2006.

18. Ryanair had a major legal success involving a case taken by IALPA to the Irish Labour Court to have a decision by the court that it could legally set terms and conditions at Ryanair under the provisions of the Industrial Relations Acts 2001–2004. The Supreme Court found that the Labour Court had not acted in accordance with the principle of constitutional and natural justice. IALPA pilots had not given direct evidence, because

of the fear of victimization, but the Supreme Court found that if the Labour Court were issuing a binding determination then the "principles of natural justice" had to apply. Second, the Court found that the Labour Court had not given sufficient regard to evidence that Ryanair may have conducted collective bargaining.

19. International Transport Workers' Federation website, "Ryan-be-Fair," www.itf global.org/campaigns/appeal.cfm.

20. By 2006 Ryanair operated a European network covering more than thirty countries, including England, Wales, France, Spain, Italy, Malta, Morocco, Poland, Norway, Sweden, Denmark, Belgium, Germany, and Hungary; see http://peanuts.aero/low_cost_airline_news/index.php?option=com_content&task=view&id=3465&Itemid=59.

21. Wallace, Tiernan, and White, "Industrial Adaptation in Aer Lingus," 28.

22. This section draws from Teresa Poon and Peter Waring, "The Lowest of Low-Cost Airlines," unpublished case study (2007).

23. AirAsia Annual Report 2005 (http://www.airasia.com), 13.

24. AirAsia Annual Report 2005, 3.

25. AirAsia Annual Report 2005, 10.

26. AirAsia Annual Report 2005, 26.

27. "Leading in Asia: Interview with Tony Fernandes," *Wall Street Journal Asia*, May 29, 2006.

28. This section draws on Greg J. Bamber, Ryan Shields, and Kate Rainthorpe, "Virgin Blue: Employment Relations Innovations in a Low-Cost New World Carrier," unpublished case study (2007).

29. Bruce Highfield, interview at Virgin Blue Headquarters, Brisbane, October 25, 2005.

30. "Virgin Blue Recruitment: The Recruitment Process," http://www.bround.net/det-contact.aspx?jobid=32692&CoId=43&rq=8.

31. Virgin Blue, "Virgin Blue Holdings Limited Share Offer," 22.

32. J. Kain and R. Webb, "Turbulent Times," *Australian Airline Industry Issues* (2003), 8.

33. Bruce Highfield, interview at Virgin Blue Headquarters, Brisbane, February 25, 2005.

34. Bruce Highfield, interview at Virgin Blue Headquarters, Brisbane, February 25, 2005.

35. Terry O'Connell, interview at Australian Federation of Air Pilots, Melbourne, October 8, 2007.

36. Peter Paulos, interview at Brisbane Airport, February 24, 2005.

37. Bruce Highfield, interview at Virgin Blue Headquarters, Brisbane, February 25, 2005.

38. Peter Paulos, interview, February 24, 2005; John Playford, interview, December 6, 2007.

39. Mike Campbell, phone interview, March 15, 2006.

40. Campbell, March 15, 2006.

41. Judy Pate and Phillip Beaumont, "The Low-Cost Orange Flying Machine: The Case of EasyJet," unpublished case study (2007).

42. Pate and Beaumont, "The Low-Cost Orange Flying Machine," 16.

43. Pate and Beaumont, "The Low-Cost Orange Flying Machine," 14.

44. Mike Campbell, interview at EasyJet headquarters, October 9 and 10, 2005.

45. Campbell (2005).

46. Campbell (2005).

47. Campbell (2005).

48. Campbell (2005).

49. Mike Campbell, phone interview, March 15, 2006.

50. Mike Campbell, interview at EasyJet headquarters, October 9 and 10, 2005.

51. Campbell (2005).

52. Geraint Harvey and Peter Turnbull, "On the Go," *International Journal of Human Resource Management* (forthcoming).

53. Harvey and Turnbull, "On the Go," 13.

54. Mike Campbell, interview at EasyJet headquarters, October 9 and 10, 2005.

55. Interview with IALPA representative (2006), cited by Wallace, Tiernan, and White, "Industrial Adaptation in Aer Lingus."

56. Scott Droege and Nancy Brown Johnson, "AirTran Airways," *International Journal of Human Resource Management* (forthcoming).

57. Droege and Johnson, "AirTran Airways."

58. Personal communication from Loral Blinde, AirTran vice president of human resources, April 27, 2006.

59. Droege and Johnson, "AirTran Airways."

60. Joe Sharkey, "On the Road: Calling for Perspective on Low-Cost Airlines," *New York Times*, April 6, 2004.

61. Jody Hoffer Gittell and Charles O'Reilly, "JetBlue Airways: Starting from Scratch," Harvard Business School Case #8-01354 (2001).

62. Interview with Vincent Stabile by Maital Dar, August 9, 2005.

63. Stabile (2005).

64. Stabile (2005).

65. Stabile (2005).

66. Stabile (2005).

67. Stabile (2005).

68. Gittell and O'Reilly, "JetBlue Airways."

69. Gittell, *The Southwest Airlines Way*.

70. Stabile (2005).

71. Barbara De Lollis, "JetBlue Jettisons Neeleman as CEO, Promotes Barger," *USA Today*, May 11, 2007.

72. This section relies on Daphne Taras, "WestJet: Canada's Premier Rival Airline," unpublished case study (2007).

73. Taras, "WestJet."

74. Rick Westhead, "WestJet Pilots Could Be Paid More in Cash; New Pact Changes Compensation Terms: Options Less Attractive as Shares Decline," *Toronto Star*, March 10, 2006, F-8.

The Legacy Responses: Alternative Approaches

1. Much of the material in this section comes from Thomas Petzinger Jr., *Hard Landing* (New York: Random House, 1996).

2. Seth D. Rosen, "A Union Perspective," in *Cleared for Takeoff: Airline Labor Relations since Deregulation*, ed. Jean McKelvey (Ithaca: Cornell University Press, 1988).

3. Petzinger, *Hard Landing*, 233.

4. Petzinger, *Hard Landing*.

5. Gordon Bethune with Scott Huler, *From Worst to First* (New York: John Wiley and Sons, 1998); Jan Rivkin and Laurent Therivel, "Delta Air Lines (A): The Low-Cost Carrier Threat," Harvard Business School Case #9-704-403 (2004).

6. Jan Rivkin and Laurent Therivel, "Delta Air Lines (B): The Launch of Song," Harvard Business School Case #9-704-439 (2004).

7. Rivkin and Therivel, "Delta Airlines (A)," Rivkin and Therivel, "Delta Airlines (B)."

8. Jody Hoffer Gittell, Andrew von Nordenflycht, and Thomas A. Kochan, "Mutual Gains or Zero Sum? Labor Relations and Firm Performance in the Airline Industry," *Industrial and Labor Relations Review* 57, no. 2 (2004): 163–80.

9. Kirsten Wever, *Western Airlines and Its Four Major Unions* (Washington, D.C.: Bureau of Labor-Management Relations, U.S. Department of Labor, 1988); Kirsten S. Wever, "Revisiting the Labor-Management Partnership at Western Airlines," *Airline Labor Relations in the Global Era*, ed. Peter Cappelli (Ithaca: Cornell University Press, 1995); Thomas A. Kochan, "Rebuilding the Social Contract at Work: Lessons from Leading Cases," Working Paper WP09, Task Force on Reconstructing America's Labor Market Institutions (Cambridge: MIT/Sloan School of Management, 1999); Joseph Blasi and James Gasaway, "The Great Experiment: Labor-Management Cooperation at Eastern Airlines," in Cappelli, *Airline Labor Relations in the Global Era*; Petzinger, *Hard Landing*; Stephen R. Sleigh, "The Difficulty of Sticking Together in Tough Times," in Cappelli, *Airline Labor Relations in the Global Era*.

10. Petzinger, *Hard Landing*; Blasi and Gasaway, "The Great Experiment."

11. "United, Pilots Settle Up," *Newsday*, August 28, 2000, A4.

12. Susan Carey, "Independent Mechanics Union AMFA Seeks to Represent United Air Employees," *Wall Street Journal*, April 2, 2001, B8.

13. Tove Hammer and Robert N. Stern, "A Yo-Yo Model of Cooperation: Union Participation in Management at the Rath Packing Company," *Industrial and Labor Relations Review* 39, no. 3 (1996): 337–49; David I. Levine and Laura D'Andrea Tyson, "Participation, Productivity, and the Firm's Environment," in *Paying for Productivity: A Look at the Evidence*, ed. Alan Blinder (Washington, D.C.: Brookings Institute, 1990), 183–237; Joseph Blasi and Douglas Kruse, *The New Owners: The Mass Emergence of Employee Ownership of Public Corporations and What It Means for American Business* (New York: HarperBusiness, 1991).

14. Bethune and Huler, *From Worst to First.*

15. Andrew von Nordenflycht and Thomas A. Kochan, "Labor Contract Negotiations in the Airline Industry," *Monthly Labor Review* (July 2003): 18–28. Note: this excludes initial contracts, when an employee group first unionizes, which tend to take twice as long as revisions to an existing contract.

16. Bethune and Huler, *From Worst to First*; Greg Brenneman, "Right Away and All at Once: How We Saved Continental," *Harvard Business Review* (September–October 1998): 142.

17. Gittell, von Nordenflycht, and Kochan, "Mutual Gains or Zero Sum?"

18. Marc Knez and Duncan Simester, "Firm-wide Incentives and Mutual Monitoring at Continental Airlines," *Journal of Labor Economics* 19, no. 4 (2001): 743–72.

19. Knez and Simester, "Firm-wide Incentives."

20. Knez and Simester, "Firm-wide Incentives."

21. Bethune and Huler, *From Worst to First.*

22. Jody Hoffer Gittell, Kim Cameron, Sandy Lim, and Victor Rivas, "Relationships, Layoffs, and Organizational Resilience: Airline Industry Responses to September 11th," *Journal of Applied Behavioral Science* 42, no. 3 (2006): 300–329.

23. Joe Sharkey, "Big Carriers Wake Up to All-Business-Class Appeal," *International Herald Tribune*, July 25, 2007, 9.

24. Scott McCartney, "At American, 48 Hours of Drama Help Airline Avert Bankruptcy," *Wall Street Journal*, April 28, 2003, A1.

25. Trebor Banstetter, "Mechanics Help American Airlines Save Money with Innovative Ideas," *Fort Worth Star-Telegram*, April 26, 2004.

26. Margaret Allen, "Pilots Union Meets with American Airlines' CEO," *Dallas Business Journal*, January 20, 2006; Eric Torbenson, "American's Pilot Relations Hit Snag: Union Leader Calls Executives' Payout 'End of Shared Sacrifice,'" *Dallas Morning News*, April 27, 2006.

27. Melanie Trottman, "For AMR, a Pilot-Salary Fight Looms; Unions Look to Restore Pay As Airline Industry Emerges from Financial-Crisis Period," *Wall Street Journal*, February 20, 2007, A12.

28. Richard E. Walton, Joel E. Cutcher-Gershenfeld, and Robert McKersie, *Strategic Negotiations: A Theory of Change in Labor-Management Relations* (Ithaca: Cornell University Press, 1994).

29. Gittell, von Nordenflycht, and Kochan, "Mutual Gains or Zero Sum?"

30. Siobhan Tiernan with Joe Wallace and Lorraine White, "Industrial Relations Conflict and Collaboration: Adapting to a Low Fares Business Model in Aer Lingus," *European Management Journal* 24, no. 5 (2006): 338–47; Russell Lansbury and Sarah Oxenbridge, "Qantas," working paper, University of Sydney, 2007.

31. Tiernan, Wallace and White, "Industrial Relations Conflict and Collaboration."

32. Susan Carey and Melanie Trottman, "Continental Rejects Merger Overtures; Move Marks Rebuke to Rival United; Shifting Alliances?" *Wall Street Journal*, April 28, 2008, A1.

Building a More Balanced Airline Industry

1. Jody Hoffer Gittell, Andrew von Nordenflycht, and Thomas A. Kochan, "Mutual Gains or Zero Sum? Labor Relations and Firm Performance in the Airline Industry," *Industrial and Labor Relations Review* 57, no. 2 (2004): 163–80.

2. Gittell, Nordenflycht, and Kochan, "Mutual Gains or Zero Sum?"

3. For evidence of similar imprinting of founder's values and practices in other industries, see Christine M. Beckman and M. Diane Burton, "Founding the Future: Path Dependence in the Evolution of Top Management Teams from Founding to IPO," *Organization Science* 19, no. 1 (January–February, 2008): 3–24.

4. For more on the analogy to a "perfect storm," see note 2 in chapter 1.

5. See British Broadcasting Corporation News, London (2007), http://search.bbc.co.uk.

6. Jody Hoffer Gittell, *The Southwest Airlines Way: Using the Power of Relationships to Achieve High Performance* (New York: McGraw-Hill, 2003).

7. Jody Hoffer Gittell, Kim Cameron, Sandy Lim, and Victor Rivas, "Relationships, Layoffs, and Organizational Resilience: Airline Industry Responses to September 11th," *Journal of Applied Behavioral Science* 42, no. 3 (2006): 300–329.

8. *Options for Improving Negotiations and Dispute Resolution: A Report of the Working Group on Airline Labor Relations*, March 2004, 29–30.

9. *The Scotsman*, newspaper website, Edinburgh, 2007, http://business.scotsman.com/newspaper.aspx.

10. Judy Nichols, "New US Airways Making Sure Disparate Cultures Will Fly As 1," *Arizona Republic*, October 2, 2005.

11. Seth Rosen, "Consolidations, Mergers, and the Merger Process," presentation to the Airline Industry Council, Labor and Employment Relations Association, Washington, D.C., June 16, 2005.

12. IATA press release, September 3, 2008.

Index

Page numbers in italics refer to figures and tables.

Aer Lingus, 39–40, 59
  collective bargaining, *147*, 162–63
  employment-relations approach, *170*
  low-cost competition, response to, 162–63
  union partnership strategy, 172
AFA (Association of Flight Attendants), *155*
AFAP (Australian Federation of Air Pilots),
  42, 108, 109
AFL-CIO, 159, 182
AirAsia, 52, 53, 100–104
  competitive strategy, 100–101
  employment-relations approach, *95*,
    101–4, *170*
  union avoidance strategy, 59, 104
AirAsiaX, 52–53
Air Berlin, 44
aircraft productivity, 71–72, *72*, *73*
Air France KLM, 56–57, 186
Airline Employees Association (ALEA), *155*
airline industry, Asia
  challenges to, 49, *50*
  cost trends, *70*
  deregulation of, 50
  See also legacy airlines, Asia; new-entrant
    airlines, Asia

airline industry, Europe
  cost trends, 69, *69*, 70–71, *71*
  See also legacy airlines, Europe;
    new-entrant airlines, Europe
airline industry, global
  anti-competitive behavior, 199n5
  profitability of, 31, *32*
  regulation of, 30–31, *33*
airline industry, U.S.
  customer dissatisfaction, 1, 2
  deregulation, 18–21, *20*, 24–25
  employee frustration, 1, 2
  employment trends, 73, 75, *75*
  low-cost competition within, 2–3
  as national concern, 7, 189
  other countries, comparison to,
    29–30
  regulation of, 4, 16
  revenue trends, 68, *68*
  service quality comparisons, 5
  volatility of, 2–3, 19, *20*
  See also competitive strategies;
    employment-relations strategies; labor
    relations; labor strikes; legacy airlines,
    U.S.; new-entrant airlines, U.S.

airline industry, U.S., cost trends, 64–68, 65, 66, 67, 70–71, 71
  fuel cost trends, 66, 66
  labor cost trends, 64, 65
  transport-related cost trends, 67, 67
airline industry, U.S., future scenarios, 176–79, 188–93
  default option, 176–77
  government leadership, 188–93
  learning and innovation, 178–79
airline industry, U.S., path to sustainability, 179–88
  compensation equity, 183–84
  improved labor relations, 181–82
  mergers and consolidations, 186–88
  positive workplace culture, 179–80
  sustainable business models, 185–86
airline performance
  defined, 87–88
  employment relations and, 83–84
  labor relations and, 175–76
  relational coordination and, 87–88, 88, 90
Air Line Pilots Association (ALPA), 15, 93, 155, 157
Airline Pilots Association (APA), 93, 155, 158–59
airline profitability, determinants of, 169
AirTran, 115–16
  cost performance, 79
  employment-relations approach, 95, 170
  quality performance, 80, 116
  union accommodation strategy, 116
Air Wisconsin, 22
Alaska Airlines, 5
ALEA (Airline Employees Association), 155
All-American Airlines, 144
Alleghany Air, 144
alliances, international, 57–58
Aloha Airlines, 143
ALPA (Air Line Pilots Association), 15, 93, 155, 157
American Airlines
  acquisitions, 26
  collective bargaining, 147, 149, 153–55
  cost performance, 78, 79
  employment-relations approach, 170
  post 9/11 restructuring, 143
  quality performance, 5, 80
  union partnership attempt, 150–53, 172
American Eagle, 22

American Mechanics Fraternal Association (AMFA), 143–44, 155, 157
America West, 22, 26–27, 146
AMFA (American Mechanics Fraternal Association), 143–44, 155, 157
Ansett, 41
APA (Airline Pilots Association), 93, 155, 158–59
APFA (Association of Professional Flight Attendants), 155, 156–57, 158–59
Arpey, Gerard, 150, 151, 152
Asia, 49–56
  Dubai, Emirate of, 54–56
  legacy airlines, 29, 49, 50, 51
  Malaysia, 52–54
  South Korea, 51–52
Asia-Pacific Economic Cooperation Forum, 49
Association of Flight Attendants (AFA), 155
Association of Professional Flight Attendants (APFA), 155, 156–57, 158–59
Association of South East Asian Nations (ASEAN), 49
ATA Airlines, 79, 143
Australia, 41–42
Australian Airlines, 41
Australian Federation of Air Pilots (AFAP), 42, 108, 109
aviation market, global, 28

Bailey, Jeff, 5
BALPA (British Air Line Pilots Association), 36, 114
Barrett, Colleen, 92
Bethune, Gordon, 133, 139
block hours, 71–72, 72
BMI (British Midland International), 186
Bmibaby, 130
Branson, Richard, 37, 38, 41
Brenneman, Greg, 133, 139
British Air Line Pilots Association (BALPA), 36, 114
British Airways, 34–37
  anticompetitive behavior, 37, 199n5
  employment-relations approach, 34–36, 170
  union partnership strategy, 172
British European Airways, 34
British Midland International (BMI), 186

CAB (Civil Aeronautics Board), 16, 17
CALite, 129
Campbell, Mike (Continental), 133, 134
Campbell, Mike (easyJet), 39, 110–11,
    112–13, 114
capitalism, varieties of, 4–5, 29–30
    See also coordinated market economies;
    liberal market economies
Cappelli, Peter, 57–58
carrier-within-a-carrier model. *See* low-cost
    operations
Carty, Don, 150
Civil Aeronautics Board (CAB), 16, 17
codetermination, 43
collective bargaining
    Aer Lingus, *147*, 162–63
    American Airlines, *147*, *149*, 153–55
    Continental Airlines, 134, *147*, *149*, 158
    Northwest Airlines, 157
    Southwest Airlines, 157–58
    US Airways, 144–47
    See also labor relations; labor strikes
Comair, 22
competitive strategies, 9–11, *11*
    cost reduction, 10–11
    legacy *vs.* new-entrant airlines, 9–10
    See also employment-relations strategies
Condor, 44
Continental Airlines, 4, 174
    collective bargaining, 134, *147*, *149*, 158
    cost performance, *79*
    employment-relations approach, 25–26,
        135–41, *170*
    post 9/11 restructuring, 143
    quality performance, *5*, *80*, *127*
    turnaround, 133–35
    union suppression, 125–26
Continental Lite, 24
coordinated market economies, 30, 42–48
    Germany, 42–44
    Scandinavia, 44–48
    union partnership and, 59
Corrigan, Chris, 171
cost trends, 64–71, *71*
    Asian airline industry, 70
    European airline industry, 69, *69*, 70–71,
        71
    U.S. airline industry, 64–68
Crandall, Robert, 3–4, 21, 188
Cutcher-Geyshenfeld, Joel, *12*

Delta Airlines
    bankruptcy, 26
    cost performance, *79*
    employment-relations approach, 17, *170*
    mergers and acquisitions, 26, 27
    post 9/11 restructuring, 143, *147*, *149*
    quality performance, *5*, *80*, *127*
    union accommodation strategy, 172
Delta Express, 129
Denmark, 44, 45
deregulation, 18–21, *20*, *23*
    Asian airline industry, 50
    EU promotion of, 31, 33
    wages, impact on, 24–25
Doganis, Rigas, *32*
Dubai, Emirate of, 54–56

Eastern Airlines, 22, 26
    employee stock ownership plan, 131–32
    union suppression, 126, 128
easyJet, 38–39, 60, 110–15
    competitive strategy, 110
    employment-relations approach, *95*,
        110–15, *170*, 171
    union accommodation strategy, 114–15
Emirates, 54–56, 204n75
employee commitment/union accommoda-
    tion strategy, 104–16, 174–75
    AirTran, 115–16
    easyJet, 110–15
    Virgin Blue, 104–10
employee commitment/union avoidance
    strategy, 116–22
    JetBlue Airways, 116–20
    WestJet, 120–22
employee commitment/union partnership
    strategy, 174, 175
    See also Southwest Airlines,
        employment-relations approach
employee control/union avoidance strategy,
    96–104
    AirAsia, 100–104
    Ryanair, 96–100
employee morale, *81*, 81–82, *82*
employee stock ownership plans (ESOPs),
    130–33, 158
employment-relations strategies, 11–13, *12*,
    170, 170–71
    employee control *vs.* commitment, 11–12,
        173–75

employment-relations strategies (*continued*)
   See also employee commitment/union
     accommodation strategy; employee
     commitment/union avoidance strategy;
     employee commitment/union
     partnership strategy; employee
     control/union avoidance strategy
employment system matrix, *95*
employment trends, 73, 75, *75*
ESOPs (employee stock ownership plans),
   130–33, 158
Etihad Airways, 55
ETUC (European Congress of Trade
   Unions), 33
EU (European Union)
   defined, 199–200n8
   deregulation, promotion of, 31, 33
European Congress of Trade Unions
   (ETUC), 33
executive compensation, 183

FAAA (Flight Attendants Association of
   Australia), 108
Fernandes, Tony, 52, 100, 103
"Fliers Fed Up? The Employees Feel the
   Same" (Bailey), 5
Flight Attendants Association of Australia
   (FAAA), 108
flight cancellations, 79, *80*, 81
Fort Worth Star-Telegram, 153
friendliness, 76, 78, *78*
Frontier, 26, *79*, *80*
fuel cost trends, 64, 66, *66*

Germanwings, 44, 130
Germany, 42–44
Gittell, Jody Hoffer, *88*, *89*
Go!, 38
Godfrey, Brett, 41, 105, 106
Gol, 52

Hafner, Matt, 93–94
Haji-Ioannou, Stelios, 38
Hansman, John, *20*
Hapag-Lloyd Express, 44
Hawaiian Airlines, 143
high-commitment workplace relationship
   approach, 135–41
   exercise of authority, 135–38
   implementation, 139–41

   management philosophy, 138
   performance-based compensation, 139
Highfield, Bruce, 105, 106–7
human resource advantage, 14

IALPA (Irish Airline Pilots Association), 96,
   99, 115, 206–7n18
IAM (International Association of Machin-
   ists), *155*, 157
IATA (International Air Transport
   Association), 30–31, 99
IBT (Teamsters), *155*, 156–57
ICAO (International Civil Aviation
   Organization), 30, *63*, *69*, *70*, *71*
IFALPA (International Federation of Air
   Line Pilots Associations), 31
Impulse, 41, 160
Independent Pilots Association (IPA), *155*
Independent Union of Flight Attendants
   (IUFA), *155*
Industrial Relations Change Programme,
   36
International Air Transport Association
   (IATA), 30–31, 99
International Association of Machinists
   (IAM), *155*, 157
International Civil Aviation Organization
   (ICAO), 30, *63*, *69*, *70*, *71*
International Federation of Air Line Pilots
   Associations (IFALPA), 31
international strategic alliances, 186
International Transport Workers Federation
   (ITF), 31, 40, 53–54, 99
IPA (Independent Pilots Association),
   155
Ireland, Republic of, 39–41
Irish Airline Pilots Association (IALPA), 96,
   99, 115, 206–7n18
ITF (International Transport Workers
   Federation), 31, 40, 53–54, 99
IUFA (Independent Union of Flight
   Attendants), *155*

JetBlue Airways, 10, 24, 27, 116–20
   cost performance, 79, *79*
   employment-relations approach, *95*,
     117–18, *170*
   growth strategy, 119–20
   quality performance, 5, *80*
   union avoidance strategy, 118–19

Jetstar, 41, 130, 160–61
    employment-relations approach, *170*,
        170–71

Kahn, Alfred, 18–19
Kelleher, Herb, 92, 94
Kelly, Gary, 94–95
KLM Royal Dutch Airline, 184
    See also Air France KLM
Kochan, Thomas A., *83*, *155*
Korean Air Labor Union, 51–52

"Labor Contract Negotiations in the Airline
    Industry" (von Nordenflycht and
    Kochan), *83*, *155*
labor cost trends, 64, *65*
labor productivity, 72–73, *74*
labor relations, 15–18
    airline performance and, 83–84, 175–76
    Germany, 43–44
    negotiations, 15–16, 82–83, *83*
    regulation of, 15
    Scandinavia, 45
    statism of, 6–7
    See also collective bargaining; labor
        strikes; Railway Labor Act
labor strikes, 21–22, *23*
    regulation and, 22, *23*
    See also collective bargaining; labor
        relations
labor unit costs, determinants of, 169
Laker, Freddie, 37
Lansbury, Russell, 160
LCOs (low-cost operations), 24, 128–30,
    160–61
legacy airlines, Asia, 29, 49, 50, 51
    cost trends, *70*, 70–71, *71*
    stage lengths, 62, *63*
    See also specific Asian legacy airlines
legacy airlines, Australia, 41–42
    See also Qantas
legacy airlines, Europe, 29, 42–44, 45, 46
    cost trends, 69, *69*
    stage lengths, 62, *63*
    See also specific European legacy
        airlines
legacy airlines, U.S., 9, 10
    aircraft productivity, 71–72, *72*, *73*
    employment trends, 73, 75, *75*
    fuel cost trends, 64, 66, *66*

innovations, 22
labor cost trends, 64, *65*
labor productivity, 72–73, *74*
liberal market economies and, 58
low-cost competition, responses to, 21–22,
    24, 26, 128–30, 160–61, 160–63
operating margins, *145*
quality performance, *5*, 76, 77–78, 78–79,
    80, 81, *127*
revenue trends, 68, *68*
stage lengths, 61, 62, *62*
survival of, 163–64
transport-related cost trends, 67, *67*
    See also specific U.S. legacy airlines
legacy airlines, U.S., employment-relations
    strategies, 124–28, 130–41, 172
    shared governance, 130–33
    union suppression strategy, 125–26,
        128
    See also employee commitment/union
        accommodation strategy; high
        commitment workplace relationship
        approach
legacy airlines, U.S., post 9/11 restructuring,
    141–56
    bankruptcy and, 143–47
    capacity reduction, 141
    labor contract outcomes, *147*, 147–48, *149*,
        150
    union partnership attempt, 150–53
    unit cost reduction, 141–43
Leonard, Joe, 116
liberal market economies, 29–30, 33–42
    Australia, 41–42
    Ireland, Republic of, 39–41
    legacy airlines and, 58
    United Kingdom, 33–39
London Heathrow, 177–78
Lorenzo, Frank, 22, 25–26, 125–26,
    128
low-cost operations (LCOs), 24, 128–30,
    160–61
Lufthansa, 2, 42–44, 57, 59, *170*, 186

Malaysia, 52–54
Malaysian Airlines (MAS), 53–54
Marks, Alexander, 197n2
MAS (Malaysian Airlines), 53–54
McCarthy, Conor, 100
McDaniel, Thom, 92–93

McKersie, Robert B., *12*
mergers, 26–27, 56–57, 165–66
  challenge of, 186–88
Metrojet, 129
Midwest Express, 22
Morris Air, 116
"Mutual Aid Pact", 17

National Mediation Board (NMB), 16, *23*
Neeleman, David, 116–17, 120
new-entrant airlines, Asia, 50–51, 52–53
  cost trends, 70, *70*
  See also specific Asian new-entrant
    airlines
new-entrant airlines, Australia, 41
  See also specific Australian new-entrant
    airlines
new-entrant airlines, Europe, 37–39, 40–41,
    44, 47
  cost trends, 69, *69*
  stage lengths, 62, *63*
  See also specific European new-entrant
    airlines
new-entrant airlines, U.S., 9, 10, 27
  aircraft productivity, 71–72, *72*, *73*
  employment-relations strategies, *170*,
    170–71, 173
  employment trends, 75, *75*
  fuel cost trends, 64, 66, *66*
  labor cost trends, 64, *65*
  labor productivity, 72–73, *74*
  quality performance, 5, 76, 77–78, 78–79,
    80, 81
  revenue trends, 68, *68*
  stage lengths, 61, 62, *62*
  transport-related cost trends, 67, *67*
  See also specific U.S. new-entrant airlines
New York Air, 19, 21, 22, 125, 128
New York Times, 1
NMB (National Mediation Board), 16, *23*
Northwest Airlines
  bankruptcy, 26
  collective bargaining, *149*, 157
  cost performance, *79*
  employee stock ownership plan, 132
  mergers and acquisitions, 26, 27
  "Mutual Aid Pact" and, 17
  post 9/11 restructuring, 143–44
  quality performance, *5*, *80*
Norway, 44, 45

O'Leary, Michael, 40, 41, 96, 98, 197n2
Oneworld Alliance, 58
Ontario Teachers' Pension Plan, 120
Oxenbridge, Sarah, 160

Pacific Southwest Airlines (PSA), 26, 144
  employment-relations approach, 17–18
Pan Am Airlines, 22
Parker, Jim, 92
partnership agreements, 34
Patrick Corporation, 171
pattern bargaining, 17
PBGC (Pension Benefit Guaranty Corpora-
    tion), 145–46
PEB (Presidential Emergency Board), 16
Pension Benefit Guaranty Corporation
    (PBGC), 145–46
People Express Airlines, 19, 22, 26
Piedmont, 26, 144
Presidential Emergency Board (PEB), 16
PSA. *See* Pacific Southwest Airlines

Qantas, 2, 41, 42, *147*
  employment-relations approach, *170*
  low-cost competition, response to,
    160–61
Qatar Airways, 55
quality performance, *5*, 76, *77–78*, 78–79,
    80, 81, *127*

Railway Labor Act (RLA), 15–16, 159
regulation
  global airline industry, 30–31, 33
  labor relations, 15
  labor strikes and, 22, *23*
relational coordination
  airline performance and, 87–88, *88*, *90*
relational work system, 93
reliability, 76, *77*
Republic, 26
revenue trends, 68, *68*
Rhoades, Ann, 118
RLA (Railway Labor Act), 15–16, 159
Rosen, Seth, 187
Ryan, Tony, 40
Ryanair, 10, 30, 40–41, 52, 207n20
  cost reduction strategy, 10
  employment-relations approach, *95*,
    96–100, *170*, 170–71
  IALPA and, 99, 206–7n18

union avoidance strategy, 59, 96–97, 98–100

Sartain, Libby, 91
SAS. *See* Scandinavian Airline System
Scandinavia, 44–48
Scandinavian Airline System (SAS), 30, 45, 46–48
   employment-relations approach, 46–48, *170*
service quality, 13, 76
service quality trends, 76–81
Shuttle-by-United, 24, 129
Skytrain, 37
social contract, erosion of, 6
Song (LCO), 129
South Korea, 51–52
Southwest Airlines, 2, 4, 10, 18, 27, 174
   collective bargaining, *149*, 157–58
   competitive strategy, 87
   cost performance, 78, 79, *79*
   cost reduction strategy, 10
   fiscal conservatism, 93–94
   as international model, 193–94
   positive workplace culture, 179–80
   quality performance, 5, *80*, *127*
Southwest Airlines, employment-relations approach, 87–95, *95*, *170*, 170–71
   employment security, 92, 94–95
   relational coordination, 87–91, *88*, *89*
   union partnership, 92–93
   work/family balance, 91
The Southwest Airlines Way (Gittell), *88*, *89*
Southwest Pilots Association (SWAPA), 93, *155*
Spain, Al, 118
Spirit, *79*
Stabile, Vince, 117, 119
stage lengths, 61, 62, *62*, *63*
Star Alliance, 58
Strategic Negotiations (Waltor, Cutcher-Geyshenfeld and McKersie), *12*
SWAPA (Southwest Pilots Association), 93, *155*
Sweden, 44, 45
SWISS, 57

Teamsters (IBT), *155*, 156–57
Ted (LCO), 129

Texas Air, 26, 125
Texas International, 125
Tiernan, Siobhan, 99–100, 160, 162
total quality management (TQM), 76
transport-related cost trends, 67, *67*
Transport Workers Union (TWU), 108, 154, *155*, 157–58, 158–59
Turnbull, Peter, 44
TWA, 26, 132, 135
two-tier wage system, 21
TWU (Transport Workers Union), 108, 154, *155*, 157–58, 158–59

U.K. Office of Fair Trading, 199n5
union accommodation strategy, 171, 172
   AirTran, 116
   Delta Airlines, 172
   easyJet, 114–15
   Virgin Blue, 107–8, 109, 110
union avoidance strategy, 171
   AirAsia, 59, 104
   JetBlue Airways, 118–19
   Ryanair, 59, 96–97, 98–100
   WestJet, 121–22
   See also union substitution; union suppression strategy
union partnership strategy, 171, 172
   American Airlines, 150–53, 172
   coordinated market economies and, 59
   Southwest Airlines, 92–93
unions, 16
   contract negotiation durations, *155*
   strategies of, 156–59
   See also collective bargaining; labor relations; *specific* unions
union substitution, 12
union suppression strategy, 12
   Continental Airlines, 125–26
   Eastern Airlines, 126, 128
   See also union avoidance strategy
United Airlines
   bankruptcy, 26
   cost performance, *79*
   employee stock ownership plan, 132
   pilot strike (1985), 21–22
   post 9/11 restructuring, 143, *147*, *149*
   quality performance, 5, *80*
United Arab Emirates, 54
United Kingdom, 33–39
   new-entrant airlines, 37–39

Unite the Union, 38
US Air, 26, 144
US Air Express, 22
US Airways, 1, 18, 26–27
    bankruptcy, 26
    collective bargaining, 144–47, *147*, *149*
    cost performance, *79*, *145*
    employment-relations approach, *170*
    post 9/11 restructuring, 143, 144–47, *147*,
        149
    quality performance, *5*, *80*
    route network, 144
U.S. Congress, 16
U.S. Department of Justice, 199n5
U.S. Department of Transportation, *62*,
    65, 66, 67, 68, 71, 72, 73, 74, 75, 79,
    127, 145
    Lorenzo and, 128
U.S. Federal Aviation Administration, *77, 78*,
    80

ValuJet, 27, 115
Virgin Atlantic, 37–38, 62
Virgin Blue, 41, 60
    employment-relations approach, *95*,
        105–6, *170*, 171
    growth strategy, 109
    union accommodation strategy, 107–8,
        109, 110
von Nordenflycht, Andrew, *83*, *155*

Wallace, Joe, 99–100, 160, 162
Wall Street Journal, 150
Waltor, Richard E., *12*
Western, 26, 132
WestJet, 117, 120–22
    employment-relations approach, *95*,
        170
White, Lorraine, 99–100, 160, 162
Wilson Center for Public Research, *81*, *82*
Wimberly, Jim, 91